Books of Merit

AN AESTHETIC UNDERGROUND

AN AESTHETIC UNDERGROUND

A LITERARY MEMOIR

JOHN METCALF

Thomas Allen Publishers

Toronto

National Library of Canada Cataloguing in Publication

Metcalf, John, 1938–
An aesthetic underground / John Metcalf.

ISBN 0-88762-121-X

1. Canadian literature (English)—Publishing—Ontario—Erin.
2. Porcupine's Quill, Inc.   3. Metcalf, John, 1938–
4. Canadian literature (English)—20th century—History and criticism.
I. Title.

Z483.M48A3 2003   070.5'092   C2002-906164-4

Editor: Patrick Crean
Jacket and text design: Gordon Robertson
Jacket image: Ellen Carey / Photonica

Published by Thomas Allen Publishers,
a division of Thomas Allen & Son Limited,
145 Front Street East, Suite 209,
Toronto, Ontario M5A 1E3 Canada
www.thomas-allen.com

ONTARIO ARTS COUNCIL
CONSEIL DES ARTS DE L'ONTARIO

The publisher gratefully acknowledges the support of the Ontario Arts Council for its publishing program.

We acknowledge the Government of Ontario through the Ontario Media Development Corporation's Ontario Book Initiative.

07 06 05 04 03   1 2 3 4 5

Printed and bound in Canada

This book is for

Ron and Kate
Elizabeth and Ethan
Dan and Chantal

Every teaching institution will have its department of cultural studies, an ox not to be gored, and an aesthetic underground will flourish, restoring something of the romance of reading.

— HAROLD BLOOM, *The Western Canon*

It seemed unto [Don Quixote] very requisite and behooveful . . . that he himself should become a knight-errant, and go throughout the world, with his horse and armour, to seek adventures, and practise in person all that he had read was used by knights of yore; revenging all kinds of injuries, and offering himself to occasions and dangers, which, being once happily achieved, might gain him eternal renown.

— CERVANTES, *Don Quixote* (Shelton's translation, 1612)

Did I not tell your worship they were windmills? and who could have thought otherwise, except such as had windmills in their head?

— SANCHO PANZA to DON QUIXOTE

Contents

A VIGNETTE

WHEN I WAS FOURTEEN and attending Beckenham Grammar School for Boys I began spending my Saturdays hanging around in the yard of the High Street auctioneer. Viewing took place from ten until noon and the auctions started at one and went on until four o'clock when the vans started backing in. Porters in green aprons manhandled sideboards and wardrobes and held aloft at the auctioneer's "What am I bid?" the silver-plated coffee sets, the brass fire irons, the baize-lined canteens of cutlery with one fish knife missing.

What attracted me was not the auction but the two coffin-sized boxes on trestles in the yard. These were crammed with the books, spines up, which accumulated from estate sales. They were priced at sixpence each. I stood by the boxes and tidied up the rows after people had rummaged. Customers soon assumed that I was employed to stand there and started giving me their sixpences. These I took into the office.

The clerk in the office with his catalogues and lists of the lots was obviously suspicious of my motives and I'd often glance up to see him standing in his doorway, cigarette smoke curling into one eye, staring.

Touching the books gave me profound pleasure. I became so familiar with them, with their bindings, decorations, and typefaces, that I played a game Saturday after Saturday, guessing at a glance a book's probable date of publication. Mostly they were novels by the likes of

William Harrison Ainsworth, Dornford Yates, Henry Rider Haggard, Sheila Kaye-Smith, Warwick Deeping, A. J. Cronin, Enid Bagnold, Ngaio Marsh, Mrs. Humphry Ward, Rafael Sabatini, Anthony Hope, Margery Allingham, and Hilaire Belloc—literary detritus specific to that time and place. But occasionally there were older books in pictorial boards or decorated cloth, my favourite among them the endless novels of G. A. Henty. I was also attracted to the short stories of W. W. Jacobs who was much admired, I later discovered, by P. G. Wodehouse. I was drawn to the work initially by the brilliance of Jacobs's illustrator, his friend Will Owen. For years I reread *Many Cargoes, Odd Craft, Sailors' Knots, Captains All,* and *Short Cruises.*

After a couple of months the clerk grew tired of my constant interruptions to deposit coins in the old Player's Navy Cut tin and told me to keep the tin outside and give him the money at the end of the afternoon.

Some while later came the day when he suggested that I keep half a crown for myself. I somehow knew that accepting the money would change the relationship in a way I didn't want, so, fighting my shyness, I wondered if instead I might have a couple of books every week. This request seemed to confirm him in his mild contempt of me and reassure him of my harmlessness.

I wanted those Henty books. I didn't necessarily want to read them, though I did read some. What I wanted was to *own* them. Not just three or four or ten. I wanted to own *all* of them. A few minutes at the public library told me there were more than eighty. And so the collection began to grow. *Under Drake's Flag, The Lion of the North, With the Allies in Pekin, With Clive in India, With Wolfe in Canada, True to the Old Flag* . . .

This vignette suggests four motifs which seem to have played themselves out all through my life. The first is books themselves. The second is collecting things. The third is a certain independence of mind and judgement illustrated in my indifference to the clerk's contempt. The fourth is the almost magical inability to acquire money.

THE CURATOR

MANY AUTOBIOGRAPHIES of writers present a picture of a shy and lonely child delivered from solitude and unsympathetic surroundings by the power of the Word, the child's mind captured, for example, by the illustrations in Foxe's *Book of Martyrs* or struggling with the text of the only book in the house, *Pilgrim's Progress*. Good examples of this typical experience are recorded in James Laver's *Museum Piece* and in Jocelyn Brooke's *The Military Orchid*.

My own childhood was nothing like this. I cannot remember a time when I was not surrounded by books. My father, a Methodist minister, had a fairly large library, most of the volumes, to be sure, theological, but he also had most of the standard poets and first editions of the novels of Conrad and Hardy. Among the more "modern" poets, he owned Masefield, Housman, Chesterton, Belloc, Yeats, and Blunden.

After he died and I was looking through what books my mother had not promptly donated to Oxfam, I was amazed to find Wilde's *De Profundis*. I'd probably seen it when younger but thought it to be a work of theology.

My mother read all the time. Her reading wasn't literary. Her favourite material was historical novels and detective stories. These came from the Public Library, from Boots Library, and Timothy White's Lending Library. The historical novels were of the Georgette Heyer variety, bodice rippers but "nice" bodice rippers, the detective stories by Dorothy L. Sayers, Agatha Christie, Margery Allingham, and Ngaio Marsh. I associate all these writers, whom I loathe, with the smell of bath salts and talc, doubtless an early memory of trips to Boots Chemists.

These detective story writers seem to me, now, to mirror and perpetuate the nastiness of British class preoccupations. The superintendent or the well-bred amateur sleuth was always assisted by the comically lower-class and utterly thick but throbbingly loyal sergeant or manservant. So it was in the 1930s, the Golden Age of detective fiction, with Margery Allingham's Albert Campion and his "gent's 'elp," Magersfontein Lugg, and it *still* is seventy years later with Colin Dexter's rather highbrow Inspector Morse and funny old Sergeant Lewis, dim but devoted as a Labrador.

When I was a child I read quickly, usually taking about two hours to finish a book. On wet days I read my ration of library books in one gulp and often returned in the evening for three more. On the other hand, I was eleven before I could tell time. I can still see the tears of exasperation and rage starting in my mother's eyes as she moved the cardboard hands on the cardboard face and asked me what time it was if the little hand was on one and the big hand was on nine. She might as well have been talking to me in a foreign language.

———————————

Oddly enough, all this reading did not mean that I was "bookish"; quite the reverse was true. School always baffled me. I'd like to pretend that I was so brilliant I was bored by school. But that isn't true. I was baffled. The only subjects in which I did well were English and history. English because I did it automatically. When it came to grammar and parsing, I had no idea of what people were talking about. It took lessons in Latin years later to drive home what was meant by "adjective" and "adverb." History fascinated me because I felt lapped in it. Lord Macauley said that history must be "burnt into the imagination before it can be received by the reason," and it was certainly seared into mine. Long barrows, dolmens, hill forts, standing stones—all sang to me of where I had come from and who I was.

I passed what was called the eleven-plus exam—an instrument for sorting out grammar school hopefuls from secondary modern fodder—only because my mother drilled me in sums and suchlike.

It quickly became apparent that if I were ever to do anything at all in life it would be on the "arts" side of affairs, though any prospects whatsoever seemed more than doubtful. At thirteen I was declared ineducable in math and I stopped taking the subject altogether. The fact that my math teacher that year was abnormally small and looked like a Japanese sniper as drawn in American comics and drove home his points with the rung of a chair may have had *something* to do with it. But not much. The truth is that numbers cause a pain in my forehead.

It's interesting that if I'd been educated in Canada I'd never have reached university because I'd never have passed the requirements in math. In England it was permissible to replace math by a science. Physics and chemistry were as incomprehensible to me as math. Math, I could see, did somehow relate to life; there were all those problems about how much wallpaper you'd need to paper a room eighty-three feet long with eight dormer windows. But physics! As far as I could see all it involved was lowering weights on bits of string into calibrated tubes of water to see how much overflowed. I couldn't understand why anyone would *wish* to know that. Chemistry was a touch more entertaining because of the fire and smoke but I never seemed able to grasp the *motives* for these activities.

Physics and chemistry, then, being incomprehensible, left only biology. I spent most of my free time—alone but not lonely—watching animals, hunting for snakes, searching for fossils, and fishing in the Avon and Stour. I could have taken the biology teacher to the one locality in Hampshire where smooth snakes were to be found, where bee orchids grew, where the lampreys gathered, where there were the sets, earths and holts of badgers, foxes, and otters, but all this, I quickly realized, was nothing to do with biology. Biology was copying diagrams.

School ground on towards my fourteenth year. I did badly in everything except English and history. Even my toast-rack in woodwork took two years and about three hundred feet of lumber.

The English teaching I received between the ages of twelve and fourteen was, I realize now, superb. Our only activities were précis, paraphrase, exercises in comprehension, and essay writing. In other words, we were drilled in logic, in the steel structure of the language. Literature was dealt with in the following way: each term we were given a list of twelve novels to read at home. This meant that in a school year we read a minimum of thirty-six novels. At the end of each term we were given a test cunningly designed to reveal if we had in fact read them.

"With whom did Jim Davis shelter after the fight with the revenue officers?"

The following books were on those lists and suggest the general flavour of the reading: *Jim Davis, Treasure Island, Kidnapped, King Solomon's Mines, The History of Mr. Polly, A Tale of Two Cities, Tarka the Otter, Oliver Twist, Allan Quartermain, Kim, David Copperfield, Three Men in a Boat, Prester John, The Thirty-nine Steps, Rodney Stone, The White Company, The Cloister and the Hearth, Rookwood,* etc.

All good stuff for boys and entertaining. The idea of discussing such things as plot and characterization would never have occurred to my teachers.

And a damn good thing too.

(I suspect that nowadays these books would be considered far too difficult in syntax and vocabulary and entirely lacking in *relevance*. I prefer them, however, to the books with titles like *Jennifer's First Period* tailored to the supposed interests of adolescents.)

This, then, was my "official" life until I was fourteen.

But I have another set of memories covering the same years which I realize now, groping back, are the *really* important ones.

They are disjointed.

Very early, being with my father in Foyle's. He is searching along the bottom rows of second-hand tomes in theology. We are in a basement, in a canyon of books. Our hands are glazed black with that peculiar kind of muck that grows on old books. My father has bought me a book to keep me quiet as he roots and rummages. It is *Struwwelpeter* with the horrifying illustration of the leaping man cutting off the child's thumb. Afterwards, we have tea in a Lyon's Corner House.

Another memory of my father, a man I wish I'd known. He was a distant figure, not given to conversation, eccentric. He silenced quarrels between my brother and me by a prim clearing of his throat. As he was a Methodist minister, he was relatively impoverished. Money was never thrown around. It was, in fact, pinched. On a rare summer holiday in Swanage we were walking past a junk shop. In the window hung a blown-up, varnished blowfish, a prickly globe of wonder. In we went. The fish was two shillings and sixpence. My father bought it for me. He also bought me some bound folio volumes of an illustrated magazine which formed a history of the First World War. And, as we were about to leave, he pointed out the sword of a swordfish and suggested that it was, if not rare, then at least unusual, and precisely the sort of thing that, if passed up, would remain a source of regret forever after.

This was not condescension on his part nor, I suspect, a desire to please a small boy. He was never "nice" in that way. It was a seriously held opinion.

Later, a collection of *Superman* and *Combat* comics, real American ones with glossy covers, not the dowdy British reproductions. These desirables were the stakes in games of marbles and nearest-to-the-wall with cigarette cards.

Later, still, *Boy's Own Paper*, all kept in severe order by volume and number.

Collecting, then. My father collected obscure books on theological matters. My brother collected coins—a harmless hobby which led eventually to his becoming Keeper of the Heberden Coin Room at the Ashmolean Museum. His bibliography lists over two hundred publications and his reputation is international.

When he was eleven and I was six my parents gave him an unused room for a museum. It had been a pantry. He filled it with coins, fossils, mineral specimens, pottery shards, a hair from an elephant's tail, a clay oil lamp from Palestine, medals, a Prussian dragoon's sword, an embroidered Chinese slipper. He charged ½d admission. He also put out a weekly newspaper printed purple on a gelatine pad. This too cost ½d. One copy of one issue remains. The newspaper was called *The Curator*.

When he retired from the Ashmolean in 1998 he gave a speech at a farewell lunch and said in part: "We try to share our knowledge and our enthusiasm generously and freely, with undergraduates, with graduates, with our museum colleagues in this country and elsewhere, with amateur collectors, with the public at large, with children . . .

"In a clamant world, we need to know what we stand for, we need to be always ready to share our values, while insisting on the disciplines of exact learning and rigorous argument; and serenity of judgement."

The word *clamant* suggests him exquisitely.

All sorts of antiques and curios were cheaper when I was a boy and far more readily available than now. I had small collections of swords and pistols. At about the age of ten I had acquired, by swapping, a "horse pistol"—a battered percussion cap job—and a bullet mould. I began an obsessive manufacture of lead bullets in the kitchen using one of my mother's saucepans. I have scars on my hands to this day from molten lead. I cycled all the way from Southbourne to Ringwood to buy a tin of percussion caps from a compliant gunsmith. But the powder defeated me; I couldn't get the mixture right.

My passion for bullet making led me into crime. I was apprehended removing lengths of lead plumbing that were still attached to houses.

My brother grew copper sulphate crystals in pie dishes and mineral gardens under waterglass in casseroles.

My father steeped his vile home-grown tobacco in other kitchen utensils and "cooked" it in the oven.

My mother bewailed the state of her pots and pans and, I suspect, suffered something close to a breakdown as the house filled with coins, books, snakes, nature specimens, hedgehogs, ammonites, belemnites, trilobites, caterpillars, butterflies, setting-boards, nets, killing jars, stone-age hand axes, slow worms, green-throated sand lizards, *Observer Books* of Trees, Wild Flowers, Birds, Reptiles . . . volume after volume in the *British Naturalist* series, owl pellets, fishing tackle, seething tins of gentles, hypodermic syringes, and cloudy jars of formaldehyde containing newts, leeches, ticks, internal organs.

My mother claims that she came home from shopping one day to find me and two friends about to open up a squirrel we'd shot. Her horror was not that we'd dispatched the poor creature but that we had it pinned down for dissection *on the bread board.*

Setting-boards for butterflies and moths, the rustproof black pins, the cork-lined exhibition cases—all came by mail from an emporium in South London. The store's catalogue featured treasures beyond the dreams of avarice—fossils, arrowheads, scrapers, neolithic hand axes (the *polished* ones), Roman terracotta lamps, sundry wondrous antiquities. The very *name* of this store, which I've never visited, had the same effect on me as Chimborazo and Cotopaxi had on the boy in Walter J. Turner's poem "Romance"; it was called Watkins and Doncaster.

(On my first return from Canada to visit my mother she confided one afternoon that she was very worried about some shotgun shells that the tide of collecting and slaughter had deposited in a cupboard some twelve years earlier. She was worried that they would explode. She said they often made her feel low and that she wept thinking about them. Amazed, I asked her why she hadn't thrown them out. She said that she hadn't wanted "the blood of the dustbin men on her conscience." And if that isn't a detail from a Thurber story, I don't know what is. For some obscure reason it reminds me of the black Thurber maid who always referred to the fridge as "that doom-shaped thing in the kitchen.")

Collecting is intimately connected with writing. With mine, certainly. There is an affinity between the two activities. The *kind* of knowledge that comes out of collecting differs from purely formal knowledge. It is informed by love and lust. Collecting sharpens and trains the eye. It forces contact with the particular. Collecting is conservative, historical, archival. Collecting is evaluative. It demands judgement. It leads inevitably to ever-expanding interests. Collecting, then, is not mere accumulation. The creation of a collection and its tending is an intricate aesthetic affair. The knowledge gained can be gained in no other way.

The collector is usually seen by the non-collector as obsessive and harmlessly loony but I hold that whether he collects Regency furniture or hand-painted chamber pots, the collector's real is more real than yours. Simply, he *sees* more.

MR. WHITE AND BERNARD HALLIDAY

THE NEXT TWO PHASES of my adolescent reading were dominated by the external examinations, the Ordinary Level exams and the Advanced Level exams. The Ordinary Level exams were equivalent to Canadian high school matriculation and were usually sat at the age of sixteen. Advanced Levels were sat two years later and were used to regulate entry to universities.

At sixteen I was still mutedly unhappy and unsuccessful at school. I was used to being told I was dim and thick and had come to believe it. My brother, Cambridge now behind him, had been and continued to be unbelievably brilliant. My school career was compared at all points with his and was found wanting. My body was flooded by naughty hormones and the air was heavy with rebellion.

I claimed I wanted to be a professional boxer.

Under the guidance of an ex-sergeant from one of the more thuggish branches of the British Army—"Partial to 'im, are you? Don't 'ug 'im, 'it 'im"—I learned, as Henry Cooper put it, to "work downstairs."

My mother's anguish and pressure increased as the exams drew nearer. The forecasts for my future were grim—on good days I might, if lucky, aspire to become a plumber's mate, on bad days the gallows beckoned. My father grew more grimly silent. And so, perhaps to please my parents, perhaps simply infected by the prevailing hysteria, I started to work. Everyone was impolitely amazed when the letter arrived from the Ministry of Education. I had passed the Ordinary Level examinations in every subject I had sat. My mother, typically, wondered aloud if they'd got my name confused with some other Metcalf.

I had had no patience with school or schoolwork up to the time of the Ordinary Level examinations simply because my interests were passionately engaged elsewhere. I was in a constant and what felt like holy connection to the natural world. My time was spent with the intensity of dream fishing for roach and perch, chub, dace, rudd, bream, and tench, names which are a poetry still. School was an abstraction to me many levels removed from the thrill of the red-and-black caterpillars of the cinnabar moth feasting on goldenrod, or the tense but fluid coiling of an adder about to strike.

But I was beginning to waken from that dream; it was becoming less intense, less consuming as the sexual current pulled me more towards the social world. I began to realize that I had arrived at a cross-roads. My mother nagged and urged, wanting me to stay on at school. I countered with odd schemes which drove her to the very verge. One proposal I remember making was that she stake me the passage money to Georgetown, British Guiana, where I would become a pork-knocker high up the Orinoco River working illicit diamonds. My father while these battles raged—for that is what they were—sucked on his pipe and did his sage-nodding-in-silence thing.

I *said* I wanted to become a club fighter because this caused maximum annoyance and distress but even I knew that I was indulging in fantasy. I didn't have the weight, the height, or the reach. I'd seen the life, seen the pugs in the gyms. And I wasn't hungry for it. For me it was a kind of playing. When I sparred with Dell Latter in a Croydon club I was on the receiving end of a controlled violence I knew I couldn't muster.

But there were things going on in my mind I *wouldn't* talk about. I was reading confusedly and with odd motivations. I read a lot of books about art and art history. I had a strange conviction I might become a painter, strange because I was utterly incapable of drawing. In the odd state I was in this did not seem to matter. I also read books about religious subjects, hoping to discover compelling arguments for becoming an atheist because painting and atheism and drinking the turpentine from your paintbox like Utrillo seemed to fit together inevitably.

I read Jessie L. Weston's *From Ritual to Romance* and Frazer's *The Golden Bough* because of the footnotes in *The Waste Land* and this was the first time that the idea of footnotes and bibliographies dawned on me. Before I had resolutely ignored them. But then, I was unable to grasp the idea of telling time until I was eleven. So perhaps this was simply another instance of weird wiring. My reading began that meandering course it's followed ever since.

From D. H. Lawrence to Katherine Mansfield to John Middleton Murry, to Frieda's ex-husband Ernest Weekley, to Gurdjieff, Ouspensky, Mme Blavatsky, and Annie Besant's *Wisdom of the Upanishads*, to Roger Fry and Clive Bell and Vincent's letters to Theo. From the gibberish of "significant form" forward to the gibberish of Herbert Read and back to Ruskin and Pater and then forward once again to Whistler's *Gentle Art*—on and on unendingly and, in large part, uncomprehendingly.

I was sullen and rude at home. I felt myself too refined, too sensitive to endure the narrow rectitude of the manse. These comic pretensions were doubtless fostered and "swollen"—and "swollen" is very much the word—by my discovery of Oscar Wilde and Huysmans' *A Rebours*.

Not very deeply hidden in the preposterous stew of adolescent rebellion and desire and aspiration was the desire to escape the pietism of my mother and live a life more generally louche and rowdy.

I wrote about this time in my life in a mock memoir called "Private Parts" in the book *Girl in Gingham*.

Irving Layton wrote for Michael Macklem, Oberon Press's publisher, a lavish blurb.

"Many thanks to you and Metcalf for the pleasure 'Private Parts' has given me. It's almost as great as that given to me by my own."

Well, the novella isn't *that* good but here's an extract:

I haunted the local library in my quest for knowledge. Not only was it a very good library but I lusted after one of the younger librarians who had a nice smile and breasts which gave the impression of great solidity. I spent hours wondering how much they weighed, what one would feel like hot and unconfined.

It was in the library that I found one day a book called *The March of the Moderns* by the art historian William Gaunt. I have never seen or read the book since. It struck me with the radiance and power of revelation. The mundane world fell away; I was oblivious to the smell of floor polish and damp raincoats, the click of the date-stamp, the passage of other browsers along the shelves. I read standing up until closing-time and then took the book home and finished it in bed.

The book revealed to me a world where brilliant but persecuted people drank champagne for breakfast and were pissed by lunch, took lobsters for walks on leashes, shaved off half their moustache, sliced off their ears and gave them to prostitutes, possessed women by the score, consorted with syphilitic dwarves, *lived* in brothels, and were allowed to go mad.

Somewhere in the sun, D. H. Lawrence was at it.

Hemingway was giving them both barrels.

Ezra was suffering for the faith in an American bin.

All painters were everywhere possessing their exotic Javanese models.

I, meanwhile, was in Croydon.

But Art was obviously the answer; it was just a question of finding my medium. The problem with the novel was that writing took a long time and nothing interesting had happened to me. I tried poetry for a time being particularly drawn to the Imagists because they were very short and seemed easiest to imitate. H.D. was one of my favourites. Painting, because of the models, attracted me most but I couldn't draw anything that looked like anything; abstraction was the answer, of course, but secretly I thought abstraction not quite honest. I had a go at a few lino-cuts but gouged my hand rather badly. Drama was soured for me by memories of endless pageants and nativity plays where kids tripped over the frayed carpet and I had to say:

"I bring you tidings of Great Joy."

But I was not depressed.

I settled down to wait. I lived in the manse, ate scones, and went to school, but I was charged with a strange certainty that I was somehow different, chosen, special; my Muse, in her own good time, would descend and translate me from Croydon to the richer world where women and applause were waiting.

My career crossroads was solved not by a choice but by a command. After the results of the Ordinary Level exams were known I was summoned by the headmaster. All previous visits had involved a cane. The headmaster's name was Mr. White. I have no idea of his Christian name; everyone was so in awe of him that I suppose we thought he hadn't got one. We were in such terror of his besuited bulk, his jowls, his massive *presence* that if he appeared in a corridor boys moved to the walls and froze like cars getting out of the way of a blaring ambulance. Though the terror was in his silence.

I tapped on the door.

"You wished to see me, sir."

"Ah, *Metcalf.* The boy pugilist. Sit."

Flowers in the cut-glass vase in the window behind him, sun dazzling on the glass-fronted bookcases, two white marble busts on columns of men in wigs.

"Our first encounter, Metcalf, was concerned with your putting pieces of carbide in inkwells. Producing a stench—methane, was it?—which forced classrooms to be vacated. Highly amusing. Highly amusing."

He hooked his thumbs into his gown.

"Your career subsequently has been marked by obstinacy and obduracy."

He shook his head slowly and as if in sorrow.

"The Bunsen burner? Hmmm?"

"Yes, sir."

"The machete-thing?"

"Bowie knife, sir."

"I am not interested in the *detail* of your armaments."

"No, sir."

"That playground altercation. An ugly exchange of blows for which I had the honest pleasure of thrashing you. Hmmm? Hmmm?"

"Yes, sir."

"What are we to do with you, Metcalf?"

"I don't know, sir."

"Annealing, wasn't it? When you attempted to burn down the metalwork shop."

"It was an accident, sir."

"One might observe that a disproportionate number of accidents seem to happen in your vicinity. Hmmm? Hmmm?"

"Yes, sir."

"And nagging at the edge of my mind is something to do with a pipette. A pipette and another boy's blazer pocket. Also you?"

"Yes, sir."

"You seem to have an antipathy towards science, Metcalf, but I have been looking at your Ordinary Level results and your marks in English were extraordinarily high. I have spoken to Mr. Rule who rashly used of you the word 'brilliant.'"

He stared at me.

"I sense in you, Metcalf, abilities untapped. But tapped they will be. I will myself tap them. And I will tap them very hard. We'll see how 'brilliant' you are. I have decided that you will win a State Scholarship and go to a decent university where you will take an Honours degree in English. All schools of English require Latin at the Ordinary Level as a prerequisite. You have no Latin as your appalling behaviour and lack of effort precluded entry into the Latin stream. It is therefore my intention to teach you Latin in one year. I shall take you from your present state of numb ignorance to an ability to sight translate the set books—Caesar and Ovid next year."

He regarded me.

"This will require of you a great deal of hard work."

"Yes, sir."

"No time for games with carbide or machetes."

"No, sir."

"That then is settled. You'll need . . . Blue and yellow, the cover."

"Pardon, sir?"

"The primer, boy. The primer you'll need. *Teach Yourself Latin.* That's it. Now away out of my sight and buy one."

I entered upon my final two years of secondary education known in England then as the sixth form. I was studying only two subjects, English and history. I had only two classes a day and spent the rest of the time reading. I could come and go as I wished and no longer was required to wear school uniform. On the first lordly day of the new term I rolled into school late, wearing a deadly elegant pair of suede shoes.

"Good God, Metcalf!" exclaimed my history teacher. "Those are the shoes of a Nigerian pimp!"

Why, I wondered, Nigerian?

Every lunchtime I reported to Mr. White's study where he corrected my exercises in grammar and translation. I learned enough Latin to develop a keen regret that I hadn't been taught Greek and Latin from my elementary school years. I came to love the discussions about the connotations of words, the propriety of diction. I also came to understand that Mr. White was infinitely kind and his verbal *harrumphing* an act to amuse himself.

There were only seven students in the English class, all of them very bright and intense, and we were fortunate in our English teacher, a newly minted double first from Cambridge. He had been a student of F. R. Leavis's and so taught us the close reading typical of what was then called New Criticism. When I did go to Bristol University my tutor was L. C. Knights, the founder of *Scrutiny*, which was edited largely by Leavis; so the man had, indirectly, a considerable influence on my life. So closely did we read in that sixth-form class that we came to look on William Empson's *Seven Types of Ambiguity* as light entertainment.

The set books for the Advanced Level exam were works by Chaucer and Shakespeare and a representative clutch of writers from the Romantic period—Wordsworth, Blake, Keats, Byron, and Jane Austen. But these were merely the skeleton of what we studied. I read more in those two years than I'd ever read before. It is impossible to convey the intellectual excitement of those two years. The cliché of being in a pressure cooker is exactly right. Nearly everything that has come afterwards has been an anticlimax.

We read the texts minutely. The placing of the texts in a larger framework was left entirely to us. It was simply *assumed* that we would read literary histories, other books by the set authors, their contemporaries, literary criticism, and period history. I read unceasingly, all day and far into the night; the weekly essays on subjects of our own choosing provided an opportunity to marshal new information and ideas.

I'll try to suggest the breathless, careering quality of the reading. Starting *Northanger Abbey*, the teacher suggested the obvious point that one couldn't really approach it without knowing what was being parodied—which led to *The Castle of Otranto*, *The Monk*, Lewis's *Tales of Terror*, *Vathek*, *Rasselas*, *The Mysteries of Udolpho*, *The Italian*, Charles Maturin's *Melmoth the Wanderer*, and *The Fatal Revenge, or the Family of Montorio*, dire tomes such as Praz's *The Romantic Agony*. Which led to Byron. To Quennell. To revolutions: to Garibaldi, Bolivar, Marx, Proudhon, Bakunin, and Kropotkin. Background books like Watt's *The Rise of the Novel* led, in turn, back to previously unread novels—lesser Defoe, tedious Samuel Richardson, the minor Fielding, Smollett, the *other* Sterne. And somehow forward to the diaries of the Austen period—marvellous gobs of gossip—to Captain Jesse's *Life of Brummel*, the mystic doings of Lady Hester Stanhope, to T. H. White's *The Age of Scandal* and then, of course, like a homing pigeon to White himself who led back to Malory who led to the *Mabinogion* which somehow led to Robert Graves who in turn led back to the Greek myths and *The White Goddess* and to archaeology —Mortimer Wheeler, Sir Arthur Evans, Michael Ventris and Minoan Linear B which led to Jean-François Champollion, Cycladic figures, the Rosetta Stone, Napoleon, fast detour through the French Revolution with side trips to Sade and a glance at *Venus in Furs*, back to Arthur Bryant's popular history of the Peninsular War Campaign and on and on and on.

The same sort of thing with Blake. Off to Swedenborg. To engraving. Back to Hogarth. Forward to Samuel Palmer and Stanley Spencer. Back to British Israelites, to Sir Joshua Reynolds's *Discourses*, to the 1831 *Life* of Henry Fuseli, to Gilchrist's *Life* of Blake himself, to Fuseli's *Reflections on the Painting and Sculpture of the Greeks*. Side trips to John Wilkes—what *was* the connection?—to Fox and Pitt. Stubbornly back to the texts themselves. Baffled.

What a relief it was when an eminent professor at university said in a seminar group, "What would you say was the *key* to approaching Blake?"

My God! I thought. Is there a key? Something vital I *haven't* read?

Into the thick silence, he said, "Well, the key thing about Blake was that he was a bit potty."

I've often thought of those two sixth-form years and wondered where the energy came from. I can only suppose it was repressed sexuality. There were heated rivalries amongst the boys and we were all devoted to our teacher and I think he too felt for us a kind of love. I'm not implying that this was homosexual but there was certainly some kind of sexual current. I think there always is in good teaching.

But current or no current and current of whatever nature, I would have traded away all this intellectual passion, the pleasure of a perfectly landed right hook, the ooziness of thick paint on canvas, the astonished joy on first reading "though moles see fine tonight in the snouting velvet dingles," I would have traded away all this and any imagined future for the possibility of touching the breasts of the girl who lived next door but one away. Her name was Mary.

My real initiation into the world of books happened just before I went to university. My father had been transferred from Beckenham to Leicester, an unlovely city. Although it had been an important Roman administrative centre little of any antiquity had been spared. The factories were brutal, the streets and housing mean. Guidebooks describe the city as: "Noted for its bulk manufacture of boots and shoes."

I fell into the habit of walking every day to the museum. They had on display a small collection of oils and watercolours by Edward Ardizzone whose work as an illustrator I'd been drawn to some years earlier when I'd seen his cramped and spiky drawings in H. E. Bates's two story collections, *My Uncle Silas* and *Sugar for the Horse*.

Strolling back home one afternoon along New Walk, trees and shrubbery on one side, small houses on the other, I saw a sign in a window: Books. I opened the front door and found myself in a small hallway which was stacked with books on either side. Books almost blocked the staircase to the second floor. I edged along the hall until it opened onto what must once have been a sitting room. It was now a cave of books. Shelved floor to ceiling but most of the floor stacked perilously with thousands more books. Most of them were leather bound.

Sitting at a desk in the middle of the room was a Dickensian figure in rumpled cardigan, *muffler*, pipe ash and dottle. Behind thick glasses his eyes were swimmy as raw oysters. He wore woollen gloves with the fingers cut off. There was a strong suggestion about him of a Peter Sellers character. I asked if I might look round. Although it was full summer the gas fire burbled and popped in the room's silence. On the desk top were a packet of Chocolate Wholewheat Digestives and a large magnifying glass.

Most of the books were eighteenth and early nineteenth century, bound in full calf, but here and there standing out because of their lighter colour were earlier books bound in vellum. I had not had the opportunity before to handle so many old books. On the bottom shelves massive leather-bound folios. I was mesmerized. I felt excited and in some way upset. I was unable to take it all in. *Flustered* is perhaps the word. Titles appeared out of the blur of leather and cloth. Dugdale's *Antiquities of Warwickshire*, William Camden's *Britannia*, Layard's *Nineveh and Its Remains*, Surtees's *Jorrocks's Jaunts and Jollities*, Thomas Love Peacock's *Headlong Hall*.

It felt to me like uncovering a treasure trove, a Sutton Hoo of books, one glittering marvel after another. The room was very hot and the smell of leather heavy. I felt almost as if I were sinking into the books, swooning. I found a three-volume leather-bound edition of *The History of Tom Jones, a Foundling* and asked how much it was. He opened the first volume and peered through the magnifying glass at the title page.

"Are you a local boy?"

"No, we've just moved here."

"I don't get many boys in here local *or* otherwise."

"The books are beautiful."

He looked up at me with swimmy eyes.

"Beautiful," he repeated. "Hmm. Well, well. You're a rum one and no mistake."

"Why rum?"

"And what will you do with our Mr. Jones?"

"Well, I like the story," I said and then, shy and blushing but somehow compelled, rushed on, "but I'd like to own a book that someone held and read in the eighteenth century."

He twisted his head round and up and opened his mouth and made a caricature of astonishment.

"'Pon my soul!" he said. "*Upon my soul!* Ten bob."

I was soon going to see Bernard Halliday nearly every day. It was a fortunate conjunction for both of us as I was eager to learn and he was lonely and longing to teach. He instructed me to buy John Carter's *ABC for Book Collectors* and his *Taste and Technique in Book Collecting.* Then I was to read Lowndes's *Bibliographer's Manual of English Literature.* Later he guided me through the gruelling terrain of Ronald McKerrow's *An Introduction to Bibliography for Literary Students.* He taught me to read catalogues and gave me old catalogues from Maggs and Quaritch.

"Always read catalogues," he'd say. "Catalogues are where all the knowledge sifts down to."

If I made mistakes he would say sternly, "It behooves you to know what's o'clock." The tea I brewed for us he dismissed as "maiden's water." Modern first editions were anathema. "No different from gambling." And then with shaking shoulders he forced out, "Some bloody pillocks collect . . . *detective stories!*"

I soaked up Mr. Halliday's outpouring of information. How to clean dust-soiled vellum bindings. Better than any gum or rubber eraser was white sliced bread. How to straighten bowed boards. Leather soap. Neat's-foot oil. The uses of lighter fluid.

I wallowed in bindings and leathers and fonts, in all the lovely jargon of the trade, half-titles, colophons, blind stamping, foxing, black letter, washed leaves, cancels . . . I came to believe that there were few things in the world more beautiful than the deep burning black of Baskerville type on crisp rag paper.

The best part of this education, however, was simply handling the books in their hundreds, coming to an understanding of the meaning of condition. I would take volumes to him excavated from the filthy piles and he would say, "So *that's* where that went. Well! Well! Interesting old book that. Russian. St. John Chrysostom. Know what that means? 'Golden Mouth.' Homilies, these are. Parchment and written in a nice hand. How much? Oh, I don't know. I could let you have it for nine thousand . . ."

He would then break down in rheumy mirth and mop at his eyes with his grubby handkerchief.

He did give me what are called "reading" or "working" copies of various of the well-known eighteenth-century novels. Both terms mean "damaged" or "in non-collectible condition." I remember taking to Canada Mackenzie's *The Man of Feeling*, Graves's *The Spiritual Quixote* (much appreciated because it is a satire on Methodism), and Smollett's *Roderick Random*. He also gave me "reading" copies of anonymous eighteenth-century novels typically written "By a Lady."

Anonymous novels are catalogued, incompletely, in a work by Halkett and Laing entitled *A Dictionary of the Anonymous and Pseudonymous Literature of Great Britain*. I've never read any kind of survey which talks about them *as literature*. During those visits to that filthy house with the musty smell of old leather and old paper in my nostrils, I imagined reading those novels in Halkett and Laing and writing about them as the matrix, as it were, from which rose the peaks of Richardson, Fielding, Smollett, Sterne . . .

That germ of an idea never left me and many years later in Canada, after various false starts, and with some guidance from the Vancouver book dealer William Hoffer and with the almost fatherly advice and encouragement of the Ottawa dealer Richard Simmins, I did form a collection of over five thousand volumes which documented the short story in Canada in the twentieth century. I also built collections of Contact Press and the House of Anansi Press, both of which were bought by the National Library of Canada.

ALMA MATER

DISSOLUTE would perhaps be the best word to describe my university years. I left home at eighteen to go to Bristol and never went home again. Set free for the first time in my life and entirely lacking any form of supervision I began to lead a life of excess. I was celebrating my escape from my mother and her cheerless and puritanical background which firmly equated sex with sin. I was also celebrating my escape from a suffocating and numbing middle-class existence.

In the story "Single Gents Only" I wrote:

> But he found it easier to approach what he would become by defining what he was leaving behind. What he most definitely *wasn't*—hideous images came to mind: sachets of dried lavender, Post Office Savings Books, hyacinth bulbs in bowls, the *Radio Times* in a padded leather cover embossed with the words *Radio Times*, Sunday-best silver tongs for removing sugar-cubes from sugar-bowls, plump armchairs.

My years at Bristol seem to me now sunlit and lazy and always expanding and deepening in new pleasures. The intellectual aspect of the university did not weigh on me. It was all something of an anti-climax after the intensity of those sixth-form years. There were gaps to be plugged, of course, and I plugged them; I endured the tedium of Chaucer's supposed translation of *The Romaunt of the Rose*, Malory's *Morte d'Arthur* and Burton's *The Anatomy of Melancholy* and suchlike—the sort of works that Philip Larkin would have dismissed as "ape's bumfodder."

The main chore at Bristol was having to attend weekly seminars for three years in Anglo-Saxon. After having ground through the vocabulary and grammar I was able to translate such gripping fragments as remain: *The Battle of Maldon*, the poems of Cynewulf, the voyages of the intrepid Ohthere and Wulfstan, and *The Battle of Brunanburh*, a poem of 73 lines about a battle between an army of Norsemen and Scots and an army of West Saxons and Mercians. The location of Brunanburh is unknown but it was apparently near the sea.

Oh, wens and thorns!

It was not enough to keep the mind alive.

The only other constraints on a carefree life were a Shakespeare seminar with L. C. Knights and occasional meetings with my Moral Tutor, the poet Charles Tomlinson. He was myopic and morose and kept the blinds and curtains in his office permanently closed so that meetings with him were like sitting in a gloomy tent. It surprised me that this frail little man rode a motorcycle. He kept it in the office beside his desk because he claimed his landlady's dog had once bitten it. I was supposed to write essays for him but he hadn't sufficient energy to invent titles and I really couldn't spare the time. After a few visits I stopped going regularly and just popped in occasionally to see that he was all right.

Insofar as I could, I let the university fall away from me. I was supposed to wear a gown at all times, not only in the university but in the streets. I did so for the first couple of weeks, then stopped as I looked and felt daft. On colder nights I wore it in bed.

Pubs became my second home. Rough pubs sold Somerset "scrumpy," a still cider, somewhat sour and of ferocious potency. Really rough pubs sold a truly disgusting Bristol speciality, a half-and-half mixture of draught bitter and draught port. I became so accepted in my local that I was asked to join the darts team, a great honour in a pub where students were barely tolerated. Many of the clientele were Bristol-born Jamaicans, street-fighting men who lived by breaking and entering and extortion and, in one case, because of the girth of his appendage, by starring in extremely rude movies.

The landlord's wife produced such typical pub fayre as cheddar cheese cobs, Scotch eggs, Cornish pasties, pork pies, and pickled eggs in a jar of cloudy liquid. Someone had printed on the jar's label: No Farting. She it was, rather than her husband, who waded into altercations; even the Jamaicans were frightened of her. It was the sort of pub where on the evening opening hour of six, old men with the shakes would say, "Just pick that up and hold it to my lips, boy." Others would wag a fatherly finger and say, "You take after me, lad. Never more than thirteen pints a night."

My other consuming interest was, of course, girls. I went from the famine of a single-sex school to feast. It seemed I was never without female companionship, none of it serious on either side in a long-term kind of way but always generous and affectionate and often torrid. The most extraordinary of these liaisons happened in Jersey where I was by accident working on a farm and sleeping in a barn with peasants brought in from Normandy as casual labour. Among them were identical twin sisters, largish girls, and I ended up in bed with both of them at the same time. There had been nothing Casanova-ish on my part. They just came and got me.

I had deliberately delayed applying for a room in a Hall of Residence in the hope that by the time I did they'd all be taken. A Hall of Residence sounded institutional to me and unlikely to tolerate what I vaguely had in mind. I was more interested in what the university called Alternative Accommodation and alternative accommodation I certainly got. My story "Single Gents Only" has more than a tinge of autobiography in it. "The Lady Who Sold Furniture" also has a basis in fact. In the first weeks of that first term I moved four times. I stayed in a succession of peculiar places. One was actually a boarding house with long-term non-student residents who addressed each other as Mr. and Miss. They were variously weird—a walleye, a toupee, tics—and all behaved with a creaking formality. Dinners were eaten in mincing, lip-dabbing silence. The owners of this mausoleum exhibited a ghastly gentility, the husband, cavalry twill trousers, Viyella shirts, and lemon silk cravats, his having been a pooh-bah of some sort in Uttar Pradesh. I thought of him as "The Major." Mrs. Major draped herself in ankle-length Paisley-pattern material. At night she left out in the dining room festive thermos flasks of cocoa and biscuits on doilies for the inmates.

In the hall suspended from a mahogany frame hung a huge Benares brass gong chased and enamelled in red and green. On the frame's mahogany ledge lay a padded striker, a long mahogany handle and a fleece-covered head the size of a baseball. Arrived back from the pub on my fifth night of residence and standing in the silent hall I could no longer resist the golden invitation. I gave the gong a two-handed BONG. The sound was astounding. The sound waves shimmered on for ever. In a panic I put the striker back on its ledge but it fell and as I stooped to pick it up my head hit the edge of the gong again. The inmates began to come down the staircase in their dressing gowns and leather slippers and stood whispering and sibilant. Mrs. Major appeared horribly without makeup and wearing a hairnet. I started up the stairs towards my room.

Someone said, "One can't just . . ."

I could feel all their eyes on my back.

I got the boot in the morning from The Major.

I found a room in a house of students the next day through an advertisement in the Students' Union building. Settled in, I fell into the habit of reading into the small hours and getting up at about 11:30 in the morning. Breakfast was usually scrumpy and Madras beef curry.

At a party one night I met a first-year student called David Hirschmann. He was taking an honours degree in philosophy. Standing in the kitchen, David pouring wine for revellers, we started chatting in an idle sort of way. After a couple of hours the conversation had become deeply personal. We left the party and walked and talked, sat in a park on a bench and talked. Talked until dawn surprised us. By breakfast time we had agreed that we had to move in together as soon as this could be arranged. It was a relationship that lasted for many years. I was very shaken last year when other Bristol friends, Charles and Penny Denton, wrote to tell me that David had cancer of the brain. He had been given, they said, about three months. I was making preparations to go to see him when Penny Denton wrote again to tell me he had died.

David was gentle, kind, quick-witted, but at the same time rather clumsy and goofy. One Sunday evening four of us decided that we wanted to go to a restaurant in Clifton but we had no cash. David was the most respectable-looking of us, so we decided that he should put on his suit and see if the owner would accept a cheque. The restaurant had about eight tables and the owner cooked on an open grill at the far end of the room. David opened the door, did something Tati-like with his umbrella, and quite literally *fell* into the restaurant, landing heavily on his back. Guido, the owner, hurried between the tables and stood looking down. David, bright red in the face and still supine, said, "May we pay by cheque?"

David's father was a doctor in Hampstead. His mother had been a matron in a large London hospital. Perhaps because of this background he was fastidiously clean and when we were living together he would actually dust things and put books into piles and hold wineglasses up to the light to check them for cleanliness. He used to nag me.

"Surely you don't expect her to sleep in *those* sheets, do you?" We were in a way like the Odd Couple. David would listen to Pablo Casals playing the unaccompanied cello suites; I would then claim the record player to listen to the majestic misery of Ma Rainey singing "Deep Moanin' Blues" and "Daddy, Goodbye" along with jugs booming and kazoos blatting.

David's girlfriends continued to be hopelessly neurotic. We suffered through a girl who appeared far too frequently in the middle of the night weeping and accusing David of base infidelities, a girl who swallowed pills and had to be pumped out, a kleptomaniac on probation, a girl who was quite enthusiastic about sexual intercourse but who refused to remove her bra, saying only that she "couldn't," and a girl who cut herself. I think he was attracted to the idea of helping them.

Eventually a small group of us, David, Charles Denton, Penny Player, and Walter Smith lived together in various combinations. Wally had two great enthusiasms—wine and bullfighting. Hemingway's *Death in the Afternoon* was a Bible in whatever rooms we were occupying. Harvey's, the famous Bristol wine merchants and purveyor of Harvey's Bristol Cream, held an annual sale of half bottles of discontinued wines; Wally spurred us on to buy dozens of these. We were, he said, to taste them and make notes about each in an attempt to educate our palates. To Wally's distress we drank the entire "cellar" over a two-day period, in a fug of cigarette smoke, and shot pigeons from the window with my Belgian .410 shotgun.

One of David's great enthusiasms was films and we went every week to the university film society. I watched all the classic material, not realizing at the time that I was getting an education in writing. We watched Sergei Eisenstein's *The Battleship Potemkin, Alexander Nevsky*, and *Ivan the Terrible*, Erich von Stroheim, Luis Buñuel, Vittorio de Sica, Robert Bresson's harrowing *Diary of a Country Priest*, all the early Bergman—*Summer with Monika, Smiles of a Summer Night, The Seventh Seal, Wild Strawberries, The Magician*.

I was particularly attracted to the silent comedies, to Buster Keaton, Harold Lloyd, Harry Langdon, and Charlie Chaplin. I loved the timing and grace of these performances. But perhaps my favourite films were Jacques Tati's *Jour de fête, Les Vacances de Monsieur Hulot*, and *Mon Oncle*. There are scenes in all three films which I've treasured for most of my life. Who could be unaffected by the postman in *Jour de fête* diverging from the Tour de France to cycle full-tilt into a lake? What could be funnier than Monsieur Hulot being catapulted into the sea by the sudden tightening of a tow-rope he is stepping over? It is the *delicacy* of Tati that enraptures me. I believe profoundly in the Hulot world.

The best was yet to come in the sixties and early seventies. In Montreal I used to go regularly to the Elysée theatre, which showed Bertolucci, Fassbinder, Fellini, Antonioni, and Satyajit Ray. Then suddenly I lost interest in films. The world had changed. Films shrank towards cartoons. The last film I had any relish for was Fellini's *Amarcord* in 1973.

David's death brought me back into contact with Charles and Penny Denton. After university Charles went to work as a freelance television producer. He then became ATV controller of programs. He was head of BBC TV Drama for three years. Governor of the British Film Institute. He is a member of the Arts Council of England and a Fellow of the Royal Society of Arts.

I have a memory of coming home one afternoon to hear Charles playing his saxophone. The sound seemed to be coming from the bathroom. He was sitting in a tub of hot water, sax over the side.

I said, "Why have you got your jeans on?"

He said, "It's solid, man. It's concrete."

Who can foresee the future?

One enthusiasm I didn't share with David or any of the others was rock climbing. I had joined the university club in my first week. I have no idea why. Experienced climbers taught beginners the mysteries of belaying, of feeding rope to the leader of the pitch, and the uses of slings, pitons, and carabiners. We climbed in the Avon Gorge on a cliff face very close to the Clifton Suspension Bridge. The club had a handbook of the various climbs and graded them for difficulty. One nightmare was called Dawn Walk, a traverse pitch which was completely unprotected. A tiny fault perhaps an eighth of an inch wide led upwards across the rock face. The only holds were flakes, cracks, and crimps. It was essential to keep moving as there was nowhere to rest.

After a few months I started going to Wales with some of the other club members. We went to the Llanberis Pass and climbed the gloom of the Idwal slabs. I wonder sometimes why I suffered the terrors of Idwal. The pitches were cruel, the bruising from the ropes after coming off the face was Technicolor. Nowadays, the prospect of mounting a stepladder induces mild hysteria and nausea. Changes with age, someone told me, to the inner ear.

In 1958 Wally Smith was agitating for a visit to Spain. He performed veronicas and naturels with sheets and raincoats; he begged us to charge him; he accepted ears. He practised that arms-wide, defiant thrusting out of chest and loins towards the bull known as an *adorno* until we reminded him that Hemingway had considered it vulgar. We decided that as true believers in Hemingway we'd go to the fiesta of San Fermín in Pamplona. We planned to hitchhike down through

France and cross into Spain at St. Jean de Luz, take a bus to San Sebastian, and a train from there to Pamplona. We planned not to hitchhike in Spain because the word was that the Guardia Civil were erratic.

David and I hitchhiked together and made good time towards Bordeaux. We were dropped off one lunchtime on the outskirts of Angoulême. I was ravenous and we found a small café with outside tables alongside a chicken run. The owner came out and we ordered omelettes and salads.

"It's not very clean, is it?" said David.

Who'd been tiresome for two days about toilets.

Clean it wasn't and it stank of chicken shit but it turned out to be the site of a miraculous event.

The omelette was runny inside. The salad was slices of tomato in a vinaigrette dressing with fresh-ground black pepper. This was the first omelette I'd ever eaten. It was superb. I was astonished. I had eaten things before that my mother *called* omelettes but compared with *this* delicacy they were like shoe soles.

Food in England in the fifties was as bad as food is now in the Balkans. My mother's cooking was good but it was narrowly traditional. To this day she cannot envision rice or pasta; they are too deeply foreign. The British are capable of almost any culinary perversion: curry on chips, spaghetti on chips (or toast!) Chip butties. English awfulness about food can undermine the strongest ethnic traditions; in a Chinese restaurant in Soho I was once served sweet-and-sour Brussels sprouts.

My wife, Myrna, remembers the childlike wonder with which the British greeted eggplants. The Sunday colour supplements carried photographs of them, articles explained what they were, recipes suggested what might be done with them. This was in 1965.

Unless one were wealthy or had travelled widely I don't think many young people in the fifties in England had much idea of what food might be. The war years had been grim. Compulsory cod-liver oil and concentrated orange juice for children, the residue of the tablespoon of oil reacting with the sweetness of the juice to produce daily and instant nausea before school. School dinners. Powdered milk. Powdered eggs. Strawberry jam made of turnips.

The B.C. novelist John Mills grew up in London. He told me that they used to have a version of spotted dick for school dinners. It was made from flour and water and steamed in a cylinder which opened in half lengthways. The resultant grey-white tube of pudding was then cut into rounds. The children called this dessert "dead man's leg."

This simple meal in Angoulême was momentous for me; it was the first time I grasped the *idea* of food.

When I think now of Spain I think always of being in the *plaza de toros* after the *paseo* but before the first bull has erupted from the *toril*. In my mind's eye I see the first matador's *cuadrilla* flaring out the yellow-and-magenta fighting capes and sprinkling them with water to weight them against even a flip of evening breeze.

Workmen preparing to work.

The fiesta in Pamplona is rather frightening if one is sober. The entire town is drunk for days on end. It vibrates with crazed energy. From early morning when the signal rockets go up to announce that the bulls have been released, are coming *now*, six Miura bulls jostling along the streets with four steers to calm them, the mob of runners glancing back to see the horns swaying behind them, until 5 p.m. when the *corrida* starts, the entire town drinks.

Sometimes a bull gets separated from the herd and the police yell and scream warnings as a solo bull is dangerous and will kill. Many of the young *aficionados* are still drunk from the night before when they pile into the *plaza de toros* ahead of the running bulls. After the bulls are herded into the *toril* a young heifer with padded horns is loosed into the ring. The *aficionados* perform self-absorbed, exaggerated passes with jackets, shirts, or sheets of newspaper.

A very tall boy from California takes the heifer by the horns and dumps it on its side rodeo-style. The Spanish boys are outraged at this insult to taurine dignity and mob him and beat him rather badly.

Many of the peasants in their traditional white clothes with red neckerchiefs and red cummerbunds and nearly all the hundreds of American and British students carry the traditional wineskins from which they drink all day. The skins are coated inside with pitch which renders the wine even more vile than it naturally is. In the restaurants, the waiters, unasked, put on every table three opened bottles of wine—red, white, rosé. The stacks of saucers rise on the outdoor café tables which are haunted by sellers of lottery tickets and beggars hawking postcard photographs of Franco. Shoeshine boys crawl under tables grabbing at feet until they are heaved away.

In this alcoholic haze things happen. A brass band appears playing a *paso doble*, a procession of giant puppets meanders past, figures representing Kings and Queens and Moors. Groups of peasants spring suddenly into one of the local dances. A statue of the Virgin Mary is borne about the town seated on a throne; the throne is carried on the shoulders of young men all wearing blue blouses. A large open car drives up and down the streets. In the back sit three young women in white ruffled dresses who throw the heads of fresh flowers into the crowds. No one knows who they are. In the middle of the square a priest in a black soutane, gravely drunk, is conducting a series of *verónicas* with an American flag.

None of this seems peculiar.

We were lucky that year to see graceful and heart-stopping fighting by Paco Camino. The choreography and rhythm of the passes was thrilling; he was fighting so close to the bulls that their withers bumped him pass after pass smearing him with blood. He was taking his *alternativa*. We saw fights on the way home in the hills in Huesca, the buildings still pocked with Civil War bullet holes, in Bilbao, in San Sebastian, and then over the border in Pau and Dax, all getting progressively worse.

I went to Pamplona again in 1959 with a girlfriend. It was the year Hemingway was writing *The Dangerous Summer* for *Life* magazine. He was following the mano-a-mano fights by Antonio Ordóñez and Luis Miguel Dominguin. On one of the days of the fiesta Hemingway was seated at the *barrera* with his entourage of about seven people. The first matador spread a fighting cape over the *barrera* in front of Hemingway and dedicated to him the Miura horror that had just trotted out into the sunshine.

Walking back into town from the *plaza de toros* after the fights were over I saw Hemingway and his group. Two of these were young, beautiful American girls and there was a girl even younger, dark-haired and sounding Irish. I was callow enough to speak to him. I told him I loved his writing. For a famous man accosted in the street by a kid he was civil enough.

Back in Bristol these sunlit days came to an end. We had graduated and David set off to Cambridge to begin a Ph.D. in philosophy. I've always remembered his answer attempting to explain to me what philosophy was all about if it *wasn't* about what constitutes living a good life. "Well," he said, with a certain exasperation, "it's about what we *mean* when we say 'I posted a letter.'"

Christ!

Charles and Penny got married and Charles moved into the world of documentary films. He directed one that involved endless travel in the United States and endless nights in isolated motels. I asked him if this wasn't tedious. "Oh, no," he said. "I always travel with Trollope's *Chronicles of Barsetshire.*" Wally disappeared into the mysteries of the wine trade. I felt lonely and abandoned. I could think of nothing I wanted to do. I was reluctant to give up idleness, curry for breakfast, darts, and beer, and so, adrift, I signed up for the buffooneries of a year in the Bristol University Education Department to acquire a teaching certificate.

University departments of education seem to be universally staffed by dimwits and ninnies. I could barely endure the indignities of that year and attended lectures as rarely as possible. It was intellectually repugnant. One woman lecturer advocated the choral speaking of verse as a way of leading children towards the light. A tall bearded Quaker in Quaker sandals considered Tolkien's *The Hobbit* an excellent vehicle of moral instruction; part of his course involved drawing dragons, Orcs, Gandalf, and Bilbo Baggins with coloured pencils *on parchment*. Others favoured recorder playing and the singing of roundelays. Origami. Aquariums. Calligraphy. Hamsters. The year was like being incarcerated in a twee loony bin.

My first year of teaching was even worse. I disliked the incipient violence which brooded over what I will call Bluebell Secondary Modern School. The headmaster was obsessed with Control and gave a strong impression of being insane. I sketched a portrait of him in my novella "The Lady Who Sold Furniture."

The bus lumbered down from my flat towards Bristol city centre, through all the commerce, on through the drab streets of terraced houses and small shops—newsagents, fish and chips, turf accountants—towards the decaying prefabs and the rawness of the housing estate served by Bluebell School. The invisible dividing line between the city I lived in and the city I worked in was marked for me each morning by a butcher's shop whose windows announced in whitewash capitals:

UDDER 9D PER POUND

I pretended an enthusiasm for teaching but could never persuade myself that each day wasn't futile. Teaching remedial reading and spelling to twelve-year-olds bored me. Reading the adventures of Nigel with a little West Indian girl leaking tears and snuffling.

"They always on at we."

"Who is?"

"Calling us nigger."

Staring blankly at her until it dawned that we were dealing here with the word "Nigel."

Added to such daily jollities as this were the supervision and consumption of school dinners and the recounting by some of the dullest men I've ever met of the nature of the previous evening's television programmes.

I'm what I'd call a Selective Viewer but honesty compels me to admit that last night's documentary on edible fungus . . .

At the end of this year I got a job in a reform school. In one of my stories I called this degrading establishment the Eastmill Reception Centre. The centre took in convicted boys from London, the Midlands, the West Country, and Wales and evaluated them for permanent placement in Borstals. In this dolorous dump I taught English. I think I reasoned to myself that if I didn't like teaching at the secondary modern level I'd move much lower academically and become something more akin to a social worker saving souls. I was infected at this time with mildly leftish sentiments and actually voted once for Harold Wilson, an act which now shames me profoundly.

I find that I often catch in fiction the essence of a place better than I do in exposition, probably because exposition is closer to reportage and fiction is a distillation.

What follows is from "The Eastmill Reception Centre," though it also captures something of Bluebell Secondary Modern.

I soon lost my nervousness of these boys under my charge. As the days passed, I stopped seeing them as exponents of theft, rape, breaking and entering, arson, vandalism, grievous bodily harm, and extortion, and saw them for what they were—working-class boys who were all, without exception, of low average intelligence or mildly retarded.

We laboured on with phonics, handwriting, spelling, reading.

Of all the boys, I was most drawn to Dennis. He was much like all the rest but unfailingly cheerful and co-operative. Dennis could chant the alphabet from A to Z without faltering but he had to start at A. His mind was active, but the connections it made were singular.

If I wrote CAT, he would stare at the word with a troubled frown. When I sounded out C-A-T, he would say indignantly: Well, it's *cat*, isn't it? We had a cat, old tom-cat. Furry knackers, he had, and if you stroked 'em . . .

F-I-S-H brought to mind the chip shop up his street and his mum who wouldn't never touch rock salmon because it wasn't nothing but a fancy name for conger-eel.

C-O-W evoked his Auntie Fran—right old scrubber *she* was, having it away for the price of a pint . . .

Such remarks would spill over into general debate on the ethics of white women having it off with spades and pakis, they was heathen, wasn't they? Said their prayers to gods and that, didn't they? *Didn't* they? Well, there you are then. *And* their houses stank of curry and that. You couldn't deny it. Not if you knew what you was talking about.

These lunatic discussions were often resolved by Paul, Dennis's friend, who commanded the respect of all the boys because he was serving a second term and had a tattoo of a dagger on his left wrist and a red and green humming-bird on his right shoulder. He would make pronouncement:

I'm not saying that they are and I'm not saying that they're not but what I *am* saying is . . .

Then would follow some statement so bizarre or so richly irrelevant that it imposed stunned silence.

He would then re-comb his hair.

Into the silence, I would say,

"Right. Let's get back to work, then. Who can tell me what a vowel is?"

Dennis's hand.

It's what me dad 'ad."

"What!"

"It's your insides."

"What is?"

"Cancer of the vowel."

The *only* good thing about Eastmill was that I met there the school's psychologist, James Gaite. Jim was my age, not long out of the University of Hull. His job was to interview the intake, administer standardized voodoo tests, and then assign the boys to particular reform schools, all meaningless, of course, since boys were always sent where there happened to be room.

Jim was very clever, funny, cynical, and stylish. He had been educated at a minor public school before university and affected a manner languid and rather snotty. He worked ambitiously to secure the most prestigious academic jobs and having secured them despised them. It became a pattern in Canada, the USA, and Australia. It added up in the long run to a peculiarly hollow life. The essence of the matter was, I think, that he believed in nothing and was bored. He died of cancer in Adelaide in 1999.

But in 1962 Jim was a lifeline in Eastmill. We were the only two men in the establishment with any education. We were the only two men who could not have been described as brutal. We amused and entertained each other. We could talk of books, music, film, and painting as an antidote to Eastmill's daily grind.

Again, from "The Eastmill Reception Centre."

Every afternoon was given over to Sports and Activities.

Cricket alternated, by Houses, with gardening. Gardening was worse than cricket. The garden extended for roughly two acres. On one day, forty boys attacked the earth with hoes. The next day forty boys smoothed the work of the hoes with rakes. On the day following, the hoes attacked again. Nothing was actually planted.

The evening meals in the Staff Dining Room, served from huge aluminum utensils, were exactly like the school dinners of my childhood: unsavoury stews with glutinous dumplings, salads with wafers of cold roast beef with bits of string in them, jam tarts and Spotted Dick accompanied by an aluminum jug of lukewarm custard topped by a thickening skin.

Uncle Arthur always ate in his apartment with the wife referred to as "Mrs. Arthur" but always appeared in time for coffee to inquire if we'd enjoyed what he always called our "comestibles."

Mr. Austyn, referred to by the boys as "Browner Austyn," always said:

May I trouble you for the condiments?

Between the main course and dessert, Mr. Brotherton, often boisterously drunk, beat time with his spoon, singing, much to the distress of Mr. Austyn:

Auntie Mary
Had a canary
Up the leg of her drawers.

Mr. Grendle drizzled on about recidivists and the inevitability of his being dispatched in the metalwork shop. Mr. Hemmings, who drove a sports car, explained the internal-combustion engine. Mr. Austyn praised the give and take of sporting activity, the lessons of co-operation and joint endeavour, the Duke of Edinburgh's Awards, Outward Bound, the beneficial moral results of pushing oneself to the limits of physical endurance.

But conversation always reverted to pay scales, overtime rates, the necessity of making an example of this boy or that, of sorting out, gingering up, knocking the stuffing out of etc. this or that young lout who was trying it on, pushing his luck, just begging for it etc.

When the Protestant School Board of Montreal recruiters placed advertisements in the local papers and conducted interviews in a Bristol hotel, Jim and I decided to sign on. We were both appalled by Eastmill, bored, restless. Montreal, we decided, could not be worse than being locked up with 160 dim, sad, smelly boys. And the pay compared with what we were getting at Eastmill seemed princely.

The formalities were simple. We merely had to furnish evidence of sobriety and moral probity attested to by a minister of religion and the results of a Wassermann test proving that we were not riddled with pox or clap. I promptly wrote a sickening letter and signed it as the Vicar of St. Michael and All Hallows and some days later took my place in a long line of subdued Jamaicans at the Bristol Royal Infirmary's VD Clinic. Two men in white lab coats were indulging in unseemly badinage with the clientele.

When my turn came, the technician said, "Well, then, where have you been sticking it?"

"I haven't recently," I said with some asperity, "been 'sticking it' anywhere. I'm not here for medical reasons. I only need a test because I'm emigrating."

He stared at me.

Then he shouted, "Hey, George. Come over here and listen to this one."

During these years I'd been living in rooms rented from Robert Giddings, a university friend. He had found a small house secluded at the end of a laneway and had rented it immediately. He called this house Quagmire Lodge. Bob had had the misfortune of contracting polio at the age of eleven and was confined to a wheelchair but such was his vitality and enthusiasm that one tended to forget entirely that he was crippled.

We shared a non-Leavisite passion for Dickens, Smollett, and Fielding, and Bob later in life went on to publish books on all three. This passion for the eighteenth and early nineteenth centuries meant that the house was festooned with late-state pulls of Hogarth's *Harlot's Progress*, *Rake's Progress*, and *Marriage à la Mode*. These and the caricatures of Thomas Rowlandson were then fairly cheaply available. Bob's other, slightly eccentric, passion was for German military marches. I would sometimes come home to find Bob wearing a German infantry helmet and rows of Wehrmacht medals, red in the face with the exertion of conducting records of the Berlin Military Police Band.

I chose not to probe into this enthusiasm.

We lost touch when I came to Canada but Bob phoned me last year around the time of David's death and we caught up with each other's doings. He had just retired from Bournemouth University which he claims has the distinction of being absolutely the worst university in the United Kingdom. He mentioned that he'd published an autobiography which was concerned with his life in schools and academe as a disabled person. He sent me a copy of *You Should See Me in Pyjamas* and I read with fascination of his childhood years in residential hospitals. And then I came to his years as an undergraduate at Bristol and was very surprised to read the following:

> One of the most entertaining characters I met at Bristol was my friend John Metcalf. He was a vicar's son, but none the worse for that. Going around with John was a laugh and a nightmare at the same time as you never knew what was going to happen next. In those days there was a great working-class thing on the go, Richard Hoggart had only recently published *The Uses of Literacy* and among the vogue books were *Room at the Top*, *A Kind of Loving*, and *Saturday Night and Sunday Morning*. We went about completely Sillitoed most of the time. It was all donkey jackets, football, Anger and Centre 42 (with exhibitions of workers' tools arranged in backgrounds by Feliks Topolski). John had a flat cap he called his Sou'Wester. When we were not actually out banning bombs, or compelling the government to resign, or bringing the South African economy to its knees by refusing to eat their rotten old pineapple chunks, we were in pubs swilling the plebeian natural cider. One Friday, having achieved some sort of

physical parity by encouraging friends to get paralytic, we left for home. John didn't make it back to his flat. His flat-mate assumed that he had picked up some bird, and went to bed. He'd be home the next day. But he wasn't. Nor the next day. No one saw him for two weeks. Then he suddenly reappeared. He'd fallen off the docks, landed in an open boat and finished up—penniless—in the Channel Islands where he'd had to get a job packing tomatoes to earn his fare back.

One of his relatives gave him a pocket-sized radio as a birthday present. It never worked properly but by turning the volume up suddenly you could get a sound like a burst of applause in radio programmes. John always carried it with him to provide instant approbation for wit and repartee. He eventually became literary editor of *Nonesuch* and soon we were in hot water, which resulted in our being brought before one of the university's most senior administrators.

We wanted to publish John's review of *Lady Chatterley* (just published unexpurgatedly by Penguin) in the university newspaper. The authorities had hit the ceiling. We were threatened with rustication, suspension and all the terrors of the earth. John stuck it out. The interview was, as they say, a stormy one. The authorities insisted that nothing should appear which might bring a blush to the cheek of a young person. Some of the short words used had, it seems, caused offence. We were interviewed by a man called Landless. In the course of this scene, without batting an eyelid, John called him Landslide, Landscape, Landgrave, Landlord, Landwehr, Landlubber and Landmine. The result was a compromise. The review appeared but contained such gems as "Lawrence overworks his vocabulary, especially the words ____ and ____."

But his finest hour was on teaching practice. Taking a class for the Napoleonic wars he was interrupted by a boy who said: "We got one of they cannon things at home. Our dad's in the Navy and they use them for warnings an' that. I'll bring it in tomorrow." The next day the boy duly appeared, staggering under a weighty load. "I got it, sir! And all the gubbins that go with it. Okay if we fire it out the window?" To his everlasting credit, John decided to go and ask the headmaster first.

The school was a vast modish glasshouse and after several long corridors and staircases John reached the headmaster's office. He knocked on the door. "Come in!" As he entered there was a dull boom in the distance. "My God!" exclaimed the startled headmaster. "What on earth was that?"

"That's just what I came to see you about," said John calmly.

They rushed to the scene. In the classroom they found a large black circle on the wall, surrounded by an irregular pigmented mosaic of all the colours of the rainbow. The young cannoneer explained that they had decided it would be too dangerous to fire it out the window and to fire shells, so they had filled it with a box of coloured chalks and fired it at the classroom wall. Several windows had shattered. The whole episode caused quite a stir in our university department, but then great emphasis had been placed on the value of visual aids in those days. John went on to become a very successful teacher. Abroad.

A TERRIFYING LEGACY

JIM HAD CHARGED ME with securing us an apartment. He had flown from England to visit some friends in the States where he was busy philandering. I was limp and exhausted when the Cunard liner *Carinthia* docked in Montreal. I'd been throwing up for days; my stomach had first contracted in Liverpool when they'd switched on the engines.

I walked from the docks to the YMCA. Montreal was a throb and an exotic blur. I was bemused by size, speed, noise. An English eye could hardly make sense of it. Skyscrapers, huge cars, signs in French, police with sunglasses, paunches, and unthinkable *guns*, not a chemist's in sight but drugstores as in Raymond Chandler, crazed drivers, on Ste Catherine Street crushes of people seemingly from all over the world, neon signs, air conditioning, a sense everywhere of unimaginable affluence, shimmering heat, abominable beer . . .

I soon found us an apartment on Lincoln at Guy and thought it palatial compared with student digs in Bristol. I was later to realize it was verging on slummy but couldn't see that then.

Jim bowled into town driving a vast and vulgar red car with white upholstery.

August rolled into September and school started.

I was teaching English at Rosemount High School in the city's east end. I found out on the first day that I was also teaching Canadian history which was unfortunate for the students as I didn't know any. After Bluebell and Eastmill, Rosemount was like a rest home.

The students were polite, tolerant of the idea of learning, and mostly able to read. No one threatened me with a knife. It was refreshing.

The England I'd just left was a homogeneous society and one simply didn't come across many non-English people even at university. My most exotic racial experience at Bristol was sharing a room for a few weeks with Mrs. Bandaranaike's nephew. So I was fascinated with classes of such disparate backgrounds—Italian, Greek, Lebanese, Latvian, Chinese . . . I suddenly had a great deal to learn.

The students were pleasant and co-operative. The staff in the English department, however, were in the main gruesome. I wrote about them in an essay in my 1992 anthology *The New Story Writers*.

The head of the English department was a faded lady of ghastly, dentured gentility who wrote poems and had published a volume of them at her own expense. I can see that little book in my mind's eye even now; it was bound in nasty blue fabrikoid. One of the poems was called "Modern Menace" and warned the reader about the dangers of alcohol. My favourite lines ran:

For ways we have against this Brute,
If offered sherry, say, "Make mine Fruit!"

Once a term she would correct a set of essays from each of my classes to discipline me and to show me how a seasoned professional did the job. All her corrections were neatly written in the margins in red ink. She once ringed in red in a student's essay the sentence "My father just grunted" and wrote in the margin: "Only *piggies* grunt!!!"

Even now, some thirty years later, I still remember the mind-numbing meetings of the department. One of the compulsory textbooks contained Hemingway's story "After the Storm" and it baffled them. How could one teach it? What, Miss Perkins wanted to know, constituted a correct answer about it on the exam? Why couldn't he *say* what he wanted to say? *Exactly!* Quite right. *Get his point across.* Whatever the point might *be.* What in God's name, demanded Mr. Lumley, was it *about.* It was like watching frowning chimps trying to extract a peanut from a medicine bottle.

Jim adjusted to life in Canada far more quickly than I did. The one area where I found it impossible to adjust was language. When people spoke of "a bunch of the guys" I had to repress chidings about flowers and bananas. The spelling *gray* for *grey* distressed me for years. It was decades before I could substitute *aluminum* for *aluminium*. But when I did submit to Canadian or American usage I felt like a ham actor.

In my first Canadian spring one of the teachers said to me, "A bunch of the guys are going sugaring off. Want to come?" I gave him a *very* old-fashioned look.

The problem with these people as teachers was that they were not very well educated, remained incurious, didn't read, had no love of what they taught. They were simply doing a job. They were plonk-ingly *ordinary* and they inevitably turned out ordinary students who inevitably went on to swell Canada's dullness.

In 1972 I published a novel called *Going Down Slow* which drew on my experience of Rosemount High School. The novel's protago-nist, David, is having an affair with a student, Susan. The following lavatorial scene which declines and deflates into one-line paragraphs and silences suggests, I hope, the emotional and intellectual desola-tion of that school.

He looked out over the white-painted glass on the bottom part of the high window. It was snowing again, light flakes drifting. The air was yellow with the gloom of a storm. Goal-posts stuck black out of the snow-covered playing field. Just below in the yard, three men in overcoats were standing around Mr. Cher-ton's new Sting Ray. Mr. Davidson. Mr. Monpetit. The flow of water gurgled back into silence.

David mounted the stand and stood in the middle of the three stalls. He unzipped his trousers. Rubber footsteps squelched in the cloakroom. The swing-door banged open and Hubnichuk came in. They nodded. Hubnichuk was wearing a shabby blue track-suit.

He mounted the stand to David's left. Standing back, he pulled down the elastic front of his trousers. He cradled his organ in the palm of his hand; it was like a three-pound eye-roast. Suddenly, he emitted a tight high-pitched fart, a sound surprising in so large a man.

Footsteps.

Mr. Weinbaum came in.

"So this is where the nobs hang out!" he said.

"Some of them STICK OUT from time to time!" said Hubnichuk.

Their voices echoed.

Mr. Weinbaum mounted the stand and stood in front of the stall to David's right.

"If you shake it more than twice," he said, "you're playing with it."

Water from the copper nozzle rilled down the porcelain.

There was a silence.

David studied the manufacturer's ornate cartouche.

The Victory and Sanitary Porcelain Company.

Inside the curlicued scroll, a wreathed allegorical figure.

Victory?

Sanitation?

Mr. Weinbaum shifted, sighed.

"I got the best battery in Canada for $18.00," he said.

If "David" was having an affair in *Going Down Slow* with "Susan," John was having an affair with a student called Gale Courey. Gale was not in any of my classes but I'd noticed her in the halls not only because of her lushness but because she was always carrying jazz records. We talked together about jazz.

I had been a jazz fan since the age of twelve and during my Beckenham years had gone regularly to the London club at 100 Oxford Street where Britain's top traditional bands played—Humphrey Lyttleton, Chris Barber, and Alex Welsh. I had a large record collection of the classic material, King Oliver, Louis Armstrong, Jelly Roll Morton, and Johnny Dodds. I had a particular liking for Morton's trumpet players, Bubber Miley and Ward Pinkett. Tommy Ladnier, too. I also owned all the usual blues singers, Ma Rainey, Bessie

Smith, Ida Cox, Bertha Chippie Hill but came early to the heterodox judgement that it was hard to better Morton singing "I'm the Win'ing Boy" or Jack Teagarden shlurping and mushmouthing his way through "Stars Fell on Alabama."

England and Europe were far more receptive to the traditional jazz revival than were the States and we enthusiastically bought all the recordings. Someone—was it Lomax?—found Bunk Johnson in the parish of New Iberia and bought him teeth and in New Orleans Sharkey Bonano, Papa Celestin, George Lewis, Paul Barbarin, and Percy Humphrey recreated bands to play the old music. Much of this music came out on a label called Good Time Jazz and a good time it certainly was. I saw the last of it in 1963 in New Orleans. I wrote about that visit in my novella "Private Parts."

> I drove to New Orleans through the increasing depression of the southern States, illusions, delusions lost each day with every human contact, until I reached the fabled Quarter, and sat close to tears listening to the Preservation Hall Jazz Band—a group of octogenarians which as I entered was trying to play "Oh, Didn't He Ramble"; the solos ran out of breath, the drummer was palsied, the bass player rheumy and vacant. The audience of young Germans and Frenchmen was hushed and respectful. Between tunes, a man with a wooden leg tap-danced. I knew that if they tackled "High Society" and the clarinetist attempted Alphonse Picou's solo, he'd drop dead in cardiac arrest; the butcher had cut them down and something shining in me with them.

Gale told me one day about a Montreal club she frequented called Tête de l'Art and where she was going that evening. She suggested I join her.

As I walked into the club that night the compère was at the microphone introducing the band. "*Messieurs, Mesdames,*" he said and then turned and gestured at the pianist. "*Orace Sil-vair!*"

And Horace Silver it was, a blistering quintet with Blue Mitchell on trumpet and Junior Cook on tenor sax. It was the first time I'd heard hard bop. I was transfixed.

I ought to say something here about music in the sixties in Montreal because it was both burden and delight to me. It was, of course, a Golden Age, though I didn't quite realize that at the time. There were three currents of music flowing through the city's clubs at once. The first current was the blues/folk current or blues-packaged-as-folk.

This played at a tiny club on Victoria Avenue called the Finjan which was owned by an Israeli named Shimon Asch. Later, the same people would play at the Seven Steps on Stanley Street. There one could hear such performers as Sonny Terry and Brownie McGee. I remember one night shortly before Christmas being in the Finjan with perhaps six other people in the audience listening to John Lee Hooker. I remember the evening vividly because he sang a song entitled "Black Snake Sucking on My Woman's Tongue" and in the intermission had a screaming match on the phone with a woman in the States.

The second current flowed through the Esquire Show Bar. The Esquire featured weird rock bands like the Blue Men who all had their hair dyed blue but it also featured quite regularly the Chess label bands from Chicago. So it was nothing special to drop into the Esquire to hear Bo Diddley, Muddy Waters, and Howlin' Wolf. Bo Diddley was always a delight because he was consciously a *show* with the two maracas girls in skin-tight gold lamé jumpsuits displaying lots of jolly cleavage.

Muddy Waters and Little Walter singing "Long Distance Call," "Honey Bee," and "Standing Around Crying" were already a transcendent experience.

Howlin' Wolf was not as subtle as Muddy Waters but I think in the end he was a better bluesman. There was a *ferocity* about his band that left the listener seared. He had an almost sullen, glowering presence on stage, visibly impatient while others soloed, prowling with his harmonica, tense to be back in the fray. He never, ever gave the impression that this was just one more gig in a dirty, pissy-smelling bar. When he played, he played balls out.

His usual crew in Montreal was Willie Dixon on double bass, Jimmy Rogers and Hubert Sumlin on guitars, Otis Spann on piano, and usually Fred Below on drums. To have heard the band play "Little

Red Rooster" and "Spoonful" is to have had the bar set very high for this kind of music.

I once took Alice Munro to hear Howlin' Wolf and asked her afterwards what she'd thought. She said rather faintly, "I couldn't have imagined it."

The third current of music flowing through the city was jazz. First at the Tête de l'Art and later at the Casa Loma. At these clubs through the sixties I heard most of the jazz giants—Horace Silver, McCoy Tyner, Hank Jones, Sonny Rollins, Stitt, Monk, Dizzy, the Modern Jazz Quartet, Zoot Sims, Pepper Adams, Stan Getz, Cannonball Adderley, Art Blakey, the Basie band playing the Neal Hefti charts . . .

The list was endless.

All this was delightful but it was also nearly killing me as I had to be in school at 8 a.m.

When I came to draw on the experiences of that first year in Canada in my novel *Going Down Slow* I used as the book's epigraph a line from a Howlin' Wolf song: "The men don't know what the little girls understand." Gale certainly understood more than most; she was the *oldest* student I've ever encountered.

We had not been particularly discreet that year. Rather, we had been publicly frolicsome frequenting restaurants, jazz clubs, and movies. My insouciance suddenly started to feel dangerous. What was that sound? Could that be the Presbyterian posse not far behind? I resigned from the School Board at the end of the year and got a job in another jurisdiction.

Sometime during that second year one of my students brought into class a flyer advertising a CBC short story writing competition designed to find and encourage New Canadian Writers. She must have left it on my desk and I must have inadvertently gathered it up along with a stack of exercise books I was taking home to correct over the weekend.

Something, probably everything cumulatively thus far in my life, prompted me to enter the competition. I spent the weekend writing my first short story. It was called "Early Morning Rabbits."

It was a special *kind* of story that many writers write at the start of their careers. These stories are always about childhood and place. For some children some places are experienced as holy. For some writers, sights and sounds, these profound surfaces, survive pristine in memory into adulthood.

"Early Morning Rabbits" was about my young self on my uncle's farm in Cumberland. It was to me a magical place. I knew every inch of Low Bracken Hall, the run of its drystone walls, its warrens, its woods, the stream that dropped pool by pool down from the tarn on the fells to join the beck in the valley bottom. Even the barn and my uncle's workbench with its Gold Flake tins of wire, solder, washers, spark plugs, and split pins burned in memory. The grease gun for the tractor with chaff stuck to it . . .

Alice Munro has a couple of stories, "Images" and "Walker Brothers Cowboy" in *Dance of the Happy Shades*, which are precisely of this type. Mary Borsky's shimmering evocation of Salt Prairie in *Influence of the Moon* contains such examples of the type as "Ice" and "World Fair." In Clark Blaise's *Southern Stories* "Broward Dowdy" is another gem. Their stories are achingly beautiful and sophisticated while "Early Morning Rabbits" was, I'm afraid, rather florid. I chose to include it in my first book, *The Lady Who Sold Furniture*, in 1970 but I had by then recognized this fruity quality and toned it down. I'd probably derived it in part from "The Peaches," a story in Dylan Thomas's *Portrait of the Artist as a Young Dog*.

I sent this effort in to the CBC and was astonished when it won a prize. Two hundred dollars, as I recall. A base part of my mind calculated that I'd only need to write three a month to live like a lord. And indeed I began to scribble away.

I realized, however, that I knew very little about the genre. I had read Katherine Mansfield and Ernest Hemingway and Dylan Thomas and obviously Chekhov and Guy de Maupassant but the short story had not been taught as a form at school, and literature much past the end of the nineteenth century had not been encouraged at Bristol University. The attitude there, and a reasonable one, was that contemporary and recent writing was what one read for entertainment and as part of being a civilized person. The short story was perceived as being basically an *American* enthusiasm and therefore really beyond the purview of Britons.

I launched myself into an intensity of self-education. I read Ring

Lardner's *You Know Me Al*, lapping up that vernacular. Followed by *The Love Nest* and *How to Write Short Stories (With Samples)*. I read Sherwood Anderson's *Winesburg, Ohio*, which was brilliant, followed by several of his dreadful novels. I read, and was ravished by, Flannery O'Connor. Was overwhelmed by Eudora Welty and read and reread her. Tried to read Faulkner but couldn't. Read in rapid succession Katherine Anne Porter, Caroline Gordon, John Updike, Grace Paley's *The Little Disturbances of Man*. Returned to *Dubliners*. Meandered off into Saroyan, Joseph Mitchell, Nathanael West, Irwin Shaw, Peter Taylor . . .

What I was after, beyond the aesthetic experience itself, was to gain some idea of what possible shapes stories could take. I was also feeling out the shape of the tradition.

At the same time I was trying to acquaint myself with Canadian contributions to the form. This turned out to be simple. The only story writers at the time with published collections were Hugh Garner and Morley Callaghan. Both were touted within Canada as giants and both were unreadable, Garner because of his sentimentality and crudeness, Callaghan because his writing was flatly ludicrous.

(Unknown to me then there were two further collections of Canadian stories just published, Hugh Hood's *Flying a Red Kite* and Ethel Wilson's *Mrs. Golightly and Other Stories*.)

Robert Weaver and William Toye wrote of Callaghan in *The Oxford Anthology of Canadian Literature*: "Today he is admired by most younger writers of fiction in Canada as their only true predecessor in this country . . ."

This judgement is hilariously wide of the mark. Most "younger writers of fiction" would tend to fall about laughing at a writer capable of perpetrating: "She stood on the corner of Bloor and Yonge, an impressive build of a woman, tall, stout, good-looking for 42, and watched the traffic signal."

Although everything I was reading was new to me I had at the same time a sense that I was engaging with the past. Wonderful as Eudora Welty's *A Curtain of Green and Other Stories* was, it had been published in 1941. I had a sense of John Updike as a near-contemporary and read with great pleasure and attention *The Same Door* and *Pigeon Feathers and Other Stories* but Updike was associated with the fabled

New Yorker and moved in a world which was not the world of *The Canadian Forum* and *Fiddlehead*.

I had no sense of there being a great literary presence in Montreal, Toronto, or Vancouver; there was no Canadian tradition or body of work I could hope to join. The country lacked what would be called today an "infrastructure"—the literary equivalent of roads, sewers, electric power, railroad tracks—and I've spent nearly all my life in Canada editing, writing, anthologizing, publishing, exhorting, teaching, and collecting in a probably vain attempt to help put the necessary infrastructure into place.

The smart writers did exactly the reverse; they positioned their work in England and the United States.

I had by now piles of stories and mounting piles of rejection slips. It is usual to submit stories to magazines singly; in desperation, I sent a bundle of sixteen to *Prism International*. I was astonished when they wrote back accepting eight. And they made a fuss about them, too, saying how the stories stood out from the general ruck of submissions. They were published in the Summer and Autumn issues of *Prism International* in 1964. The person instrumental in all this was Earle Birney.

When his *Collected Poems* came out years later he inscribed a copy for me and wrote: "To John Metcalf whose fiction I've admired and continued to read ever since he sent Jake Zilber and me a stack of his short stories which we were happy to publish in *Prism International* back in the sixties when that journal was still international."

I reread those stories before writing this and found them, not surprisingly, to be no better than most juvenilia, though the themes that were to occupy me for so many years were already there. I reworked "Early Morning Rabbits" and I took some material from "Just Two Old Men" and used it in the novella "The Lady Who Sold Furniture." The rest of the stories I'm happy are forgotten. I winced at the ghastly pretentiousness of the title I'd given to the group of stories: *The Geography of Time*. I can only beg that I was young. But I was pleased to note that George Johnston had a poem in that Summer issue; he is one of Canada's finest poets and in *The Cruising Auk* wrote one of Canada's most elegant books. Years later at the Porcupine's Quill I had the honour of bringing out his collected poems,

Endeared by Dark, which George, until I dissuaded him, had wanted to call *From a Rhyming Brain*.

Gale and I were still going out together but we seemed to be quarrelling rather pointlessly. I think looking back that we were both unsure of what we wanted next. Gale was also under pressure from her parents. They were Lebanese Canadian and seemed to my WASP stolidity excitable and volatile. I had been to their apartment for meals on various occasions and the evenings passed in uproar and cacophony which seemed friendly in intent. But her parents blew hot and cold. Her father would from time to time work himself up into tirades about the nasty anatomical things he was going to do to me with his bare hands while her mother would leave block-lettered notices in the fridge reading: NONE OF THIS GOOD FOOD FOR GALE.

At the end of term I was having a beer at a neighbourhood bar and fell into conversation with a man at the next stool. His name was Meunier, from Alberta, visiting family. He, too, was a teacher. Principal of a high school. While in Montreal he was going to run some ads to secure a teacher of English. Several glasses of beer later, seduced by the high salary, I signed on the dotted line. I think that I was unconsciously simply putting some distance between me and a situation about which I wasn't decided.

This impulsive and rash act landed me the following September in Cold Lake, Alberta, honorary second lieutenant at the Cold Lake RCAF base. The base itself was featureless, a bland suburb set down in the wilderness. The nearest patch of civilian civilization—the *only* patch—was about three miles away. It was called Grand Centre. Grand Centre comprised three or four houses, a trading post that exchanged little wooden kegs of nails and the like for pelts, a laundromat, an RCMP lock-up, and a tiny Chinese restaurant that offered Canadian-Chinese food in red gooey sauce.

The contiguous Indian reserve with its abandoned cars and tumbledown hovels patched with sheet tin was a persuasive argument for assimilation.

The long winter began. Teachers drove to school from the barracks, plugged their cars into block heaters, and left the engines running all day. The cold was beyond description or belief.

I spent most of the year playing billiards and darts and going slowly stir-crazy. One was not supposed to win at darts or billiards if playing against an officer senior in rank; it was not done; it was considered bad form; I became unpopular.

The Wing Commander suggested I get my hair cut. My hair was, apparently, setting a bad example.

To whom and of what?

Did I not respect the feelings of the mess?

Not so's you'd notice.

Had I no respect for his rank?

Not a jot. Not a tittle.

Midmorning every day a Thunderbird fighter flew to the base in Comox, British Columbia, to pick up salmon for lunch.

Every day at lunchtime the Americans landed to refuel; they were flying the H-bomb around the world.

For lunch they ate the four-bean salad and the salmon.

Some people used to drive to Grand Centre to wave at the train.

Others watched the clothes tumbling in the laundromat.

Some drove to Grand Centre to eat toast at the Canadian-Chinese restaurant.

I was writing to Gale almost daily and phoning her as I could. Her letters became increasingly important to me. I was still worried about the amount of dope she smoked; she was still impatient with my "square" disapproval. I was irritated by her vocabulary, the *shit* she *scored*, the *smoke* she *toked*. Little did I know that it was soon to become a lingua franca. I remained irritated by her contempt for a university education; she was concerned that I might become an academic. She wanted me always to be "free." Never, she begged me, become *boring*. The gathering of rosebuds while she might was her general plan of action.

When the snow and ice reluctantly disappeared to be replaced by mud and mosquitoes and my servitude ended, I returned to Montreal, and Gale and I, despite the tensions between us, were married in a rather hugger-mugger fashion by a United Church cleric who obviously regarded the union with reservations but needed the money.

After a few days we left for England where we intended to stay. For a year at least we were going to live on the money I'd saved at

Cold Lake. I was going to write. We went to Bristol and stayed for a while with David Hirschmann and his wife, Jill, while looking for a flat. Gale seemed to have difficulties distinguishing between pounds and dollars and kept coming home with dismaying "bargains." I was also improvident, buying at an auction one day a Victorian chaise longue and a Regency mirror six feet high with gilded columns and capitals and gadroon beading. The end of the money was in sight.

I got a job teaching English in a Catholic comprehensive school which served a nearby housing estate. It was a grim employment. The school was staffed by teachers whose main qualification was their faith, rural Irishwomen who as they sipped their orange-coloured tea in the common room would say into the silence, apropos of God knows what, "And a blessing it is, a blessing it is."

The principal was saintly and ineffectual. When it was reported to him that the children had *again* poured their free milk into the grand piano, he murmured, "We live in an imperfect world."

The school was openly violent. Classes were searched for knives. Mr. Murphy, the deputy head, kept a cane down the leg of his trousers and would draw it like a sword, cutting at the legs and hunched backs of troublemakers. A boy in one of my "slow learner" classes set fire in his desk to a Bible and Lamb's *Tales from Shakespeare* which my predecessor had used as a remedial text. The female school-leaving class flatly refused to work, claiming that they attended only "for the cooking." After lunch, police cars and a Black Maria returned the apprehended shoplifters.

My decision to go to Canada for the first time in 1962 had been made without much thought. Neither Jim nor I at the time had any idea of leaving England permanently. We were simply bored and looking for new experience. My life was split between a decaying past which exercised a great power over me and a present which was unbearable and stretched ahead like a life sentence. Even then, I suspected that it was dangerous to live for the past and I knew I had to get out of England and escape from its dream. Joyce Cary's novel *To Be a Pilgrim*, a volume in *The Horse's Mouth* trilogy, brilliantly portrays a man in thrall to that dream of Englishness.

Had my job been interesting and comfortable, I'd doubtless have succumbed to the dream and lived out the rest of my life clad in tweed with vacations spent taking brass rubbings in medieval churches. But life at Bluebell Secondary Modern and the Eastmill Reception Centre was neither interesting nor comfortable. The staff were caricatures, the headmasters clinically insane. The pupils ranged from the merely drooling to the psychopathically loutish.

Bluebell Secondary Modern was the sort of school where homework was never assigned because the pupils returned with notes written on torn brown bag paper which said:

Dear teacher,
He have not done his sums because
its bad for his "nerves"
Thanking you, I Remain
Signed Mary Brown *(Mrs)*.

The remedial mornings were divided by school dinner from the remedial afternoons.

From a utensil of medieval aspect and proportions, greasy stew studded with emerald processed peas was ladled by the grubby monitor. The stew was followed by steamed pudding and aluminum jugs of custard topped by a thickening skin.

Leaving was no difficulty.

Return to Canada was a relief. Canada, after England, seemed filled with rising hope. Expo 67 in Montreal marked some kind of high point. My writing career was soon to get under way. My daughter was born in 1969. Looking back now, I would say that the euphoria everyone seemed to be feeling began to fall apart in about 1975.

I suffered from the delusion that Canada could be improved. Since then, I feel that year by year Canada has been in continuous cultural decline. Our schools are a disaster. Our public life is a grim farce; the present minister of defence was unaware of Dieppe and confuses Vimy with Vichy.

The leaching away of knowledge, taste, and sophistication might be well suggested in this June 1989 *Ottawa Citizen* column by Marjorie Nichol.

Pierre Juneau, the retiring president of the CBC, has had an eventful public career. It is doubtful, though, that Juneau will ever forget the events of the afternoon of May 24, 1989.

On that day Juneau appeared, probably for the last time, before the Commons committee on communications and culture, which examines CBC policy and spending.

The main topic of discussion, not surprisingly, was the draconian cuts to the CBC budget meted out in the new federal budget. Over the next four years $140 million will be lopped off the corporation's budget.

Juneau painted an extremely bleak picture of the CBC's future, predicting that "a slaughter" will be required to keep the broadcasting behemoth afloat.

Committee members badgered the president to say how he would deal with the corporation's fiscal crises. He demurred, stating repeatedly that salvaging the CBC will be a task for its next president to be appointed next month by Brian Mulroney.

The newly appointed chairman of this prestigious Commons committee is Felix Holtmann, a two-term Conservative MP from the Manitoba riding of Portage-Interlake.

What follows is a verbatim excerpt from that committee meeting.

Chairman Holtmann: ". . . I have listened to CBC radio, CBC television back home and you have programming that sometimes goes on for hours without any advertising in it at all. Either there are no listeners or you are afraid to advertise. I do not know what the darn reason is.

"But I think if you advertised even a little you would wake some people up who were listening to some of these long, drawn-out musicians from some other country . . ."

John Harvard (Lib-Winnipeg/St. James): "You are talking radio?"

Ian Waddell (NDP-Port Moody/Coquitlam): "What is it, Bach or something like that?"

Chairman Holtmann: "Something like that. Why should they get to listen to that for nothing?"

Harvard: "Nothing?"

Chairman Holtmann: "Why are you afraid to advertise and recover, well, the money. Of course the taxpayers are paying for it, if you are not advertising. Why are you not throwing an advertisement in every once in a while to pay for that programming?"

Harvard: "My God."

Pierre Juneau: "Mr. Chairman, since I said CBC management would present to the CBC board a list of every possibility, no doubt that one will be included. I would not call it an option, because I personally would be against it."

Chairman Holtmann: "You personally would be against it?"

Juneau: "Yes, I would."

Chairman Holtmann: "I do not understand that."

Juneau: "I will explain why, but never mind. As I said, I will not be there when the decision is made . . . There is a condition of licence, and if you read the Broadcasting Act, a condition of licence is like law. There is a condition of licence that prohibits advertising on CBC radio except in very, very few cases . . ."

Chairman Holtmann: ". . . You said you are against it; I suppose your board is against it too, or something like that."

Juneau: "I would say the majority of the board are."

Chairman Holtmann: "What is the rationale for being against something like that? What is cultural to Canada's culture to listen to Beethoven? Is it because you are interfering with our culture? You guys have lost me on that one."

At the close of the committee hearing Chairman Holtmann confessed that culture and communications are not his first area of expertise or interest.

As he put it, "Hogs and cows are things I have been associated with more." He then wished Juneau "good luck in any retirement that you get involved with."

But it is not simply living in cultural desolation which is turning my thoughts again towards England. It is the pain, more heartfelt every year, of not living in history.

The English past still grips me. The parish church, Norman, with its yew trees and lichened tombstones, the pub, the village green or square, behind the high stone walls the manor house . . . I am still a captive of the dream.

Momentous as getting married and moving to England and then returning to Canada had been, something equally momentous had occurred in my artistic life. In 1964 I had happened upon a book which exploded upon me. It overwhelmed me. I was *consumed* by this book. It was so big, so perfect, so merciless that I could live inside it. The book was Richard Yates's story collection *Eleven Kinds of Loneliness*. Years later *Esquire* wrote of him, "Richard Yates is one of America's least famous great writers."

The book had been published in 1962. It was a first book of stories. The author was older than me but not by much. The stories were dazzling. It wasn't the writing itself which excited me so much. Yates had a simple and unadorned style. What excited me was that someone had produced a work of art which was within striking distance of perfection and they'd done it not in 1941 but *now, today*. The book opened up the possibility that someone else could attain the same distinction. It gave me a mark to aim at. It also validated the entire genre for me, made me feel intensely that a lifetime spent in achieving just one such book was more than justified. With at this point just a handful of juvenile scribbling to my name, I consciously dedicated the rest of my life to achieving that book and to the service of literature in general in my time and place.

This zeal may sound priggish but I was in a state of exhilaration. Yates made me feel what Philip Larkin felt on hearing Sidney Bechet:

> On me your voice falls as they say love should,
> Like an enormous yes.

By the end of 1999 all of Richard Yates's novels and story collections were out of print. Writing of him in the *Boston Review*, the novelist Stewart O'Nan said:

> Across his career he was consistently well-reviewed in all
> the major places, and four of his novels were selections of the

Book-of-the-Month Club, yet he never sold more that 12,000 copies of any one book in hardback.

If his work was neglected during his lifetime, after his death it has practically disappeared. Of the tens of thousands of titles crammed into the superstores, not one is his . . .

To write so well and then to be forgotten is a terrifying legacy. I always think that if I write well enough, the people in my books—the world of those books—will somehow survive. In time the shoddy and trendy work will fall away and the good books will rise to the top. It's not reputation that matters, since reputations are regularly pumped up by self-serving agents and publicists and booksellers, by the star machinery of Random House and the *New Yorker*, what matters is what the author has achieved in the work, on the page. Once it's between the covers, they can't take it away from you; they have to acknowledge its worth. As a writer, I have to believe that.

This is the mystery of Richard Yates: how did a writer so well-respected—even loved—by his peers, a writer capable of moving his readers so deeply, fall to all intents out of print, and so quickly? How is it possible that an author whose work defined the lostness of the Age of Anxiety as deftly as Fitzgerald's did that of the Jazz Age, an author who influenced American literary icons like Raymond Carver and André Dubus, among others, an author so forthright and plainspoken in his prose and choice of characters, can now be found only by special order or in the dusty, floor-level end of the fiction section in secondhand stores? And how come no one knows this? How come no one does anything about it?

THE YEARS WITH ROSS

IN 1966 I WAS CONTACTED by Earle Toppings, then senior editor at the Ryerson Press. He was working on an anthology entitled *Modern Canadian Stories* selected and edited by Giose Rimanelli and Roberto Ruberto. Earle Birney contributed a foreword and had been influential behind the scenes. They wished to include two of my stories previously published in *Prism International*. This was an important publication for me for a variety of reasons. The book represented only the fourth time since Raymond Knister's *Canadian Short Stories* in 1928 that Canadian story writers had been anthologized. I had been placed in the company of people whose work interested me—Mordecai Richler, Alice Munro, Hugh Hood, Ethel Wilson, and Irving Layton. It also introduced me to Earle Toppings, who became a friend. Lastly, it had given me an entrée to the Ryerson Press.

I used to send Earle stories which he read and discussed with me but wisely refused to publish. He thought I needed a book from a smaller press first. He took it upon himself to take a group of my stories to Stan Bevington at Coach House. Stan accepted the book and I was set to become the first collection of fiction that Coach House published. I knew nothing much about Coach House or Stan Bevington other than that he was a honcho in the Toronto counterculture. After a couple of months had gone by I phoned Stan to inquire about progress. Everything, apparently, was fine, just fine, but there hadn't been any, well, you know, man, actual *physical* progress, though . . .

About three anxious months later, still no news, I phoned again. My tentative questions were followed by a silence as of profound thought.

"Hello?" I said.

"Look, man," said Stan, "if you're going to hassle me I'm not doing the book."

And he didn't.

My writing life was absorbing me to the point that I realized I could no longer afford to work full-time. I resigned from Northmount High School and looked about for part-time work. Just before the term ended I was visited by the board's consultant in English, Charles Rittenhouse. Charles had been very active in amateur theatre —always a bad thing—and was given to gesture and noisy recitation. He was related by marriage to the Holgate family and had several of Edwin Holgate's prosaic canvases in his apartment. He sat on the edge of my desk and said that he considered me the most interesting young teacher in the system and asked me to work with him on five textbooks for which he had a contract with J. M. Dent and Sons.

The series was called *Wordcraft* and books 1 to 3 were written by Charles, me, and Juliette Dowling. *Wordcraft Junior* and *Senior* were written by Charles and me alone. Actually, largely by me with Charles acting as taskmaster. The purpose of the books was to interest children in the history of words, to build vocabulary, and to provide exercises in precise usage.

We wrote *Wordcraft 2* and *3* in 1968 and they and other textbooks I compiled were to prove very important in my writing life. They sold astonishingly well and brought in just enough in royalties each year to persuade me that I had enough "base" money to risk one more year without full-time employment.

I had also been earning money by editing school text editions with notes, questions, and exercises for Bellhaven House. I prepared editions of *The Razor's Edge*, *The Daughter of Time*, and *Flight of the Phoenix*. These appeared in 1967 and 1968. Also in 1968, I put together with Gordon Callaghan, a fellow teacher, a textbook called *Rhyme and Reason* to teach children how to read poetry. *Wordcraft 1* appeared in 1969. In 1970 Gordon and I compiled a poetry anthology for high school use called *Salutation*. Also in 1970 Rittenhouse and I put out *Wordcraft Senior*. Again in 1970 I published *Sixteen by Twelve*.

The idea behind this old warhorse was simple. I chose twelve writers and asked them to write a piece about writing to accompany their story or stories in the book. I wrote brief biographies and included an informal photo of the writer. These devices seemed to give the book a certain intimacy and personality. The writers I chose were Morley Callaghan, Hugh Garner, Margaret Laurence, Hugh Hood, Mordecai Richler, Alice Munro, Shirley Faessler, Alden Nowlan, George Bowering, David Helwig, myself, and Ray Smith.

The book is still in print and still selling well after more than thirty years. It ought to have been scrapped and updated years ago. When I did attempt to present different writers in a similar collection called *New Worlds* in 1980—such writers as Merna Summers, Alden Nowlan, W. P. Kinsella, Jack Hodgins, C. D. Minni, Norman Levine, and Terrence Heath—the book didn't sell well and the reports from the McGraw-Hill Ryerson salesmen were that the teachers hadn't heard of any of these writers.

Year after year *Sixteen by Twelve* has underwritten my fiction and criticism. It typically produces four thousand dollars a year. The Dent *Wordcraft* books used to bring in fifteen hundred to two thousand a year but sales are more or less finished; I suspect the books are now too challenging for the students' dwindling abilities.

It is for me rather saddening to look at *Sixteen by Twelve* today. Seven of those twelve writers are now dead, four of the seven from drink. Given Canada, perhaps not surprising. Frederick Philip Grove wrote: "There is no greater curse that can befall a man than to be afflicted with artistic leanings, in Canada."

That comma might be the best thing he ever wrote.

The royalties rolled in as a delightful extra. The motivation for compiling these and later books was less financial than educational. I was at that time interested in teaching and I believed that Canadian children ought to be in contact with Canadian art. *Sixteen by Twelve* was, apparently, the first Canadian textbook of Canadian stories ever. Gordon Callaghan and I put together *Rhyme and Reason* and *Salutation* simply so we'd have intelligent material to teach. Very little infrastructure had been put into place by the early sixties and we both felt a need to shape and civilize. Only years later did we realize that it was like throwing stones into a bog.

In 1963 W. H. Auden wrote: "The dominions . . . are for me *tiefste Provinz*, places which have produced no art and are inhabited by the kind of person with whom I have least in common."

Difficult not to concur.

I have often thought about this surge of publishing at the beginning of my career and of the textbooks that came later—*Kaleidoscope: Canadian Stories* (1972), *The Narrative Voice* (1972), *The Speaking Earth: Canadian Poetry* (1973), *Here and Now: Best Canadian Stories* (1977), *Stories Plus* (1979), *New Worlds* (1980), *Making It New* (1982), *The New Story Writers* (1982) and *Canadian Classics* (1993).

Had I remained in England a similar surge of publishing would not have occurred because I could not have imagined it. Textbooks in England were written by heads of department in famous public schools or by lecturers in departments of education and certainly not by lowly toilers at Bluebell Secondary Modern. There was besides a resource pool of thousands of educated minds on which publishers could draw. Also to the point, there was no *need* of new textbooks.

Canada offered me the freedom to do anything I could imagine. The negative side of this freedom was that it was a freedom which arose from ignorance and indifference. There was certainly little competition. In the sixties Canada was an intellectual and creative wasteland with a large percentage of its population functionally illiterate.

Royalties fluctuated and it wasn't possible to rely on them and so a part-time job was necessary. Irving Layton suggested to me that I try Ross High School. At that time it occupied the upper floor of a takeout Bar BQ chicken joint on Decarie near Vezina. It was a private institution that catered to students who had failed in the state schools or who were disaffected, stoned, or simply idle. Classes were small as were the four rooms into which they were crammed.

Mr. Ross also had a sideline of rich immigrant students mainly from Taiwan and India.

"What I am not understanding, sir, is the whereabouts of your motorcar."

Preceding me as heads of the English department had been the proletarian layabout poet Bryan McCarthy, author of *Smoking the City*, layabout novelist John Mills, and Irving Layton. Whenever

I asked Harry Ross for a raise he always replied, "Who do you think *you* are? Irving Layton?"

Myrna once told me that years before I knew her, McCarthy, a boozehound and notorious wastrel, had taught her dancing "by the binary method." I've never had the moral courage to press her on what "the binary method" actually entailed.

I sketched this curious school in a story called "The Years in Exile" and again fiction feels more accurate than fact.

Rosen College Preparatory High School occupied five rooms on the floor about the Chateau Bar BQ Restaurant and Takeout Service. There were three classrooms, the Library, the supplies locker, and the Office. The staff was all part-time and so in my five years I came to know only the morning shift—Geography, Mathematics, and Science. At recess, the four of us would huddle in the supplies locker and make coffee.

Mr. Kapoor was a reserved and melancholy hypochondriac from New Delhi who habitually wore black suits and shoes, a white shirt, and striped college tie. His only concession to summer was that he wore the gleaming shoes without socks. I remember his telling me one day that peahens became fertilized by raising their tail feathers during a rain storm; he held earnestly to this, telling me that it was indeed so because his grandmother had told him, she having seen it with her own eyes in Delhi. He taught science in all grades.

Mr. Gingley was a retired accountant who taught Mathematics and wore a curiously pink hearing aid which was shaped like a fat human ear.

Mr. Helwig Syllm, the Geography teacher, was an ex-masseur.

Mrs. Rosen, who drew salaries as secretary, teacher, and School Nurse, would sometimes grip one by the arm in the hall and hiss: "Don't foment. My husband can fire anyone. *Anyone.*"

Mr. Ross was actually a genial man but with marked eccentricities. He lived to do battle with the education department bureaucrats in Quebec City who were continually finding him in violation of codes and attempting to close him down. They claimed he had no gymnasium; he countered that he had an arrangement with the Y. They announced an inspection of the library; he gave me taxi money to transport suitcases of my own books into the library cupboard for the duration. They claimed the school afforded no toilets for the students; he countered that the school had a toilet arrangement with the Bar BQ management. On and on it went, Mr. Ross in wheezing chuckles as he recounted his latest coup against the faceless ones.

The years with Ross were the happiest years of my teaching career. I remember going to him on the first day I worked at Ross High School and asking him for chalk. He took two sticks from a box and wrapped them in a twist of paper. Next week I asked for more. He looked astonished and said, "You've *had* your chalk for this year!" But he wasn't always penny-pinching and if I was late in the morning and had had to skip breakfast he would go to a nearby restaurant and bring me coffee and hot buttered toast in waxed paper which I'd eat while teaching Chaucer.

I taught in the mornings and walked home at midday. I usually then corrected essays for an hour or so. I was correcting class sets for the Protestant School Board of Greater Montreal for fifty cents an essay. I liaised with the English department head at Northmount High School, a charming Englishman who wore silk suits and who used to say to his students, "If you don't be quiet, I shall go *quite rigid.*" We liked each other. In the late afternoons and early evenings I worked on fiction.

My writing was going well. I was getting stories published in the literary magazines and there were signs and portents everywhere. I was awarded a Canada Council grant in 1968. I remember taking that cheque to a branch of the Banque Nationale near our apartment. The teller examined it and said, "We don't cash cheques from foreign countries." A hint of things to come.

I was awarded the President's Medal of the University of Western Ontario in 1969 for the best short story of the year. That was "The Estuary." Mordecai Richler selected "Keys and Watercress" for his Penguin anthology *Canadian Writing Today*. During these years Professor Alec Lucas at McGill was working on an anthology for the American paperback company Dell. The book was called *Great Canadian Stories* and it finally appeared in 1971. I had met Alec Lucas at a launching party for a young protégé of Louis Dudek's. Drink was flowing abundantly and Alec endeared himself to me eternally when Louis Dudek rose and quieted the uproar, saying, "And now I think the time has come to listen to our young poet." Alec said loudly into the silence, and in a *petulant* tone, "They always have to *spoil* these occasions."

Alec had fallen into the habit of summoning Ray Smith and me to the McGill Faculty Club at lunchtime to pick our brains for his anthology. He was going to include both of us but wanted our opinions of our contemporaries. These lunches were nearly always purely liquid as the food in the faculty club was disgusting. One day someone wrote in chalk on the club wall: *The poor hate you.* I picked up the nub of chalk and wrote underneath: *They wouldn't if they'd eaten here.*

Most excitingly, I was selected for *New Canadian Writing 1969*, the second volume of a series published by Clarke Irwin. The year before, they had published *New Canadian Writing 1968* with stories by David Lewis Stein, Clark Blaise, and Dave Godfrey.

In the publisher's foreword to the 1968 book Bill Clarke wrote:

> The stories in this collection are representative of the current trends, of the move away from the old established patterns towards new methods of conveying impressions. They are not necessarily the *best* stories that will appear in this decade but they are important in that they are indicative of the work being done by young Canadian writers today. It is the publisher's intention to continue this programme with the publication of other volumes of a similar nature.

New Canadian Writing 1969 was the final volume in the series.

Clark's stories were "The Fabulous Eddie Brewster," "How I Became a Jew," "The Examination," and "Notes Beyond a History." Bill Clarke was exquisitely mannered and perhaps excessively genteel. He felt that "How I Became a Jew" had in its blunt usage of the word *Jew* the potential to offend. Clark and I were vastly amused when he proposed that Clark change the title to, "How I Became a Jewish Person."

New Canadian Writing 1969 also contained stories by D. O. Spettigue and C. J. Newman. I had five stories in the book: "The Children Green and Golden," "Walking Round the City," "Robert, Standing," "Our Mr. Benson," and "The Estuary." These stories caused quite a stir and were singled out in reviews. As a result Clarke Irwin proposed that I publish a collection with them. This appeared in 1970 and was entitled *The Lady Who Sold Furniture.*

But many other changes were accompanying these little literary triumphs and trophies. The most momentous event in these years was the birth of our daughter, Elizabeth, in 1969. I went with Gale to the hospital, of course, but the usual happened. I cannot stand other people's pain and I usually faint or vomit. Receiving pain while falling off cliffs or in the boxing ring is somehow different; one is to a degree immune, perhaps because charged with adrenalin. Gale was in labour and extremely vocal. I was distressed and lurched out into the corridor, my vision a migraine-like blizzard of white mesh. I bumbled along the wall and fell through a pair of swing doors and then fell down a flight of stone stairs. After I had come to and after my vision returned to normal I ignominiously got a taxi and went home to bed.

Elizabeth was a great joy to me and especially so when she was learning to talk, which she did early. She used to deliver long, excited monologues with many repetitions attempting to describe or explain such things as thunder. She sounded oddly like Lucky's speeches in *Waiting for Godot.*

There was something irresistibly delicious about a two-year-old standing staring at a large toy lion and saying admiringly, "My word!" Though usually sunny, she had cross days and on one of these I'd taken her to a zoo. I said to her with forced parental enthusiasm, "Oh, look, Elizabeth! A llama!"

She glowered at the beast.

Then said plonkingly, "What's it for?"

There were changes, too, on the job front. I stopped marking exercise books partly because I was busy writing texts and partly because I couldn't stand any longer changing *their* and *there* and *its* and *it's.* The increasing frequency of the publication of my stories meant that I was building a small reputation and that reputation was opening up new employment possibilities. I was beginning to review for the *Montreal Star*. By strange chance, I was to review Eudora Welty's lovely last novel, *Losing Battles*. Mr. Ross remained intransigent about wages, so with considerable regret I left the old bugger to his comic machinations. By 1970 I had acquired two part-time jobs, one teaching writing at McGill for Bharati Mukherjee, the other teaching literature at the Loyola CEGEP.

There is for a writer nothing quite like the experience of a first book. No subsequent book means quite as much. To hold that first book in one's hands is to hold proof that one indeed is what one has for years dared and hoped to be. I was so elated by *The Lady Who Sold Furniture* that I put copies in every room in the apartment so that I could see it and stroke it wherever I was.

The book contains five short stories and a 102-page novella. Although I still quite like the stories the meat of the book is the novella. In the novella I managed to deploy what I'd been struggling to teach myself in the preceding years. I'd wanted to get away from plot and towards a story that moved forward in a different way. What I was after, though I couldn't quite articulate it, was a story that was powered through images that generated strong emotion. I wanted a story propelled by a series of emotional jolts. This, in turn, implied a close observation of surface and detail. In acutely observed surfaces are depths. To deliver the emotion the language had to be utterly clean and sharp, cuttingly precise. Dialogue, too, had to make demands on the reader. It had to be fast, full of implied tone, utterly lacking in "stage directions"; in brief, the dialogue had to be a performance in which the reader took part.

It was here perhaps that everything collecting had taught me was brought into play. Everything that paintings had taught me. Everything I'd learned from the Imagist poets. Everything I'd thrilled to in the theatre.

My short stories had been tending in the right direction—"Keys and Watercress" and "Dandelions" move forward in intense images —but I could not then have expressed as a theory what I was grappling with. I was listening to CBC *Anthology* one evening when an actor started reading a story called "Images" by a writer named Alice Munro. I think this was in 1968 but it might have been 1967. It certainly preceded publication of *Dance of the Happy Shades*. I was galvanized by this story. I recognized immediately what she was doing. She had succeeded brilliantly at the very thing that I was still messing with and by using the title "Images" she'd pointed out the method of her fiction. She allowed my own thinking about these technical problems to expand. I wrote to her in great excitement and we entered into a correspondence which lasted for years.

In 1985 *The Malahat Review* (Number 70) put out under the editorship of Constance Rooke "A Special Issue on John Metcalf." I was immensely flattered by Alice Munro's contribution and immodestly quote it here. It refers back to the sixties and the story "Images."

On John Metcalf: Taking Writing Seriously

I think John wrote to me for the first time after a story of mine was read on the radio, before I had published any books. Or maybe it was just after the first book came out. I was living in Victoria then. I had absolutely no status as a writer. A creative writing teacher at the University of Victoria had told me that I wrote the kind of things he used to write when he was 15. So I was quite surprised by this letter of appreciation. I was stunned by it, really—it was a bouquet, a burst of handsome praise. He had taken the trouble to do this—to write so generously and thoughtfully, to a writer he didn't know, a writer of no importance, no connections. He didn't do that out of kindness alone, though it seemed to me so wonderfully kind. He did it because he believes writing is important.

I didn't meet him until three or four years later. We wrote letters. We wrote about what we were working on and what a hard time we were having with it and what we thought about each other's writing, and other people's, too. We developed then what I hate to describe as a literary friendship—that sounds to me too pretentious and genteel for the letters we wrote—but I suppose that's the kind of friendship it was, and is. He was bracing and encouraging and not always uncritical. I was learning that remarkable respect for his opinion that many of his writer friends have. I've never lost it. Praise from him, you feel, is real gold. Once he is your friend he will back you up and make allowances for your quirks and problems and refrain from blabbing your confidences, he will be kind and loyal and affectionate, but he won't tell you he likes your writing if he doesn't. I have the feeling—and I'm sure there are other writers who have it—that he is one person who can tell where the soft spots are, where the words are pasted over the cracks, can tell what's fake, what's shoddy, what's an evasion, maybe even mark the place where a loss of faith hit you, not momentously like an avalanche but drearily like a dry trickle of clods and stones. It won't matter what compliments you've been getting from other quarters.

This makes him sound like one of those mentors people idealize from the past—a wise ironical fellow, incorruptible, never fooled. It's absurd to make him into anything like that. He never set himself up to be anybody's literary conscience—that's a rickety business you have to develop for yourself—and he has a blind spot or two, like the rest of us. If I do think of him this way, as somebody sitting out there *not being fooled*, I probably should apologize for it. But it is very useful, and our friends all have their uses.

And it's exactly how I do think of him. I'm grateful to him, and so I should be.

He does take writing seriously, that's all it is. He has a consistent, natural respect for it, which is something a lot rarer than you'd think.

By the time I came to write "The Lady Who Sold Furniture" I knew exactly what I was doing and why. The novella still stands up for me after all these years. It hasn't lost its flavour. These are the first two paragraphs:

Purple. Purpleness with a zigzag line of black. A zigzag line of black stitching. Peter pushed the bedspread down from his face and moved his head on the pillow. He expected for a second to see above his head the raftered darkness of the barn and to hear the clatter of sabots on the cobbles, the everymorning shout of *Monsieur Anglais!* But the only sounds were sparrows on the window sill and the distant rattle of the milkman's van.

Sunlight lay over the floorboards and the worn carpet. His boots and rucksack lay where he'd dropped them the night before. The sole of one boot was grey with caked mud except where the tips of the steel cleats glinted in the sunshine.

The Lady Who Sold Furniture was published in 1970. Clarke Irwin printed 1,500 copies but bound up only 750 copies. These were bound in black cloth. Some years later they bound the rest in grey cloth. Copies of this second binding are still available from ECW Press. This means that the book has sold fewer than 1,500 copies in thirty-nine years.

The novella is also available along with two others—"Girl in Gingham" and "Private Parts: A Memoir"—in *Shooting the Stars*, published in 1993 by the Porcupine's Quill; a glance at my royalty statements shows that *Shooting the Stars* sold in 1999 0 (zero) copies with a wild surge in 2000 to 4 (four) copies, slumping in 2001 to 0 (zero) again.

Reviews in 1970 were very favourable and the book is routinely mentioned as a landmark volume in histories of literature and guides to culture. In *The Oxford Companion to Twentieth Century Literature in English*, edited by Jenny Stringer, the entry on me reads in part: "His abiding reputation as one of the finest prose stylists in contemporary Canada was established with the vividly observed and imaginatively disquieting stories collected in *The Lady Who Sold Furniture* (1970)."

Surely this critical encomium and my book's virtual disappearance require some kind of explanation?

In 2001 I wrote an essay for the *National Post* which attempted to explore the reasons for the similar neglect of Blaise and Levine; the conclusion I arrived at was that Canadians merely parroted American estimations and as a society were incapable of informed, independent judgement. This provoked a vicious, personal letter to the *Post* from Douglas Gibson of McClelland and Stewart.

My piece was called "Canadian Classics" and I'd like to quote from it:

Let us probe a little deeper into my contention that Canada cannot elect "classics" by considering the careers of two other writers,

Clark Blaise and Norman Levine. If I had to pick the best six story writers in Canada I would certainly select Alice Munro and Mavis Gallant and I would with equal certainty select Clark Blaise and Norman Levine.

I would have to admit that Blaise and Levine are lesser writers than Munro and Gallant. They have written fewer and less complex stories and both have a narrower range both of subject matter and emotion. Yet they remain so obviously in the same league as Munro and Gallant. Both men have written stories which are at the centre of Canadian achievement in the short story form. Both voices are wonderfully individual and alive. I cannot imagine Canadian literature without thinking of such Levine stories as "A Small Piece of Blue," "Something Happened Here," "By the Richelieu," and "Champagne Barn." Nor can I imagine Canadian literature without thinking of such Blaise stories as "A North American Education," "The Salesman's Son Grows Older," "Eyes," "How I Became a Jew," and "Meditations on Starch."

Despite the bizarre inclusions and the even more bizarre exclusions we must put *some* weight on the fact that both Clark Blaise and Norman Levine are given entries in *The Cambridge Guide to Literature in English* and *The Oxford Companion to Twentieth Century Literature in English*.

The Oxford Companion says: "Levine's spare, understated prose style is seen at its best in his short stories. Predominantly first-person narratives, they exhibit a keen eye for external details, but their prime concern is with the subjective experience of the outsider."

Of Blaise's work *The Oxford Companion* says: "The autobiographical dimension in much of his highly regarded fiction is integral to his treatments of the impermanence and relativity of personal identity . . . His short stories in *A North American Education* (1973), *Tribal Justice* (1974), and *Resident Alien* (1986) are widely considered to represent his central achievement."

All this is to say, then, that thus far Blaise and Levine have survived the process of literary winnowing and were picked to represent Canada in two international compilations that survey world writing in English. As were Alice Munro and Mavis Gallant.

Why is it, then, that Clark Blaise and Norman Levine are largely unknown or ignored in Canada? Why is it that Norman Levine's stories have so long been out of print? Why is it that Norman Levine's work is not taught in any Canadian university? Why is it that Blaise's *A North American Education* and *Tribal Justice* languish in the respectable ghetto of New Press Canadian Classics *still in the first issue of the first printing sixteen years after publication?*

"Place him with Alice Munro and Mavis Gallant," declares *Maclean's Magazine* of Blaise.

What happened?

Because Blaise's career did not flourish in the USA there was no pressure on Canada to recognize a compelling writer in our midst. *A North American Education* and *Tribal Justice* remain two of the most glowing and obviously important volumes of stories ever published in Canada. And this is to make no mention of the delights of *Resident Alien*, *Days and Nights in Calcutta* and *Man and His World*.

Although Blaise was well reviewed, the *New York Times Review of Books* describing the stories as "glittering," *The New Yorker* did not adopt him and his publisher, Doubleday, did little to promote him. Canada remained deaf to his prose, and to the prose of his wife, Bharati Mukherjee.

Norman Levine's obscurity in Canada is even more curious than Blaise's. Ron Corbett, an *Ottawa Citizen* columnist, wrote a profile of Norman Levine recently and said: "Today, how Mr. Levine will be remembered in Canada is a question not only unknown, it is one largely unasked. None of his books or stories are taught at a Canadian university . . . Viking-Penguin, the last company to publish a new Levine book, says it has no plans to publish another one."

Corbett then goes on to quote Penguin Books Canada publisher Cynthia Good. She had published *Champagne Barn* and, later, *Something Happened Here*.

Corbett quotes her as saying: "At the time, we considered Norman to be on a par with Alice Munro or Mavis Gallant. We weren't alone. That's how many people viewed him at the time."

Norman Levine remains the writer he always was, a writer of central importance, one of Canada's best.

Here is a suggestion of the way Levine's work has been received elsewhere: ". . . passionate and brilliantly rendered" (*New Statesman*), ". . . masterly . . ." (*Times Literary Supplement*), "Impressive and fascinating . . ." (*Frankfurter Allgemeine Zeitung*), "Timeless elegance . . ." (*The Times*). "Norman Levine is one of the most outstanding short story writers working in English today" (*Encounter*).

Levine has been only nominally published in the USA.

Clark Blaise *has* been published in the USA but by a low-key publisher which treated him as a "mid-list" writer; he was not, in other words, heavily promoted.

It is curious that European and British praise for Levine has not been echoed in Canada. Such praise seems no longer to carry as much authority for Canadians as American praise. When one considers the careers of all four writers it is difficult to avoid the conclusion that the success of two of them and the relative obscurity of the other two centre upon publication in the USA and more particularly in *The New Yorker*. Further, it is difficult to avoid the conclusion that, were it not for American endorsement, Alice Munro and Mavis Gallant would languish in exactly the same Canadian obscurity.

Norman Levine and Clark Blaise are nearing the end of careers; they have behind them achieved bodies of work. What is there to say to brilliant writers nearer to the beginnings of careers? What is there to say to Caroline Adderson, to Terry Griggs, to Annabel Lyon, to Michael Winter? And to all the other writers who are part of our current flowering in the Canadian short story?

The fame you are so properly seeking cannot be conferred in Canada or by Canada. Canada cannot hear you. Canada cannot recognize you. Canada will not read you unless you are validated elsewhere.

THE MONTREAL STORY TELLERS

I CALLED HUGH HOOD at the end of 1970 and proposed to him that we put together a group of writers to give readings in high schools and colleges. The group came to consist of Hugh, Ray Smith, Ray Fraser, Clark Blaise, and me. I won't go into great detail about the Story Tellers because there is a book edited by J. R. (Tim) Struthers called *The Montreal Story Tellers: Memoirs, Photographs, Critical Essays*. The book appeared in 1985 and was published by Montreal's Véhicule Press.

I would, however, like to reminisce about Hugh Hood. Noreen Mallory, Hugh's wife, phoned us on Tuesday, August first, 2000, to tell us that Hugh had died. He had for some years been suffering from Parkinson's disease. The funeral service was held on August third. Myrna and I drove to Montreal. The congregation was sparse. Only two other writers were present. Joel Yanofsky was there to report for the *Gazette* and W. J. Keith and his wife, Hiroko, had come down from Toronto. The Montreal writing community was conspicuously absent.

The *Globe and Mail* asked me to write an obituary. An excerpt follows:

Hugh Hood, who died on Tuesday in Montreal, was a man of vibrant and engaging eccentricity. He was a cornucopia of information which he imparted relentlessly. The range of his knowledge was astonishing: history, literature, theology, Haydn,

Canadian politics, hockey, baseball trivia, the names of the sidemen in every obscure band Bing Crosby sang with, the names of the scriptwriters on every *Carry On* film.

He had something like a photographic memory and when we were driving to readings in Montreal during the 1970s, he would unreel for us long quotations from P. G. Wodehouse, Anthony Powell, Evelyn Waugh and Raymond Chandler. Our task was to guess the title and date.

Hugh was eccentric variously. His dress was usually casual. He sometimes invested in new sneakers. He organized his writing life under strange numerical schemes which made vital sense to him but which were incomprehensible to his listeners. He boasted that his car was the cheapest new car that it was possible to own in North America. At that point, this was a Russian Lada with holes in the dashboard where the instrumentation would have been had he taken those options.

My wife and I were once driving with Hugh to Toronto to read at Harbourfront. As we pulled out of the drive, my wife asked Hugh why he had not put on his seat belt. Taking in a comprehensive survey through the ages of the doctrines of Free Will, Salvation, Law, and the nature of the Social Contract, the answer lasted until we were approaching Oshawa.

I recall, too, with great affection, a cross-country reading tour that Hugh and I did with Leon Rooke when the three of us were published by ECW Press. Leon and I used to trade our Air Canada chicken for his wine. He loved the chicken and would talk at length about the cleverness of its packaging, the beauty of plastic, form and content, Marshall McLuhan, *Japanese* packaging . . . a typical Hoodian arabesque.

Hugh ate vegetables only from tins. His soup of choice was Campbell's. He described most cuisines as "foreign muck." He insisted his coffee be instant.

I shall miss him.

Ray Smith wrote an obituary for the *Gazette*, opening with the following anecdote:

It was 1971 and the five Montreal Story Tellers were taking Canadian literature to a West Island high school, one of a series of school readings we did over two years. I think Raymond Fraser was on stage when in the wings John Metcalf told the rest of us that his marriage had collapsed.

We sympathized, offered beds, names of lawyers, shrinks. Hugh Hood privately slipped John a piece of paper.

"You'll need this," Hugh murmured.

When he looked at it later, Metcalf found it was a cheque for $400.

That would be about $1,800 today. John was amazed, but only briefly. Of course Hugh would do that, not because he was rich, for he wasn't, but because he was Hugh.

All of the Story Tellers wrote memoir pieces for the book Tim Struthers compiled and I'd like to quote excerpts from Ray Smith's. It gives an affectionate portrait of Hugh and suggests something of the hilarity of the Montreal Story Tellers expeditions.

The five of us are in Hugh's car driving to a reading. Probably along some ghastly six-laner like the Decarie Expressway. Known as "The Big Ditch," it has concrete walls fifty feet high. A dangerous and depressing place. Hugh gleefully extols freeways, concrete, and the Decarie.

"Yessir," he exults, "they ought to pave the island from end to end. Concrete is civilization."

He goes on in this vein. I never know if he is being serious or trying to get a rise out of someone. John plunges in. "You are being deliberately perverse, Hugh." John's ideal landscape is perhaps filled with the barren hills and green valleys of Yorkshire or Cumberland; he looks upon a life which includes the Decarie Expressway as something from Hieronymus Bosch, and his life here as a punishment for an adolescence spent in furtive wanking.

"Perverse?" Hugh cries. "Shit no. Do you realize that if the Romans . . ."

Given half a chance, Hugh will talk on the history of concrete all the way to the reading, be it in Rosemere or be it in Vancouver. Long before that, John will have thrown himself screaming from the car; or will be in paroxysms of hysterical laughter. But neither is given a chance: Clark interrupts with an apt quotation from Rilke, Schiller, or Pushkin; someone whose work I have never read. Clark quotes in the original language.

In the back seat, I murmur to Fraser: "Bring out the Argentine brandy."

"Bulgarian this week," says Fraser as he digs the mickey from the inevitable Air Canada bag. "Bulgarian was only 19.6 cents an ounce."

Fraser uses a housewife's calculator to buy his booze. We each take a pull and Ray offers it around but all refuse. Fraser and I are, of course, the only Maritimers in the group.

Hugh and Clark are now fully into the discussion about concrete.

"Those nineteenth-century romantics are ontological arseholes," Hugh is saying.

In rebuttal Clark summarizes Bergson.

Another car comes close to ours. Hugh rolls down his window and yells, "Watch out, you stupid fucker, the future of Canadian literature is in this car."

Metcalf says, "Quebec drivers are all either suicidal or drunk. Probably both."

Clark quotes Alberto Moravia on Italian drivers. In Italian.

I remark that I once skimmed a Moravia novel. The cover had promised steamy sex, but the text was a philosophical working out of exquisitely attenuated ennui.

Clark quotes Anouilh on ennui.

Fraser's nerve breaks and we get another pull at the Bulgarian.

"Moravia is a teleological arsehole," says Hugh. In illustration he quotes two pages of a Moravia novel he read in 1947. He quotes in English.

Now John reaches for the bottle. "I saw a great line yesterday in *The High Window* by Raymond Chandler: 'large moist eyes with the sympathetic expression of wet stones.' Superb."

Hugh quotes the next two pages of the novel.

I interrupt to point out a girl standing at a stop light and wearing a see-through top and no bra. Hugh sings a song he has written about lingerie. I never did learn the words, but something like:

Your girdle is a hurdle
I never want to jump
But your garter belts send me
And bikini panties rend me
And black stockings bend me
Into a hump-hump-hump!

On the last line Hugh bounces vigorously in his seat. A good thing we are no longer on the expressway, for the car swerves into the next lane and heads for a lamp post. As Hugh nonchalantly regains control, John remarks in tightly controlled hysteria: "Hugh, if I might make a small suggestion . . ."

Hugh ignores him; he has noticed a fellow in jeans and jean jacket staring in amazement from the sidewalk. Hugh rolls down the window.

"Hump-hump-hump!" he bellows. "Culture!" He guns the car around the corner. "And why don't you get a haircut, you long-haired hippie freak." He rolls up the window. "That's telling him."

Clark quotes Yukio Mishima on lingerie. This time he quotes in English.

Fraser flourishes the bottle. Metcalf grabs it in desperation.

I reflect that whatever Hugh's estimable qualities—and they are many—if he wore a hat it would inevitably bear a card reading: "In this style, 10/6."

Ray is referring here, of course, to the Tenniel illustration.

We are probably too close to Hugh's novel sequence *The New Age* to form a judgement yet. I feel that some of the novels are more successful than others but I have not yet been able to absorb all twelve books and see them as one. Many readers have problems with Hugh's meanderings down byways of information, his asides, his digressions, feeling that these are blemishes on the books' artistry and destructive of the suspension of disbelief. Other readers feel that Hugh's disquisitions are an essential part of his charm. The novella *Five New Facts About Giorgione* would be a good starting point for coming to some decision about this argument. I found the book maddening.

I feel much clearer about Hugh's early work perhaps because I have lived with it for so many years. In any literature there are certain works which seem obviously to stand in the national canon. I am convinced that Hugh's *Around the Mountain* is one such book. It is my favourite among his short fiction. It was conceived and written as a cycle of twelve stories which together capture Montreal as it was in 1967. Exhibiting an endearing innocence Hugh thought it would sell to American tourists wanting a souvenir of Montreal and Expo 67.

Since Hugh's death I have put together for the New Canadian Library a selection of his stories with an Afterword. The selection is entitled *Light Shining Out of Darkness*, that title being the title of one of the selections. I like to think the title expresses the essence of Hugh's life and writing.

CONDUCT UNBECOMING

AUNTS AREN'T GENTLEMEN is P. G. Wodehouse's last complete novel. It was published in 1974 when he was ninety-three. He died in 1975 leaving behind a first draft of *Sunset at Blandings*. During the sunset years of the late sixties and seventies it seemed to me that many women stopped behaving like gentlemen.

Sisterhood was relentless. Bastions were stormed, institutions toppled with maenadic energy. Women were joining consciousness-raising groups and, once raised, were everywhere forsaking their husbands for electric toothbrushes. Men, meanwhile, were wagging around like bewildered golden retrievers unable to figure out their transgression and dispirited by the mistresses' permanent scowl.

I once saw a Margaret Atwood novel on offer in a dealer's catalogue which was described as being inscribed: "To ____ in feminist frenzy." "Frenzy" aptly describes those heady days. By coincidence, it was Margaret Atwood who gave me my first personal encounter with the feminist schtick. We had been reading together one evening for David Helwig at Queen's University and a group was going on to Toronto the next day by train for some other literary event. I asked people in the group who wanted coffee or soft drinks and went to the serving hatch. On return, I handed a coffee to Margaret Atwood who asked me how much it had cost. I did my gentlemanly mumble saying it was of no import. She *demanded* to know what it had cost. I had no idea as I'd paid for various drinks with a twenty-dollar bill. Why, Margaret Atwood demanded to know, should I pay for her coffee? What was my motivation? Was I really unaware that I was patronizing her? Demeaning her? Belittling her? Was I unaware that I was showing contempt for women . . . I received the full nine yards.

What I'd *thought* I'd been doing was getting her a cup of coffee.

Ah, well.

Loyola, along with every other campus in the country, throbbed with radical energy. Gale was often on campus, often in the faculty club. Aggressive feminism was central to the Zeitgeist. It wasn't an intellectual or practical feminism—equal pay for equal work, say—but rather an implacable emotionalism directed against the opposite sex. I am not meek by nature and during 1970 and 1971 our relationship became increasingly testy.

Gale was pregnant with our second child and demanded an abortion. I was strongly opposed but felt rather helplessly that it wasn't my decision to make. She found a doctor willing to claim that the pregnancy was detrimental to her mental health and the operation was performed at a local hospital. Shortly after this she started spending time with a Loyola student called Elizabeth Bateman.

Elizabeth Bateman was tall with lank and malodorous hair. She was probably mucky for ideological reasons. She called herself Bitsy. She wore boots and suspenders. She claimed to be a photographer. Gale declared herself passionately in love with this unappetizing creature. The lesbian life, she announced, was the life for her. And she intended it, she said, for our daughter, Elizabeth, too. I objected to the situation and left the house, moving into what amounted to a commune of Loyola faculty members whose marriages had gone awry. Gale referred to this house as Heartbreak Hotel.

I sued for divorce. Gale did not even attend the hearing and I was granted the divorce and custody of Elizabeth. I was preparing to move to Fredericton where I had been offered a year's work as writer-in-residence. Elizabeth was still living with Gale and Bitsy as I hadn't wanted to move her into temporary accommodation. In Fredericton I was going to share a house with my friend Douglas Rollins, a fellow teacher who was studying for a Ph.D.

Gale came to see me one afternoon and said that she had changed her mind about the divorce and wished to go to Fredericton with me. The decree was not yet absolute and she asked me to cancel the action as a demonstration of my general faith and devotion. This I did because I still loved her and was distressed about Elizabeth's emotional state. We went to the Palais de Justice and I filled in the paperwork.

My friends were incredulous.

My lawyer was apoplectic.

A few days later while I was picking Elizabeth up to take her out to play Gale told me that she had no intention of going to Fredericton, that she had had no change of heart, that she had deceived me just to have another chance at custody. She also allowed that she thought I was simple.

I again sued for divorce, this time being granted the divorce but denied custody. Gale's parents committed breathtaking perjury. It was a sour day. The judge, too, seemed to think that I'd acted rather irresponsibly in cancelling the first divorce.

Various people have asked me how I could have been so stupid. It *was* stupid, I suppose, in the terms of the workaday world. But what had been at stake was very important. It was the right *sort* of mistake to make, and I'm not sure I wouldn't make a similar sort of mistake again.

What does this sad catalogue leave me feeling thirty years later? My position is close to the sage words of P. J. O'Rourke, who in *Age and Guile Beat Youth, Innocence and a Bad Haircut* wrote:

> Miniskirts caused feminism. Women wore miniskirts. Construction workers made ape noises. Women got pissed off. Once the women were pissed off about this they started thinking about all the other things they had to be pissed off about. That led to feminism. Not that I'm criticizing. Look, Babe . . . I mean, Ms . . . I mean, yes, sir I *do* support feminism. I really do. But that doesn't mean I want to go through it twice.

WRITER-IN-RESIDENCE

MY FIRST STINT as a writer-in-residence was at the University of New Brunswick in 1972–73. I was offered the appointment through the good offices of Kent Thompson, a fellow writer and a professor in the UNB English department, who argued that the university should assist younger writers instead of automatically piling honours on those already laden.

I had first met Kent when he was editor of *The Fiddlehead*, the literary magazine which has been associated with UNB for so many years and which has done so much to encourage young poets and fiction writers. In 1970 Kent organized under the umbrella of *The Fiddlehead* a conference of writers and critics to discuss the current state of fiction in Canada. It was Kent's conviction that the critics were years behind the writers and he hoped the conference might stimulate some of them to grapple with the sudden sophistication that Canadian fiction was exhibiting. Nothing of the sort happened, of course, but it was interesting and instructive to spend time with Hugh Hood, Dave Godfrey, Rudy Wiebe, and David Helwig.

Dave Godfrey was then a bright star in the firmament of Canadian letters, having helped found the House of Anansi and having written a bulky and ultimately incomprehensible book called *The New Ancestors*. He now designs computer software. He was at the time rabid with nationalism and my accent and antecedents seemed to rub him up very much the wrong way; at breakfast in the Lord Beaverbrook

Hotel he read the stock market reports in a marked manner. I was relieved to discover, however, that his rage was general; during a dull but unexceptionable paper by Professor Hallvard Dahlie entitled "Self-Conscious Nationalism in the Novels of Hugh MacLennan," Godfrey suggested that Professor Dahlie would benefit from "a good bum-fuck" administered by Scott Symons. This was a form of ideological re-education which had not previously occurred to me.

If the academic offerings were tedious, the discussions among the writers were of great interest. I can recall my enthusiasm at the time for the ideas of the Imagists and how those ideas could be worked out in the story form. I began in the discussions at that conference what has turned into the lifelong task of attempting to teach academics the necessity of an aesthetic approach to literature. I'm now convinced it's a task that's largely hopeless.

Canadian literary studies and "scholarship" have always been lax and undemanding. It is a field which attracts second- and third-rate minds. Such widely published critics as John Moss, who was a Ph.D. student at Fredericton when I was writer-in-residence, can to this day write gibberish such as the following and still retain the regard of his colleagues: "This novel, as much as any, shows why Callaghan is a significant writer in the Canadian tradition without necessarily being an accomplished artist. [WHAT?] The prose is awkwardly simplistic, but forceful and direct . . . [WHAT?] He is probably the best example we have of the serious artist as entertainer." (WHAT?)

The author of these moronic sentences is considered one of the chief adornments of the University of Ottawa's English department.

The lax and slapdash are everywhere. Three tiny examples suggestive of the whole. *Going Down Slow* concerns a teacher's affair with a student. The entire plot centres on the affair's illegality. *The Oxford Companion to Canadian Literature* describes the student, Susan, *as a fellow teacher.* Again, the new dictionary, *The Canadian Oxford Dictionary* (1998) has an encyclopedic element and carries hundreds of biographical entries. I am listed, correctly, under Metcalf but in company with Charles Theophilus Metcalf, governor general of British North America (1843–45) whose name is not Metcalf but Metcalfe.

The entry for Ethel Wilson reads: "South-African-born Canadian novelist and essayist. Her many collections of stories include *Love and Salt Water* (1956) and *Mrs. Golightly and Other Stories* (1961)."

Ethel Wilson published only six books in her career. Four of the six were novels. One was a book containing two novellas. *One* was a book of short stories. One is not "many." *Love and Salt Water*, identified by Oxford as a story collection, is, in fact, a novel.

But does any of this petty detail *really* matter?

Yes.

William Hoffer, the fabled Vancouver antiquarian book dealer, once wrote about Canadian writing: "The complicated pocket watch of literature has been replaced by a rude drawing of a watch with no moving parts."

"In Canada," he used to say, "*approximations* are good enough."

My office in Fredericton was in the old Arts Building between the offices of Robert Gibbs and Fred Cogswell. Robert Gibbs often held long discussions with students about Pre- and Post-Confederation poets, none of whom I'd read. He also had briefer and more interesting chats with his bookcase, briefcase, and filing cabinet.

Fred Cogswell used his office as warehouse and editorial centre for Fiddlehead Poetry Books, an enterprise distinct from *The Fiddlehead*. He was always extremely affable and kept me abreast of the doings of all his poetesses. These conversations were baffling because his starting point was always an outcropping of some buried lode.

An entirely typical exchange would run as follows:

"She's feeling a lot better now."

"Oh, hello, Fred. Pardon?"

"Much closer to a decision."

"Oh. Good."

"We went for a long walk on the beach on Sunday."

"I see."

Silent puffing on his pipe.

"His big mistake, you see, was to offer marriage."

"Mistake?"

"It offended her deeply."

"Oh."

I had no idea to whom these daily bulletins referred and so they all combined in my mind into a composite, into an Identikit portrait of a Fiddlehead Poetry Books poetess—youngish, good-looking, sexually unhappy or inverted, offended at elemental levels by the world's *coarseness*, terribly sincere, terribly sensitive, terribly intense —in sum, not unlike the Madeline Basset to whom Bertie Wooster often refers with a shudder.

These chapbooks were unspeakable. During the years of his editorship he published 307 of them. At first I thought his motivation must be the desire for contiguity with young female flesh but came to understand that, worse, he actually believed in all this jejune inadequacy. I held the position that such an outpouring of drivel was an example of bad coin driving out good, that his wretched pamphlets took away attention from the three or four good poets we should have been reading.

I had, of course, got it all wrong. Fred's contribution was of the kind Canada understood and wanted. It was a kind of "outreach," the literary equivalent of helium balloons on strings and painting the faces of children at "cultural" events. Cogswell was made a member of the Order of Canada in 1981.

A recent Canada Council jury award prompted David Solway into velvety rage and a comic tour of the stunning banality of a new book by a Fiddlehead Poetry Books veteran. I quote from his essay "Getting on the Gravy Boat."

In 1999 Sharon H. Nelson, the author of ten little-known and largely unreviewed chapbooks dating back to 1972, received a $20,000 Canada Council Arts Grant to write a book of poems. Two and a half years later an eleven page collection appeared, entitled *How the Soup Gets Made*. Not counting a 12th page of Notes in which we are given a definition of *parmentier* and a detailed recipe for its preparation, this averages out to approximately $2000 per page, a sum whose literary amortization may in this case prove highly problematic.

To get some sense of what this modest work entails, let us embark on a quick tour of its pages. The book begins with its title poem where we are initially apprised that

Today I made leek and cauliflower soup
because Brenda had dental surgery this morning . . .

—which is surely a direct if unexpected way of whetting the reader's appetite. While the soup is on the boil, we discover that the poet, speculating over the destiny of her restorative bouillon, is also thinking of

Rahel and Bella and Maureen
all of whom can't eat anything made with *allium* . . .

And of Maxiane who "no longer eats potatoes." Once we have digested these disturbing facts, however, we learn to our immediate relief that Brenda is recovering well, and soon the steamy kitchen of Nelson's culinary imagination begins to fill with ever more Goddesses of the Soup, a numinous sorority which proceeds to

cook soup against the chill,
and welcome the companionship of friends
whose presences pervade the air
with the rising scent of braising vegetables . . .

Solway's comic performance here can only *suggest* the contagion Cogswell spread for so many years.

Long after my stint at UNB was over I was chatting to Kent Thompson about the general *looniness* of Fredericton and the astonishing marital frolics of the English department; he corrected me sharply, pointing out that the loony one had been me. And I suppose there's truth in that too; I was distraught about my wife and daughter and Fredericton offered few distractions from grief.

In fact, as far as I was concerned, Fredericton had little to offer at all. Its pizza parlours featured pizzas studded with turd-like mounds of hamburger and signs proudly claimed: Topped with Genuine (Mild) Canadian Cheddar. All Chinese restaurants served things in red sauce. I loathed the pretentiousness and *awfulness* of the vast Salvador Dalí painting in the Beaverbrook Art Gallery, so I rarely went there. I was banned for life from the River Room of the Lord Beaverbrook Hotel for unplugging two amplified Spanish singers from Saint John. I felt isolated, aware always of the oppressive miles of forests black and dripping.

Years later when we were living on a farm in Ontario, Myrna and I were part of a group sponsoring some young refugee men from Vietnam. One of them, Cuong, said one day, "In Hong Kong . . . lights! . . . music! . . . women! In Canada . . . tree, tree, tree." How deeply I empathized with his boredom!

One of Fredericton's few solaces was the presence of Alden Nowlan. He held court in a small house on the edge of campus and along with the painters Bruno and Molly Bobak and several talented musicians was one of UNB's permanent artists-in-residence.

Alden's house was a mecca for visiting writers and for troops of young poets who dropped in for encouragement, words of wisdom, beer, and the ever-present gin. Evenings with Alden always began with great affability but the emotional direction of the evening could veer as the level in the gin bottle dropped. Or on some evenings, bottles.

Alden was a very large man. Operations on his throat for cancer had left his voice growly and his face puffy and this, combined with his bulk and beardedness, suggested an obese bear as he sat in his armchair sweating and rumbling and roaring about the monarchy (he supported the Stuart Pretender) or about the paucity of scientific evidence of the world's being round (he was a founding member of the Canadian Flat Earth Society).

Alden was brought up in a small village in Nova Scotia in conditions of dire poverty. He was an autodidact and proud of the fact. But it also made him prickly. He was likely to attack and bait visitors for the relative ease and comfort of their circumstances, demanding to know how with their obvious gentility and education they could hope to understand "life."

To hear Alden's account, he never saw paper or pencil until the age of twenty-five. Some professorial visitors seemed to feel shame at their lack of humble origins and at their ordinary fathers who hadn't gnawed at the bark of trees to sustain life. Alden derived a great deal of entertainment from these exercises.

I was rather bored by the romanticism of the idea that the life of New Brunswick peasants was somehow more "real" than the life of, say, Toronto stockbrokers and I used to tell him to stop talking balls. It was at about this point that the evenings degenerated into slurred and rumbling abuse.

Patrick Toner has written a biography of Nowlan entitled *If I Could Turn and Meet Myself: The Life of Alden Nowlan*. In it he recreates the first time I went to Nowlan's house in 1970 during Kent Thompson's conference.

Kent Thompson was not a frequent visitor to the Nowlan household. The man he brought that night, John Metcalf, was a first-time visitor. He had made a good impression among the UNB faculty, so good that it was generally understood that he might soon become a familiar face. Nowlan was holding forth in the den about a topic central to his mythos: the poverty of his youth. He catalogued his various deprivations like a mantra. "We had no indoor plumbing, no running water. I didn't even learn how to use a telephone until I had moved away at the age of 19 . . ."

"Yes, I know how that is," Kent Thompson said from the corner where he had been listening. "I, too, had a pretty impoverished childhood."

The guests could not listen to Thompson; they were too focussed on Nowlan, who fixed the professor in his stare while Thompson spoke. People started looking away. There was a void of silence before Nowlan responded.

"Oh, yes, Kent," he said, his voice steady. "I know that you knew just what it was like. Take your family for instance. They were so poor they could only afford to trade the car in every second year . . ."

"Oh, come off it, Alden," Thompson protested.

But Nowlan was relentless. "You were so poor that you could only afford a party line for your telephone, so poor that you sometimes had only beans and bacon to go with your potatoes . . ." And on and on, every word twisting the knife deeper.

Thompson had not had an easy week, either, what with the stress of organizing the conference. He put down his glass in disgust and walked towards the door. "That's right, Kent," Nowlan persisted. "Go back to where you are wanted, because it's not here."

Metcalf had had enough, too. "Alden, you've obviously had way too much to drink, and have no right to subject Kent or anyone else to your blatherings."

But Thompson had already grabbed his coat, nearly in tears, muttering on his way out, "I know one thing: I'm sick and tired of taking all this shit." Metcalf followed . . .

The next day Nowlan remembered enough about the night before to know that he owed Thompson a huge apology. There were a few people brave enough to remind him. "You were wrong and I'd be a shit to myself and to Kent if I didn't say so," Metcalf wrote on Monday, after cooling down. "Which, being said, I hope we can proceed as before and that you'll reply to this. You must know that I admire your work this side idolatry."

So what had this jolly evening been about? The bellicosity of gin, anti-Americanism, and Alden's insecurity in educated company.

He was kind and attentive to the young poets who hung about the house but he rarely criticized their work or put to them the necessary steel. And not one of them has emerged as a writer of any significance. Part of this acceptance was, I'm sure, kindness and camaraderie. Part of it may also have been a lack of knowledge about the traditional forms and techniques.

The camaraderie had a special Maritime tinge and was destructive to certain of these aspiring poets. When Charlie Parker was dying in the apartment of the Baroness Pannonica de Koenigswarter from the combined effects of heroin, ulcers, and cirrhosis of the liver the attending doctor asked him if he drank. Parker is alleged to have replied: "The occasional glass of sherry." I've been known to sip the occasional sherry myself and don't object at all to taking off the edge of day at about 4 p.m., but Alden drank violently and pathologically. When I once suggested that fifty-two ounces of undiluted gin was going at it rather hard, he countered by saying that where *he* came from he was not accounted a drinker. And that remark is revealing. Nova Scotia and New Brunswick are drunken and violent societies. Drinking is equated with manliness. Alden endorsed this suicidal drinking as part of being both man and poet. The legacy he left to some of those impressionable boys caused years of suffering.

I had, of course, known his poetry before going to Fredericton. When I wrote to him after that unpleasant evening in 1970 and criticized his behaviour I rather smarmily used Ben Jonson's phrase about Shakespeare to describe my liking for his work . . . *this side idolatry*. (It is taken from Jonson's 1641 tribute to Shakespeare in *Timber or Discoveries* and I assumed Alden would recognize it.)

I must confess that these days I'm very far this side idolatry. That holds true of many other writers whose work I've liked. I think I had a longing for the work to be better than it was.

"With the passing of time," Bill Hoffer used to say, "we stand the more clearly revealed."

The poem "Palomino Stallion," though it dates from 1974, can reasonably represent what Alden was writing in the early books.

> Though the barn is so warm
> that the oats in his manger,
> the straw in his bed
> seem to give off smoke—
>
> though the wind is so cold,
> the snow in the pasture
> so deep he'd fall down
> and freeze in an hour—
>
> the eleven-month-old
> palomino stallion
> has gone almost crazy
> fighting and pleading
> to be let out.

The early poems seemed at the time to possess a spontaneity which was refreshing. The volumes I'm referring to are *The Rose and the Puritan*, *A Darkness in the Earth*, *The Things Which Are*, *Under the Ice*, and *Wind in a Rocky Country*. But what seemed spontaneous then strikes me now as lax, lacking tension, insufficiently wrought.

The simplicity and charm would later coarsen into folksiness and sentimentality. In fact, this decline began with *Bread, Wine, and Salt* which was awarded the Governor General's Award in 1967. The later poetry became far too prosy and he gave in to the desire to be warm, wise, and "philosophical." Cracker-barrel philosophy, I'm afraid, and at the end of *that* road lies the *Reader's Digest*.

The early poems remind me strongly of certain poems by D. H. Lawrence and Raymond Knister, brief arpeggios which, as Kingsley Amis might have said, do not resonate *enough*. Nowadays I'd trade reams of Nowlan for just one stanza by the ineffable Eric Ormsby.

Alden once wrote to me: "*If* there comes a time when truck drivers read poetry, mine will be the poetry they'll read."

And I'm afraid that might well be his work's epitaph.

The term ground on. Eager students with manuscripts did not appear. In the endless hours, I wrote some short stories, "The Strange Aberration of Mr. Ken Smythe," "The Practice of the Craft," "The Years in Exile"—collected with others, and published in 1975 in a volume called *The Teeth of My Father*.

During that year I also helped to found the Writers' Union of Canada. I chaired a committee made up of Margaret Laurence, Alice Munro, Fred Bodsworth, and Timothy Findley which was responsible for drawing up the criteria for membership. There was a deep split from the very beginning between those who wanted a union and those who wanted something close to the idea of an academy. Everyone, however, feared that the proposed union might become merely another cozy, mushy version of the Canadian Authors' Association and any accommodation seemed worth avoiding *that* fate; the chasm between those who were frankly elitist and those who were unionist was papered over. We compromised eventually by making membership dependent on having published a trade book (i.e., a non-textbook) with a non-vanity press. Acceptance or rejection of an application for membership, however, lay with the Membership Committee.

I loved the euphoria of the first meetings, the sense of community, but the Union grew larger and its ranks filled with people who had published genuine trade books but *what* books: cookbooks, bizarre litcrit, kiddylit, how-to, Saskatchewan on $5 a day. The union soon bulged with people I'd never heard of and didn't want to know. Pierre Berton even tried to bully the membership into closed-shop politics.

I served on the national executive of the Union for its first three years but quit in umbrage over Graeme Gibson's proposal that the Union supervise the putting together of a series of anthologies for school use. I had nothing against missionary work, but I argued that if this were done the contents of the anthologies would seem to have Union imprimatur, that it would seem as if the Union were saying, "This is Canadian literature." My other strong objection was that the anthologies were thematic in structure. Producing a book called, say, *The Immigrant Experience* reduced the stories and poems in it to mere illustrations of sociology and history. In other words, I felt that the thematic approach to literature was anti-literary.

Irving Layton once wrote to me in a letter about the publication of some of his poems, ". . . there's lotsa love in you John, and that puts us roaring and clattering on the twin rails of glory." And, indeed, glory has always been my desired destination.

Poor Irving! He himself has been effaced by Alzheimer's, he's been abandoned by his publishers, largely forgotten by the public, his books entirely out of print except for the Porcupine's Quill version of *Dance with Desire*. Not much glory there, Irving, old love.

Accomplishment and glory need their rewards and in the arguments leading up to the founding of the Union, Kent Thompson and I had a vision of the institution's headquarters, a large stone mansion in Ottawa or Toronto, a somnolent library—literature, history, reference, with a sprinkling of *erotica*—log fires, deep leather chairs. A silver handbell which, when rung, brought forth Scrotum, the wrinkled old retainer, with his silver salver. Thinly sliced caraway cake and fino sherry in the mornings. Or oloroso if you *must*. Hot canapés in the afternoon. Savouries in the evening featuring the Gentlemen's Relish, Patum Peperium.

I found my favourite clubland story in A. D. Peters's autobiography. He was Evelyn Waugh's literary agent. Peters's club was closing for refurbishment and its members were farmed out to other clubs for the duration. When the club re-opened, A. D. Peters and another man were standing at the urinal having a pee and gazing round at all the glittering brass, the gleaming porcelain, the roseate copper tubing. Peters's companion said to him: "Makes the old cock look a bit shabby, doesn't it?"

Memo to Kent: *We'll have to get Scrotum a green baize apron to wear while polishing the silver and I also feel quite strongly that we ought to force the shifty old sod to iron the daily newspapers as well. Would white gloves be going too far?*

Our visions of elitist pleasures soon paled into the boring realities of rules of procedure, contract clauses, royalty rates, kill fees. "Glory" didn't get a look-in. And then, year after year descending into the bile of "gender," "race," "appropriation of voice," "women of colour." Most good writers left this snakepit or simply did not attend. It was not an appropriate context for the women who'd written "Labour Day Dinner" and "Speck's Idea" or for the men who'd written "A Small Piece of Blue" and "A North American Education."

In more recent years the Union has generated the moral fervour of a revival meeting. Their righteous antics delight. The Union newsletter presented this unintentionally hilarious account of the activities of one of their earnest and doleful Committees.

On February 1, Ontario writers and the National Council wined and dined with members of the Racial Minority Writers' Committee, at 21 McGill Street. Jill Humphries, TWUC's Ontario Co-ordinator, and Jillian Dagg, the Ontario Rep, had arranged for a very nice dinner, good wine (a bit expensive), and had managed to attract a record number of people (76) to the event. It was a good evening.

But can you imagine? A women's club, a club of well-to-do women, preserves, in two corners of the auditorium/banquet hall, gilded plaster sculptures of children carrying baskets of fruit on their heads. Not just any children, no, little black children, little slaves.

Neither Jill nor Jillian had inspected the hall prior to the dinner, nor could they have suspected the presence of imperialist or colonialist works of art there. I must admit that I myself perceived the statues only after the salad . . .

After the meal, I gathered my courage, went to their table and asked them how they felt about these objectionable objects. They were angry, of course, outraged. No, they said, such things cannot even be sold to an antique store or some place like it, "they must be destroyed!" A copy of this letter will go to the McGill Club and I hope its Board of Directors will do away with all mementos of shameful times. I did not inspect the place from top to bottom, but who knows, there may be more such things in other nooks and crannies.

How marvellously *relaxing* it must be to have a mind so basic!

The choice of Union over Academy was an inevitably Canadian choice. Leftish rather than rightish, fair and aboveboard rather than snooty, no nasty or disturbing judgements needing to be made. The Union reflected the politics of Graeme Gibson and Margaret Atwood and their set; they've always believed in organizing and melding literature and institutions and directing them towards nationalist ends.

One of that year's few pleasures in Fredericton was meeting John Newlove. He came to UNB to give a public reading and I was keenly interested to attend. I knew the poetry he'd already published and was reading his current work as we were both appearing in the same magazines. He loomed large on my horizon. I loved the *tone* of his writing.

I produced a version of our meeting as the opening paragraphs of a story called "The Teeth of My Father."

Adrift one afternoon on a tide of beer and nostalgia in the River Room of the Lord Beaverbrook Hotel in Fredericton, my friend and I traded stories of our dead fathers. We drank until the bar began to fill for Happy Hour. He told me how his father had employed him every Saturday and how every Saturday evening before being allowed out his father had forced him into a game of poker to recover the day's wages. We drank until the free cheese, olives, and melba toast were wheeled away at six. I told him of my father's teeth; he, of his father's three-and-a-half-year disappearance for a drink. I, of my father and the loose box; he, of his father's contempt of court charge. I, of my father and the consequences of the VD pamphlet. We drank until shortly before his evening flight to Halifax was due.

It was Cyril Connolly, I believe, who said that drinking is a low form of creativity. A perceptive remark. Drinking also prompts my memory. Walking home on wilful legs in the cold night air, my drunkenness unlocked the smells and textures of the receding past, recalling incident and anecdote I had not thought to tell in the bar's warm comfort. Lurching up Forest Hill, I remembered my father's tobacco growing, and worse, its curing, our cinema outing; the afternoon he felled the kitchen; the tubular steel incident. And it was on Forest Hill, although I'd often told the story of his teeth, that I realized for the first time how genuinely and entirely eccentric my father had been.

(I have decided to tell the truth. My stories in the River Room were not purely nostalgic; they were calculated to be funny and entertain my friend. My friend was more an acquaintance, a man I admired and wanted to impress. And "wilful legs" was plagiarized from Dylan Thomas.)

I dedicated this story to Alice Munro. She dedicated one to me called "Home" which appeared in *New Canadian Stories 1974*. This was because we'd been talking to each other about what "autobiography" in fiction meant. Alice felt it nearly impossible emotionally to write about her mother. I think she felt also that to write about an experience was in some way to betray it. We were both experimenting with the idea of commenting *on* the story *within* the story—as I do in the bracketed paragraph above. We were attempting to make the stories more "real" or "truthful" by "confessing" to their artificiality.

In later years I came to believe that there is no such thing as autobiography. There are arrangements of words on a page. There is rhetoric. We are not recording; we are creating. I was charmed by a statement I read recently by Quebec abstractionist Claude Tousignant. He wrote: "What I advocate is the notion of paintings as beings, not representations." It immediately struck me that the finest stories are also "beings" rather than "representations," magical worlds wrought by language.

But to return to John Newlove.

In centuries past itinerant craftsmen travelled from mill to mill seeking work recutting the blunted patterns of grooves on the faces of the millstones. Over the years tiny slivers of metal worked their way into the men's hands, causing blue and black ridges and worms beneath the skin. Millers wanted experienced men and so used to say to the masons, "Hold out your hands and show me your metal." If one wanted to see John Newlove's metal one would need an MRI machine.

One ankle is held together by a metal pin, the ankle broken during a drunken fight in the kitchen of Al Purdy's house in Ameliasburg. Newlove claims that Purdy dropped on him, or threw at him, a water cooler. His thigh is held together by a large pin which was put in after a severe fall off a bar stool in Regina. One knee contains metal acquired after he fell down over a small drain in Peter Milroy's front garden after having been thrown out of the house for attempting to kick down the door of Peter's wine cellar. The scars are multiple. It seems that all John's life has been an effort to outrun sorrow and melancholy, the darkness everywhere in human life that weighs upon him. Many of his early poems are about hitchhiking; he's always been on the road escaping from and travelling to.

> Every muddy road I walk along
> I am the man who knows all about Jesus
> but doesn't believe. My fat ass
> trudges on. I am so weary. Lord;
> beer is my muse, my music.

John's drunken exploits are legion. Everyone, it seems, has Newlove stories. Newlove biting strangers at parties; Newlove putting his false teeth in a stranger's beer glass; Newlove awaking in an abandoned lot in the back of a taxi, his body heaped with empty cans of Newcastle Brown Ale. Newlove flying back to Nelson and getting off the plane drunk in Castlereagh instead of Castlegar and summoning a taxi to drive him 175 miles through the midnight Kootenay mountains. Newlove ordering vodka after vodka with the stern command: "No fruit or vegetable matter."

My most preposterous Newlove story concerns a bookstore in Toronto which was called About Books. It was on Queen Street West and was run by the antiquarian dealer Larry Wallrich. John and I had stopped in there one morning and Larry and I soon got deeply involved in some Robert Graves limited editions. Larry also brought out some prized Graves manuscript written in fountain pen on flimsy blue sheets of what looked like airmail paper. The poems were from *Fairies and Fusiliers* and probably dated from 1916 or 1917. Larry described to me the difficult research to identify the poems, difficult because Graves had suppressed the volume.

Newlove, bored with all this antiquarian chit-chat, wandered off and returned half an hour or so later with a bottle of vodka, a carton of orange juice, and three Styrofoam cups. He seemed slightly unsteady. He pulled up a chair and asked us if we wanted a drink. Both Larry and I said that it seemed a little early. The inevitable occurred. Wrestling to open the carton, he knocked over the vodka. It gouted onto the manuscript sheets and instantly the ink began to blur and fuzz. Larry and I were so shocked neither of us said anything. We just stared. John started looking shifty, then cowed, gazing up at us like a dog expecting a smack. Then, as we stared at him, he reached out and peeled off two or three sodden pages and in an act of expiation stuffed them into his mouth, chewing and painfully swallowing.

And that was in the morning.

In the afternoon, I got him back to the Royal York Hotel where I was staying. This involved John on his hands and knees in taxis, his mistakenly urinating into the clothes closet, his lying on my bed to sleep, my attempting to remove some of his clothes so he'd be more comfortable, his accusations that I was molesting him homosexually, his attempts to hit me. In the end I got so cross I gave him a good clout in the head and he went to sleep.

But—obviously—there was another John. Those who loved him and his poetry knew that the pain that enveloped and consumed him was real. We knew him as a soft-spoken gentleman, a technician in sophisticated verse, a voracious reader of history, a curator of anecdotes, a collector of Victorian travel books, a hoarder of ancient Syrian pottery and Athenian silver tetradrachms.

Concerning Stars, Flowers, Love, Etc.

Make it easier, they say, make it easier. Tell
me something I already know, about stars or flowers or,

or happiness. I am happy sometimes, though
not right now, specially. Things are not going
too good right now. But you should try
to cheer people up, they say. There is
a good side to life, though
not right now, specially. Though the stars
continue to shine in some places and the flowers
continue to bloom in some places
and people do not starve in some places
and people are not killed in some places
and there are no wars in some places
and there are no slaves in some places
and in some places people love each other,
they say. Though I don't know where. They say,
I don't *want* to be sad. Help me not to know.

For John's fiftieth birthday I gathered together and printed up
poems people had written in tribute. Using a line from one of his
poems I called the pamphlet "Everyone Leans, Each on Each Other:
Words for John Newlove on the Occasion of His Fiftieth Birthday."
George Johnston, now lost to Alzheimer's, one of the most important
poets Canada has ever produced though almost entirely unknown,
wrote one of his renowned occasional poems which gorgeously captures his feelings for John and speaks for all John's friends.

A Palimpsest for John Newlove's Fiftieth Birthday Party

Everyone is wise. John Newlove is
a master in his versifying and he
knows things he cannot explain to the others,
though he tries as hard as he can anyways.

God only knows what he is up to tonight
making his way to eternity, through destiny
manufacturing chaos into rhythms
and all the while observing himself

wrapped for fifty years in the cold dark cloak
of fate, and making poetry of his doubts.
How splendid, how pregnant, all his poetry,
and not composed of vegetable peels, either.

How important it makes him in our eyes.
Though we are in a land of loonies, we can feel
that he has done us all good in his fifty years
and we hope he will have many more to do us good.

It has been a long, dear association
making the alien recognizable
in ourselves—and why should it ever end?
Think of that, John, if you can bear it, tonight.

When John got wind of the publication and the proposed party
he said that he would leave town on the proposed date and berated
me bitterly when I gave him a copy of the tribute, complaining that I
had lumbered him with the unwanted task of having to write thank-
you letters to all the contributors.

Over the years after Fredericton our paths crossed continually.
John wrote a book called *The Green Plain* which he dedicated to me.
Together we published a book called *Dreams Surround Us*. He moved
back to Toronto and then after some years moved back west to Nelson,
B.C., where he taught at a community college. Letters were sporadic.
Then I heard that the college had closed and that he was without
work. Soon after this I heard that he was in a hospital there.

Late one night the phone rang and the ghost of John's voice whis-
pered, "You've got to get me out of here. You've got to get me a job."
He'd been hospitalized because of his drinking, apparently, and the
doctors had given him six months to live if he continued.

At the time Myrna was working for the Commissioner of Official Languages doing mystic things with computers. Her immediate
boss was Pierre de Blois, a *bon vivant* and *bon viveur*. She persuaded
Pierre that the Commissioner really needed an English-language
editor for the department's unspeakably dreary magazine, *Language*

and Society. We looked up and copied out reams of quotations about John from literary guides and encyclopedias and Myrna wrote up a magisterial CV.

We felt forced to say to Pierre that there *was* a tiny problem, that John had been known from time to time to, well, tipple. Pierre made a Gallic gesture and uttered a French equivalent of *Pshaw!* An interview was arranged. I went out to the airport at midday to meet the plane. John was, inevitably, inebriated. I got him home and into the shower. Made him eat scrambled eggs and toast, phoned Pierre and got the interview delayed for two and a half hours. I walked him down to Pierre's office. By this time he was running with sweat and was so nervous he was scarcely able to speak. The difficulty of the interview, I understand, was compounded by the fact that the interviewer was a weird Englishman so shy and withdrawn he could scarcely speak in public. Pierre, typically, solved this problem by asking the questions *and then answering them.*

John emerged from this strange non-interview with the job secured and at a considerable salary and dined with us every night for a month until Myrna found him an apartment which he later complained about because he said the garage it faced was ugly.

Myrna kept her eye on him and if he arrived squiffy in the morning she and a friend would take his arms and march him back into the elevator again and send him home in a cab.

Soon he burst forth in beautifully cut Harry Rosen suits and was obnoxious. He would phone me at odd hours and say, "Let's go out and cause some *serious* trouble!" Walking home from the post office one day with my mail I saw him on the street and holding up the letter said, "Hey, John, I'm in *Who's Who*." He said, "Who isn't?" John checking his stride and glancing back at the panhandler sitting with his kerchiefed dog with its one eye a spooky milk-blue and saying, "No, but I *would* be willing to assist you financially by killing your dog." Asking him on another occasion for the loan of twenty dollars which he begrudgingly withdrew from his fat wallet saying, as if in moral disapproval, "Why don't you find a fucking job, Metcalf."

In 1993 I had the honour of helping John put together a new Selected Poems. Porcupine's Quill published this volume as *Apology for Absence: Selected Poems 1962–1992.* We launched the book at a reading series I was running at Magnum Book Store. It was a delight to hear John reading with tight passion such classic poems as "Samuel Hearne in Wintertime," "The Pride," "Doukhobor," and "Ride Off Any Horizon."

I concluded my introduction of him to the Magnum audience by quoting from a review written by Robin Skelton ten years or more earlier of John's preceding selected poems, *The Fat Man.*

Skelton wrote:

The poetry itself is enormously well crafted, subtly controlled in tone, and richly various in style, even while remaining consistent to what emerges as an overall purpose to portray the human tragedy with an economy and elegance that succeed in making the whole book a tribute to courage and a statement of the awesome spiritual strength of man.

This *Selected Poems*, omitting as it does many of the poems of pure reportage and of whimsy which lessened the impact of some of the separate collections, is one of the most impressive to have been published in the English-speaking world in the last twenty years.

"What," I asked rhetorically, "would Skelton say of this even more splendid selection?"

Newlove rose, walked to the lectern, nodded acknowledgement to me, and said in his habitual sardonic manner: "The last time I saw Skelton was at a party in Victoria and he was wearing a colander on his head with feathers taped to it. However . . ."

Recently, after sporadic illness and a long period of sobriety and quiescence, John erupted again. His wife, Susan, was in Vancouver visiting their daughter and he phoned asking me to buy him a bottle of vodka and bring it to his house. He said he was too sick to go out. I debated about this for a while but decided I'd go and urge him to sober up before Susan returned. When he opened the door I could see he was shaking, sweating. I gave him the vodka and urged him to drink just enough to straighten himself out and then go to sleep. He asked me to unscrew the top of the bottle. Then he asked me to pour a shot into a glass. Then he asked me to hold the glass to his lips. The shaking became less violent, and after a few more sips, stopped. I delivered my speech sternly and turned to leave.

He smiled at me.

He said, "I can feel it singing in my blood."

"Go to bed," I said, "you horrible old bugger."

In the summer of 2001 Susan phoned us to say that John was in hospital. He had suffered a major stroke. Myrna immediately sent white orchids to his hospital room. When I walked in he was strapped into a wheelchair. All of his right side was dead. He could not speak. He looked at the orchids, then at me, and nudged with his left hand as if to say: *you, you.* I talked to him for a while, not really knowing what I was saying, until sorrow silenced me and I sat holding his hand and stroking his hair, taking liberties with his dignity for which in earlier years he'd have tried to knock me down.

RESURRECTION

WHEN THE TERM ended in Fredericton I went back to Montreal to look for work. In Fredericton I'd had the daily company and friendship of Doug Rollins. In Montreal I was alone and my depression fed on itself in the silent apartment and grew more intense and convoluted. Gale had renounced the lesbian life and, taking Elizabeth with her, had decamped to New York where she lived, serially, with members of Dave Liebman's jazz band.

I managed to get two part-time jobs teaching at Loyola and Vanier CEGEPs. It took all my energy to work and to hold myself together sufficiently to see Elizabeth and look after her in the holidays. During these two years I spent a lot of time with Ray Smith and I doubt I would have survived without his wonderful kindness and concern.

I knew that I was becoming seriously ill but couldn't see beyond where I was. I suffered suffocating dreams. I woke some mornings to find tears running down my face. I felt incessant grief. I *leaked* tears. I could feel myself becoming more and more emotionally frail. My weight had dropped to under 120 pounds.

I decided that I had to get help and I was sufficiently deranged that I sought the services of a psychiatrist. I drew on these experiences in my novella "Girl in Gingham." Again fiction is more vivid that fact. My protagonist in the novella is an antiques appraiser called Peter who is divorced and is persuaded by a friend to avail himself of the services of a dating service called CompuMate.

The woman situation had started at the same time he'd stopped seeing Dr. Trevore, when he'd realized that he was boring himself; when he'd realized that his erstwhile wife, his son, and he had been reduced to characters in a soap opera which was broadcast every two weeks from Trevore's sound-proofed studio.

And which character was he?

He was the man whom ladies helped in laundromats. He was the man who dined on frozen pies. Whose sink was full of dishes. He was the man in the raincoat who wept in late-night bars.

That office, and he in it, that psychiatrist's office with its scuffed medical magazines and pieces of varnished driftwood on the waiting room's occasional tables was the stuff of comic novels, skits, the weekly fodder of stand-up comedians.

In the centre of Trevore's desk sat a large, misshapen thing. The rim was squashed in four places indicating that it was probably an ashtray. On its side, Trevore's name was spelled out in spastic white slip. Peter had imagined it a grateful gift from the therapy ward of a loony bin.

It presided over their conversations.

How about exercise? Are you exercising?

No, not much.

How about squash?

I don't know how to play.

I play myself. Squash. I play on Mondays, Wednesdays, and Fridays. In the evenings.

Following one such session he had gone home, opened the bathroom cabinet, regarded the pill bottles which had accumulated over the months. He had taken them all out and stood them on the tank above the toilet. He arranged them into four rows. In the first row he placed the Valium. In the second, the Stelazine. In the third, the Tofranil. In the fourth, the Mareline.

Uncapping the bottles, he tipped the tablets rank by rank into the toilet bowl. Red fell upon yellow, blue fell on red, tranquillizing, antidepressant psychotherapeutic agents fell, swirled and sifted onto agents for the relief of anxiety, emotional disorders, and nausea.

The results had suggested to him the droppings of a Walt Disney rabbit.

Some nattily turned cadences there. Is this autobiography? No, as I always insist, it's art.

Though it is more or less what did happen to me.

Except that "Dr. Trevore," a pallid man who wore a tie with horseshoes on it, also tried out on me, if I recall aright, Elavil, Norpramine, Manerix, and Nardil. All of which I washed down with beer or Scotch and none of which seemed to have the slightest effect.

One day I simply stopped leaking. During this darkness I had been unable to value anything. Suddenly I was back in the world again, possibly not a ray of sunshine but able to imagine a future.

My literary life meanwhile had not been particularly productive. After *The Lady Who Sold Furniture* appeared I had moved from Clarke Irwin to what was considered *the* Canadian publisher, McClelland and Stewart, for the publication of *Going Down Slow*. The book appeared, was well reviewed, then disappeared. This was in 1972. My editor was Anna Porter (then Anna Szigethy). I had certain expectations of a publisher. I thought that editors should keep in touch with their writers. Should be solicitous. Should be aware of intentions and of work-in-progress. Should be concerned about the shape of a writer's career. I certainly had none of this from Jack McClelland. He concerned himself only with the writers of his own age such as Mordecai Richler and Farley Mowat. As far as I can recall I had no contact with Anna Szigethy for about a year after *Going Down Slow* came out. I wanted to be in a relationship and that need for support has guided me all these years later in my conduct at the Porcupine's Quill.

There's been an effort lately to posit Jack McClelland as the conscious founder of Canadian literature. He certainly did a great deal but his taste in literature was perhaps not as keenly honed as is suggested in James King's biography *Jack*. No one could deny that Jack McClelland was an ardent nationalist, and a great publicist and impresario. I've always enjoyed the story of his publicizing Sylvia Fraser's *The Emperor's Virgin* in 1980. On a blustery day, Sylvia Fraser in a shimmering dress, two centurions carrying books, and Jack in a toga paraded down Bloor Street. An onlooker was alleged to have said: "There goes Jack McClelland—only one sheet to the wind."

No one could deny that he built the careers of Berton, Mowat, Richler, Layton, Cohen, and Margaret Laurence. But he also published a much longer list of potboilers by such worthies as Richard Rohmer and Adrienne Clarkson. And some of the reputations he built are sagging badly; the best Margaret Laurence titles seem to me to be *The Tomorrow-Tamer* and *A Jest of God*. I cannot reread *The Stone Angel* or *The Diviners*. He published far more non-fiction than fiction, popular political and sociological titles which quickly mulched down to become leafmould. His lasting legacy was the New Canadian Library series.

It was in the late sixties that the small press movement was beginning to gather steam. The House of Anansi started in 1967. Oberon Press in 1966. I was attracted by the intimacy and the energy. I thought at the time that Oberon was going to become a Canadian version of the Hogarth Press in England. I wrote to Anna Szigethy, resigning as a McClelland and Stewart author, and contracted to publish with Oberon Press. Anna was both surprised and alarmed. Alarmed, apparently, at the possibility of further defections. Matt Cohen always used to say that he owed all the fuss M&S made of him to my letter of resignation.

In 1975 Oberon published the story collection *The Teeth of My Father*. The cover was a photograph of me with Elizabeth taken by Sam Tata. This was printed in teeth-gritting yellow and lime; a second printing appeared in a more pleasing plum colour.

Nineteen seventy-five turned out to be a momentous year for reasons other than literary. I got married again. Some romances are described as whirlwind; this one was more like a tornado. In December of 1974, at a dinner party, I met Myrna Teitelbaum. Christmas intervened and I was busy with Elizabeth. I phoned Myrna after Elizabeth had gone back to New York and a mere two months later Myrna and I were married by a protonotary in St. Jean, Quebec, in a civil ceremony not much of which I remember, except that Myrna had to agree to accompany me if my work took me out of the province and I had to agree that I would refrain from beating her.

We have remained immersed in each other ever since.

INCREASINGLY BAD VIBES

I CRINGE when people describe themselves as "educators." What pomposity it bespeaks! By 1975 I was going distinctly *off* education. The feel-good, feel-happy duo of Emmett Hall and Lloyd Dennis, authors of *Aims and Objectives for Education in Ontario*, a report tabled in 1968, together poisoned the Ontario school system and spread the taint of "child-centred" education throughout Canada. The *Hall-Dennis Report*, as it was called, almost immediately reduced English and history to elective subjects. Mix in with this short-sighted barbarism the fads and fashions rolling in from the States—drugs, brown rice, guitars, I Ching, flower power, Zen, primal screams, vibrators, identity crises, *You're Tremendous, I'm Terrific*, boring goddamn people *finding themselves* all over the damn place . . . this tidal wave of sloppy thinking and sloppy feeling left teachers facing students who rejected traditional bodies of knowledge as authoritarian intrusions on their rights and who were innocent of grammar, history, geography, literature, music, architecture, and painting, students who were, increasingly, far out.

This general morass is now dignified as "the counterculture"; I'm always surprised to see in catalogues the extremely high prices still commanded by sawdust books by such genuinely unlikeable writers as Jack Kerouac, Allen Ginsberg, and Richard Brautigan.

The sixties and early seventies were a sorry time.

My job at Loyola involved sharing an office with the new writer-in-residence, Al Purdy. Al wasn't actually in residence. He commuted from Ameliasburg. This involved him in early morning train rides during which he felt it necessary to fortify himself against the cold. By the time he arrived at Loyola he was usually fortified to the gills, cheerful but sleepy. He solved this problem by having a collapsible cot moved into our office and locking the door.

He surfaced at midday. He'd boom and bellow about in the English department office for a while, groping unfortunate secretaries and filching letterhead and then he'd phone a nearby grocery store to get a case of beer delivered. A pizza would follow and soon he'd have the place comfortable with a fug of cigar smoke. His cigars were rank, plastic tipped and dipped in port.

Al's classes in creative writing mainly involved listening to records of *Under Milk Wood* and Cyril Cusack's renderings of Gerard Manley Hopkins, recitations rather too fluttery for my taste.

On some afternoons I'd be further excluded from my office, facing a locked door while on the collapsible cot he plumbed the depths of one of the female department members.

With the advent of spring and the retreat of the snow under our office window, beer bottles began to surface, more and more every day as the sun gained strength, until they lay revealed on the playing field like corpses after a mighty battle.

I assigned during the second term an essay on Margaret Laurence's *The Diviners*. One numbed sophomore wrote a deranged screed comparing the novel with a song by Elton John. Naturally, I failed him. He complained to the English department. The Chair, in his wisdom, ordered me to justify my actions before three department members. This I declined to do.

The following academic year I found part-time work at Vanier College, Snowdon Campus. It was an unspeakable employment. The word *campus* is misleading; it suggests lawns and manicured flower beds. The college was housed in what had been an office block and fronted onto the Decarie Expressway. Immediately next door was a large A&W. With the windows closed, the heat was intolerable; with the windows open, it was impossible to make oneself heard over the traffic.

I taught two courses: creative writing and a course on the Canadian short story. Some way into this latter I was removed from the course on the grounds that I was not competent, lacking as I did an

MA. The year was saved by the fact that I had one good student, now in theatre in Chicago, and by my office being adjacent to that of Barry Cameron—now a professor at UNB—who was severely shaken by what had signed up for his thoughtful courses in Canadian literature. We sustained each other by mutual bemoaning as we picked our way through the ankle-deep litter in the corridors.

The chairman of the English department had retired from the fray; he used to lock himself in his office with the head of the remedial programme and gaze at rented videotapes of dubious artistic merit.

I had become disenchanted with teaching because I couldn't find people bright enough to teach. It is impossible to teach people at more than a rudimentary level if you do not share a vocabulary. I needed to be able to say to a student, What you need to do here is shape the paragraph in the spirit of the opening paragraph of Katherine Mansfield's "Miss Brill." And have the student knowing author and story and capable of picking up the hint.

I felt the same disenchantment recently at the Humber School for Writers in Toronto, a week-long course in the summer I've been teaching for some years now. A young man brought to the class sixteen stories, none of which made the slightest sense. They were shapeless and it was impossible to divine their aim. He didn't seem to understand any questions I asked him about them. Something inspired me to ask him if he had *read* any short stories. He said he had read one but couldn't remember much about it. I wrote out a long list of titles and told him to go away and start reading. He told me that same day at lunch that he was going to live in Montreal for a couple of months to see what it was like. I said that he'd find the architecture in Montreal more pleasing than Toronto. He said, "Architecture? That's not anything *I'd* know about."

I gave up my apartment and moved in with Myrna a couple of days before we got married. She owned a house in the almost entirely Jewish enclave of Côte St. Luc. I was not entirely at ease in a community of observant or even semi-observant Jews. I wouldn't have been at ease in a community of observant anything.

I felt not at ease living in the house that Myrna had lived in with her first husband. I was feeling disenchanted with teaching, oppressed by the grind of separatist politics, constricted and confined. It was as if one cycle of my life were over and it was time to launch into new experience.

The woman who lived opposite had a pale, weedy five-year-old who sometimes played with Myrna's son, Ronald, who was the same age. When he came over his mother would screech from the middle of the road, "Don't let him near anything *treyf.*"

When Pesach rolls around, the celebration of Passover, Jews are required to clean their houses and get rid of all bread and any product which is not manufactured under rabbinical supervision and designated "suitable for Passover" or *pesachdik.*

One afternoon during Pesach I was sitting on the front steps and eating a cheese sandwich. The horrid little boy drifted across and stood regarding me. In silence he broke a few twigs off a bush. He eventually said, pointing to the sandwich, "Is that pesachdik?"

"Piss off," I explained.

Côte St. Luc, I decided, was not my natural habitat.

It was to be another year before we moved.

I often daydream about my natural habitat. Bath and Clifton would serve as models. Georgian terraces clad in honey-coloured stone. Pubs with cobbled courtyards shaded by vast horse chestnut trees. Little shops filled with dubious antiques. A used-book shop where a gentle old rogue also sells fading watercolours labelled "School of Cotman 1782–1842." All a little shabby and seedy now. Once aristocratic, now déclassé, with a floating population of students, single professionals, and in the pub, the Colonel, "Call me Courtney," in his canary-yellow waistcoat drinking pink gins. There's something mildly louche about this sun-lit place, mildly raffish, Roger et Gallet savon, Eau de Cologne Jean-Marie Farina, sex in the afternoon, Spanish champagne.

At some time during this Vanier year of suffering I was invited to the University of Ottawa to give a reading. I happened to bump into the chairman of the English department, Professor Glenn Clever, who said quite casually, "Oh, by the by, would you like to be writer-in-residence here next year?"

"Yes," I said, "thank you."

"Fine," he said. "I'll send a contract."

Above: The 1971 Sam Tata photo that was used as a poster for Montreal Story Tellers. Ray Smith, Clark Blaise, Hugh Hood, and Ray Fraser. After that day's shoot we ended up in a tavern on McGill Street; we often did. (SAM TATA)

Right: About to read with Alden Nowlan in 1972 in the art gallery in the University of Fredericton. Somewhere in the background lurks Molly Lamb Bobak, who once sent me an exquisite watercolour landscape to say thank you for having written *The Teeth of My Father*. (STONE'S STUDIO, FREDERICTON)

Below: P.K. Page and Earle Birney in 1972 at the founding meeting in Toronto of the Writers' Union. (RAY SMITH)

With Hugh Hood, Doug Jones, and John Newlove at a Canada Day at Selwyn House in Montreal, 1975. What a long time ago it seems now that Canadian literature was taught in Canadian schools.

Left: John Newlove in the apartment Myrna found him that faced "the ugly garage." (SAM TATA)
Right: Bharati Mukherjee and Clark Blaise in the long-ago Montreal Story Teller days. I'm just starting work now on the fourth and final volume of Blaise's monument, the Collected Stories. (SAM TATA)

After a reading with Alice Munro at Loyola of Montreal, 1975.

Left: The Sam Tata photograph used as the cover of *The Teeth of My Father*, 1975. Mr. Klein used to ascribe inept or degenerate carving to "sub-tribes." In the corner, a statue by a sub-tribe of the Bambara. (SAM TATA)
Right: The farmhouse at Delta, 1976. As Myrna's Romanian grandfather used to say of the unmotivated indigent and to his spoiled grandchildren: "Go work CPR pick and shovel!" (DAVID HIRSCHMANN)

Above: Hugh Hood with Danny and Rangidam at Delta. He seems to have made a rare investment in new sneakers. (JACK CHIANG)

Right: William Hoffer in our kitchen in Ottawa about to snap at Myrna: "There is nothing wrong with the transmission. Check the set." (AUTHOR)

Below: The Vancouver Tanks Debate with Bill Hoffer, Andreas Schroeder, Eleanor Wachtel, and Dave Godfrey looking in some indefinable way like Richard Nixon.

Above: With Rangidam and Leon Rooke in Ottawa, 1982, on the ECW Road Show, a grueling tour on which Leon and I subsisted on our and Hugh's Air Canada wine and Hugh feasted on everyone's Air Canada chicken.

Right: A 1982 portrait by Peter Milroy, now director of UBC Press, taken in the days when I yet had vices. (PETER MILROY)

Below: With Myrna and Rangidam. In the background one of Claude Breeze's *Canadian Atlas* paintings, which ought not to work but does. (PETER MILROY)

A Sam Tata photograph for *Portraits of Canadian Writers*. I remember watching Sam "burn up" the texture of the fireplace marble to resonate with the colours and textures of the Jean McEwen painting behind me. (SAM TATA)

Left: An "environmental" portrait by Sam Tata taken in 1985. On the wall a leaf from a Kufic koran. (SAM TATA)
Right: Family group in 1982 in Ottawa. (PETER MILROY)

Above: With Al Purdy and Tony Calzetta behind Al's cottage at Ameliasburg in 1989. Sam Tata was photographing for me for *The Second Macmillan Anthology*. (SAM TATA)

Right: Tony Calzetta in the early 1980s with his friend and companion, painter Andrea Bolley. One of her constructed canvases hangs in the background. (PAUL BUER)

Below: *Regal Lane Drag* by Tony Calzetta 1979 (65" x 104"). This vast canvas hangs in our bedroom in Ottawa and each morning galvanizes us. (PAUL BUER)

Above: With Carol Shields in 1993 at the National Library's celebration of the Governor General's Awards. I was the stand-in for Don Coles, who had won for *Forests of the Medieval World* but refused to tread the boards. (UNKNOWN)

Right: Keath Fraser in Vancouver in 1988. Keath gave the royalties from his travel anthology *Bad Trips* to Canada India Village Aid Society, a charity founded by George and Ingeborg Woodcock. As an illustration of the cultural and linguistic divide, the British called the book *Worst Journeys*. (SAM TATA)

Below: Sam Tata in 1991 at the National Library launch of *Portraits of Canadian Writers*, talking to Tony Calzetta and Fran Hill, owner of the Fran Hill Gallery on Queen Street East in Toronto. (MICHELLINE ROCHETTE)

Off he pottered.

It was agreed that I would make myself available to students (as it turned out, all one of them) two days a week. I was commuting from Montreal and sleeping over in Ottawa for one night. The department had known months in advance of my arrival. When I duly presented myself on the first day of term I was introduced to the new chairman, Professor Marcotte. He informed me that my office was at the top of the old house which served as English department offices but that unfortunately the room didn't have a desk in it. Or chair. There was, apparently, something wrong with the heating system so that the temperature in the room was stuck at over one hundred degrees.

I returned to the Lord Elgin Hotel.

It took three more weeks for the desk to appear.

The chairs took another two.

Two weeks before I left, my arrival was announced.

Deskless, chairless, studentless, I was bored out of my mind. To while away the time I decided, pinching Kent Thompson's idea, to organize a conference on the short story. I invited Clark Blaise, Hugh Hood, Kent Thompson, Alice Munro, Ray Smith, Margaret Laurence, and Audrey Thomas and they gave readings to upwards of three hundred students every evening. During the day, the critics I'd invited, W. H. New, George Bowering, Barry Cameron, Patricia Morley, Frank Davey, Doug Barbour, and Michael Dixon, gave papers on the work of writers they'd been paired with. The whole affair was introduced by Robert Weaver of CBC *Anthology*.

I had scraped together the necessary money for this conference from the Canada Council and from the University of Ottawa Student Council; the English department confined its support to insisting that papers be signed indemnifying it in case of financial shortfall. At one point, enraged and sickened by the department's *pissy* attitude, I offered in writing to make good out of my own pocket any loss that might be incurred.

As the date of the conference approached, my days were spent on the run booking hotel rooms, booking the Press Club, arranging an auditorium, checking sound systems, writing letters, confirming, soothing.

The University of Ottawa had promised to publish the papers presented at the conference but, of course, reneged. I regret to this day the loss of that volume. George Bowering gave an involving and quirky paper on Audrey Thomas. Doug Barbour was entertaining and stimulating on Ray Smith's work. Frank Davey's paper on Clark Blaise was astonishing in that he seriously advanced the view that Blaise's writing was akin to journalism—this of one of the country's most *poetic* writers.

The only unhappy writer was Margaret Laurence. I'd paired her with an academic called Patricia Morley. This woman taught at the Simone de Beauvoir Institute for Women's Studies, a name that always makes me smile because it sounds like some ghastly joint in a David Lodge novel. Compared with Patricia Morley, Margaret Atwood sounds vivacious. To say that Patricia Morley talks in a relentless monotone does not even *suggest* . . . Morley had more or less *appropriated* poor Margaret who came to me in weeping complaint and had to be bought Scotch.

I was happy escaping from Ottawa. A dismal little university. A bland, parochial little town. I was not to know then that in the future I was to spend more than twenty years there. A couple of years ago Mordecai Richler asked me how long it had been and, shaking his head sorrowfully, said, "John, John, it's a long sentence."

Back in Montreal, Elspeth Cameron, then chair of English at Loyola, offered me a job as writer-in-residence for the balance of the year. Though I religiously kept office hours, not a single student came to see me. I spent a lot of time with Harry Hill propping up the faculty club bar. Harry, though camp as a line of tents, was one of the most brilliant teachers I've ever seen in action. If Loyola had not itself been a dim little college riven by vicious academic politics, it could have built round Harry Hill a very important drama school but they predictably squandered the opportunity.

Hugh Hood published *A New Athens*, the second volume of his *roman-fleuve*, in 1977 but he'd probably written it in 1976. Myrna remembers reading the manuscript in second carbon. He phoned one day in the summer and asked us if we'd like to drive with him to look at Athens and surrounding countryside. We were much taken by the countryside and we were soon scouting houses on our own. We both had the feeling that this was the move towards something different that had been ordained for us.

We drove about the area looking at Plum Hollow, Philipsville, Forfar (which sold a five-year-old cheddar called "Old Baby"), Chantry, Elgin, and one day found an old stone house just outside Delta, a village about ten miles from Athens. I was charmed to discover that Delta was in the Township of Bastard. I was also charmed to discover that Delta was the birthplace of Lorne Pierce who had been editor-in-chief of Ryerson Press. I named my press the Bastard Press and it was under that imprint that Newlove and I published *Dreams Surround Us*.

And dreams did surround us. The house had been built in about 1840. There were exposed ceiling beams, wide-sawn plank floors, a vast garden to one side, a forty-one-acre field in the back vivid with meadow flowers, and in front of the house an ancient mulberry tree laden with plump maroon berries.

STEERING THE CRAFT

BETWEEN 1976 AND 1993 I edited and
co-edited eighteen anthologies of Canadian short stories and compiled seven textbooks of Canadian stories for use in schools and universities. I did all this work with the conscious intention of changing
the nature and shape of short fiction in Canada.

In 1971, David Helwig and Tom Marshall edited a story anthology for Oberon entitled *Fourteen Stories High.* This was followed in
1972 by *New Canadian Stories,* which became the title of the annuals
that were to follow. David Helwig resigned from editing the series in
1975 because he had accepted a job with the CBC Drama Department which precluded outside work and through David's interven-
tion I was offered the job as co-editor with Joan Harcourt.

The policy of the series when I took over was to publish previously unpublished work. Helwig had started the series with the
intention of providing another outlet for new work and new writers.
Joan Harcourt and I were receiving manuscripts by the hundred.
Nearly all were atrocious. I was soon driven to begging friends for
unpublished stories—and at that, I wasn't getting the cream because
Oberon could not afford to match the payments offered by some
of the magazines, nominal though such payments were. (An entire
genre in Canadian literature was shaped by the fact that some publications paid as much as a hundred dollars for a story, others far less,
or nothing.) It dawned on me slowly that we were in direct competition with the literary magazines for a very small crop of good work.

There was not much point in this and I began to get restless with the whole policy and purpose of the series.

Although Joan and I got on well together, I began to hanker after the idea of a fresh co-editor, someone not quite so *nice* as Joan, someone harsher in judgement. I felt I needed to work with someone who really knew short fiction, who lived and breathed it as I did. I wanted someone who would understand style and elegance and who would be repelled by socially acceptable *themes*. I decided on Clark Blaise. Joan resigned by mutual agreement in 1977 and I persuaded Michael Macklem, Oberon's publisher, to change both the title and policy of the anthology.

The title was now to be *Best Canadian Stories* and the policy was to concentrate on republishing the best stories from the literary magazines. I *had* wanted an outright policy of republication only but Macklem argued that such a policy would be bad PR and would result in reviewers berating Oberon for closing off yet another publishing outlet. Under pressure, I agreed that we would continue to read and consider unsolicited manuscripts.

Joan Harcourt, in her farewell foreword to the 1978 book, said:

> I learned some things during my stint as co-editor of *New* (now *Best*) *Canadian Stories*, many of them small, some that I didn't want to know, but learn I did. Mostly I learned that this country is full of people shrouded in arctic light, trapped in their Canadian loneliness, sometimes writing badly about it, sometimes well, occasionally brilliantly. Probably I've read as many stories typed on kitchen tables in efficiency apartments and in echoing old houses in small towns as has anyone in the country. Some of the writers whose stories I read cut slightly ridiculous figures, but they were fighting the battle the best way they knew. Courage is where you find it, and I do dignify them with the title "writer" even when the stories were less than good: they had a faith and that's more important than the product.
>
> I think I learned that there is little real fiction in Canada. What we have instead are personal histories with the names changed and the facts slightly bent . . . The large run of the stories we received presented carefully crafted reliquaries, little

boxes in which were enshrined little memories. Some of these reliquaries were elaborately enamelled, but mostly they were simple, sturdy constructions.

This extract from her introduction illustrates what I meant when I said that Joan was *nice*. I found the "simple, sturdy constructions" far less "carefully crafted" than she did.

(Mavis Gallant, in a letter, described them disdainfully as "pallid little 'I' stories" though *she* was talking about the ones we'd *selected*.)

It is with Joan's first paragraph that I am in violent disagreement.

". . . they had a faith and that's more important than the product."

Although Joan is saying this of *inadequate* writers, it's an attitude which has condoned and fostered the mediocrity of all Canadian writing from its beginnings to the present.

When I was a child and aunts for my birthday gave me socks, my mother used to say to my disgruntled little self, "It's the thought that counts." I considered this argument but it seemed to me that what I was left with was, inescapably, *socks*.

My desire to change the title and direction of *New Canadian Stories* was prompted by a belief that "product" was more important than "faith."

I was tired of socks.

As I grew into the job I was able to see that by presenting what I considered the best I was promoting one kind of writing and suppressing another. I was deliberately suppressing, I came to realize, Joan Harcourt's "simple, sturdy constructions." I wasn't interested in "personal histories with the names changed." I was interested in sparkling language, in play, in glorious rhetoric. I was also promoting a fiction which was looking outwards for its models and its energy. The direction of that gaze was inevitably the United States. I set out to change the concept and shape of what a story is and how it should be read.

In *Kicking Against the Pricks* (1982) I wrote:

Where 20 years ago Canadian stories stressed content—what a story was *about*—the main emphasis now is on the story as verbal and rhetorical *performance*. Our best writers are concerned with the story as *thing to be experienced* rather than as *thing to be understood*. This more than anything else is what seems to baffle some readers—and not a few critics; it is difficult for those of us writing stories to understand why this is so since these concerns have been dominant since about 1925.

Alice Munro in a piece she wrote for me in 1982 said the same sort of thing in a different way:

I will start out by explaining how I read stories written by other people. For one thing, I can start reading them anywhere; from beginning to end, from end to beginning, from any point in between in either direction. So obviously I don't take up a story and follow it as if it were a road, taking me somewhere, with views and neat diversions along the way. I go into it, and move back and forth and settle here and there, and stay in it for a while. It's more like a house. Everybody knows what a house does, how it encloses space and makes connections between one enclosed space and another and presents what is outside in a new way. This is the nearest I can come to explaining what a story does for me, and what I want my stories to do for other people.

The 1976 Oberon volume carries a foreword which said in part:

76: New Canadian Stories is a transitional volume. It contains previously unpublished stories as well as stories that have appeared in the literary magazines. Starting next year, in frank emulation of Martha Foley's *Best American Short Stories*, Oberon's anthology will be entitled *77: Best Canadian Stories*. Though we will continue to consider unpublished manuscripts, our principal purpose will be to find and collect the best published stories of the year.

In 1976 I managed to work in among others, Norman Levine, Hugh Hood, Audrey Thomas, Clark Blaise, Elizabeth Spencer, and Leon Rooke.

In the foreword to the 1977 volume I wrote:

An anthology such as this offers some slight hope. It offers to a larger audience work that otherwise might well not have been seen; it extends the life of a piece of work; it directs the attention of readers to writers who otherwise might have been consigned to the vaults on microfilm.

The editorial task is not merely one of compilation; it is also critical. Frank Kermode described literary criticism as "the medium in which past work survives." We hope that this anthology and succeeding ones will serve this function as well as offering immediate pleasure.

Into the 1978 volume, edited with Clark Blaise, went Alice Munro, Hugh Hood, Elizabeth Spencer, and Kent Thompson. In the 1979 volume we published Mavis Gallant. In 1980 Mavis Gallant *and* Alice Munro along with Guy Vanderhaeghe and a first story from Linda Svendsen which later would be a part of her brilliant collection *Marine Life*.

Clark Blaise left Canada in 1980 because his wife, Bharati Mukherjee, could no longer tolerate the racial harassment she was enduring in Toronto. The loss to Canada was considerable. Clark Blaise, one of the handful of great story writers in Canada, was always reminded that despite his having become a Canadian citizen, he wasn't a *real* Canadian. He and I were always referred to as American-born and British-born. Clark went on to a long career at Iowa and Bharati to a long career at Berkeley and the National Book Critics Circle Award for *The Middleman and Other Stories*.

To succeed Clark as co-editor, I chose Leon Rooke, another American-born. Leon, too, had an almost encyclopedic knowledge of the short story and his own exuberantly improvisational approach to the form was doubtless a liberating influence on what remained staid in my own judgement.

Leon has been and continues to be an important and shaping force in Canadian literature, so I'd like to quote from an essay I wrote about his work recently. The essay is entitled "This Here Jasper Is Gittin Ready to Talk."

In the 1970s when I began to encounter Leon Rooke's stories in the literary magazines I recognized immediately an interesting new voice. A way of approaching the form new to Canada—though not so new in the States—was beginning to make itself heard. Or *should* have been making itself heard for it was surprisingly difficult to get people to listen.

I remember showing some of the stories in what became *The Love Parlour*, Leon's first book in Canada, to Michael Macklem, the publisher of Oberon Press. Michael has a doctorate in literature from Princeton and taught English at Yale. He declared the stories incomprehensible but said that if I thought they were good he'd publish them on my say-so but only on condition he wouldn't have to read further.

This seeming inability to read Leon Rooke, to connect with his vitality, is puzzling because looking back at *The Love Parlour* now it doesn't strike me as wildly innovative or madly experimental. It remains a good, solid collection but it is not a stylistic trailblazer.

To get Macklem to publish Leon's second book in Canada, *Cry Evil*, I had to write little explanatory notes about each story. Macklem published the book but remained unconvinced. It was with *Cry Evil* that Leon began to move towards the sort of story that was to be his major contribution to the form. With *Cry Evil* we were treated to a display of Leon limbering up for the major work ahead. This is not to say that some of the stories in *Cry Evil* are not already masterly performances. I'm particularly fond of "The Deacon's Tale," "Adolpho Has Disappeared and We Haven't a Clue Where to Find Him," and "Biographical Notes."

Another anecdote about listening. In 1980 Leon published his first novel, *Fat Woman*. It is a book which draws with intense imagination on his Southern roots. Every line of the book is instinct with the rhythms and cadences of Southern speech yet a young Canadian fiction writer, and a good one too, reviewing the book for a major newspaper, understood it as being set in Nova Scotia.

Yet another anecdote. When Leon and I left Oberon Press I wanted to move us to ECW Press because the owners, Jack David and Robert Lecker, were friends of mine and possessed of great energy and dedication to Canadian writing. I sent some of Leon's new work to Jack David who seemed unenthusiastic. Indeed, he phoned me and asked me if I really stood behind the work, if I really considered it the genuine article. I told him very firmly that I did. A short while later, Leon was in Toronto giving a public reading and Jack David went to hear him. Jack phoned me the next day in great excitement. "*Now* I get it," he said. "Now I've *heard* him. I just wasn't getting it from the printed page."

Jack David and Robert Lecker went on to publish two major books of Leon's stories, *Death Suite* in 1981 and *The Birth Control King of the Upper Volta* in 1982.

Academic neglect of Rooke's work is easily understandable. Not many academics actually read contemporary writing and many of them were unaware of his existence. Another part of the answer, less silly than it sounds, is that Leon is playful. Not a good thing to be in any of the arts in Canada. Yet another strike against him is that he moved progressively away from normative realism into fable, fantasy, pastiche of genre writing, all in scrambled shapes of his own invention. This departure from realism did not endear him to academics whose hastily cobbled canon really had no room for his shenanigans; shenanigans, furthermore, which were suspiciously American.

But the central reason for his early neglect is that most readers were not hearing what Leon was up to. Their attention was directed elsewhere, to theme, perhaps, or form. They were in a similar situation to an earnest gallery-goer standing in front of a Rothko and asking, "What does it mean?" The answer is, "Look."

To the reader who asks, "What does it mean?" of Rooke's "Sixteen-Year-Old Susan March Confesses to the Innocent Murder of All the Devious Strangers Who Would Drag Her Down" the answer is, "Listen."

Listen.

Rooke has published four or five plays and many of the stories are essentially *scripts*—monologues or voices talking, arguing. The insistent direction in his work is theatrical. Leon himself is never happier than on a stage, the rhetoric flying high and wide and often over the top. Leon is a performer. Leon is a self-confessed ham. His stories are *performances*.

He is very prolific, having published by now some three hundred short stories in literary magazines. Most are uncollected because on further reflection he felt they simply did not work. Leon doesn't brood for months over the shape and detail of what he hopes will be a masterwork; he picks up his horn and tries out a few runs, a few phrases to see if something is going to happen.

I sometimes think that Rooke's academic acceptance has been slow because academics have been slow to think of Leon as, say, a tenor sax player and the story as a jazz improvisation. If the reader *does* respond in those terms it becomes immediately obvious what Leon is up to.

Leon is leading the parade. He doesn't want a tweed-with-leather-elbow-patches response. He wants celebrants performing along with him. He wants a Second Line. At other times he wants to preach, a big Texas tenor sound, wave after wave of impossibly mounting fervour.

Leon preaching always reminds me of recordings I've heard of the Reverend Kelsey leading his Washington congregation in "Lion of the Tribe of Judah"; the preacher's voice probes at the words, repeats, hums, slides into falsetto, repeats and finds a form and then all rhythmic hell breaks loose, hands clapping, jugs grunting and booming, a trombone's urging. All rather glorious.

In the foreword to the first volume Leon and I edited together in 1981, a volume which included Blaise, Gallant, Levine, Munro, Thompson, and Svendsen, I wrote:

Now past our tenth year, in one guise or another, and still committed to presenting each year a gathering of fine fiction, it is interesting to glance back at our tracks in the snow. Despite all the annual grumbling by reviewers, it seems clear to me that over the last ten years the general standards of story writing in Canada have been rising. The art is becoming generally more sophisticated. *Best Canadian Stories* still cannot stand comparison with

Best American Stories but that is not, and should not be surprising; what is pleasing is that the comparison is no longer quite so devastatingly painful.

That this is not an entirely subjective judgement is attested to in remarks by W. J. Keith in his 1985 book *Canadian Literature in English*: "Thanks to Metcalf, whose numerous anthologies of short stories have been appearing regularly since the early 1970s, a whole generation of talented writers is emerging who find the short story a satisfying and infinitely varied form of expression."

Such forewords and attitudes and the demolition of the "simple, sturdy constructions" enraged the cultural nationalists who would have much preferred to remain in huddled celebration of the muddy achievement of Raymond Knister, Morley Callaghan, Hugh Garner, and Ernest Buckler.

Between 1980 and 1994 my writing was excluded from every trade anthology of national scope. I was excluded from *The Oxford Book of Canadian Short Stories in English* edited by Margaret Atwood and Robert Weaver. I was excluded from Weaver's *Canadian Short Stories: Fourth Series and Fifth Series*. I was excluded from Wayne Grady's *Penguin Book of Canadian Short Stories* and from *The Penguin Book of Modern Canadian Stories*. I was excluded from Michael Ondaatje's anthology *From Ink Lake*.

This list of names came to mind when I read in Adam Gopnik's *Paris to the Moon*, "The logic of nationalism always flows downhill, toward the gutter."

While the cultural nationalists were busily enshrining mediocrity and proclaiming it genius the academics were doing the same thing in *their* mausoleums. I have written of this extensively in *What Is a Canadian Literature?* And *Freedom from Culture: Selected Essays 1982–1992*. Academics damage the short story genre by maintaining a stolid silence on the alleged merits of writing which is deplorable. One example must suffice.

Morley Callaghan has been cemented into place as the father of the short story in Canada. Our only alleged ancestor more revered by nationalists is Duncan Campbell Scott, from whom, claims Wayne Grady, all Canadian story writers are artistically descended. Penguin

Books paid Grady money for writing this know-nothing twaddle and spread the shame of it all over the world.

In the seventies John Mills was reviewing frequently in the literary magazines and Myrna became an instant fan when she read a Mills review which opened, "Coarsened as I am by years of reading for pleasure . . ." John reviewed Morley Callaghan's *Close to the Sun Again* (1977) in *Queen's Quarterly*.

If *Close to the Sun Again* were a first novel by a young writer I would say of it that it shows some awareness of the technique of plot construction, that though the dialogue is inept and the prose generally abysmal, there are signs in the last two chapters that the author is beginning to slough the deleterious effects of high school training on his writing habits, and that he might also move on to themes of greater interest and importance if he could only empty his head of jejune notions of psychological realism picked up God knows where. The writer is Morley Callaghan, however, who has been around a long time and is unlikely to improve; nor would he, on the evidence of what is written about him on the dust-jacket, particularly want to . . .

Hemingway is invoked twice on the dust-jacket. Callaghan worked with him on the *Toronto Star*, then lived on the periphery of his circle in Paris where, presumably, he joined the Master's declared war against rhetoric in general and the adjective in particular, while remaining well-insulated against that peculiar electricity that used to flow through Hemingway's early writing. We are also told that Edmund Wilson called him "the most unjustly neglected novelist in the English-speaking world," and that, despite this neglect, his last novel sold more than half a million copies in the Soviet Union . . . It is good to know that 60 years after the Revolution petit-bourgeois notions of what constitutes a novel are still alive and well in Mother Russia. Apart from that I don't know why Callaghan succeeds in foreign countries. Perhaps he translates well and there is some internal evidence to suggest that *Close to the Sun Again* was translated from manuscript into, let us say, Lithuanian then back into English for Macmillan by some well-intentioned, polyglot, but tone-deaf and maladroit Pole.

A passage like the following: "The scratching little hollow ping was like the beating of a heart, only not muffled like a heart: it came throbbing in the vastness of cathedral space . . ." makes a man clutch and fumble at his chest to ascertain whether his pacemaker's working properly. My own heart, and I am speaking now as a hypochondriac, does *not* make these scratching little pinging sounds, muffled or otherwise, and in any case there is, in my opinion, a contradiction between the ideas of *scratching* and *throbbing*. It is a clumsy, sloppy metaphor but at least it represents a step, or rather stagger, in the direction of colourful prose and, in contrast to such sodden, dispiriting stuff as: "She went on to say that her father had taken her to Europe, and in Paris they had gone to one of those small clubs that had fight cards. Her father had been impressed by a good-looking boy named Robert Riopelle, a middleweight, a lonely-looking boy, a kid, with all the great natural talents. The French boy had a strangely moving, noble character. The kid took a shine to her father, too . . ." it shines "like a good deed in a naughty world." So this French boy "had a strangely moving, noble character," had he? Apart from the stylistic poverty of using an auxiliary verb instead of a proper one, the sentence with its vagueness and pomposity breaks every rule in the book of narrative art (including the Jamesian ukase that the reader must be *shown*, not *told*) while creating no new rule of its own. Perhaps this is what the dust-jacket means when he says, perhaps a little too glibly, that "the novel is told in Morley Callaghan's distinctive style—so easy and flowing that it seems to be no style at all." But the style is *there*—and it is abominable.

Mills's review and my essay on Callaghan's stories "Winner Take All" will, I predict, be entirely ignored. When the next batch of Guides, Companions, and Encyclopaedias appears a Weaver clone will have been found to extol Callaghan's nonexistent virtues.

I bring this matter up not to be contentious but to illuminate the fact that we are living a critical lie. If we are blind and deaf to Callaghan's cacophonies how can we *genuinely* respond to Alice Munro's glories? How can students trust us or our works of reference if we describe as "distinguished" writing that is stumblebum?

Nearly all the editing I did between 1976 and 1993 was, as it were, *editing against the grain*. I was suppressing the "simple, sturdy constructions" and searching for sophistication, elegance, invention, language that sang. What the public, such as it is, really wanted was W. P. Kinsella and W. D. Valgardson but it wasn't going to get them from me.

In an article by Andy Lamey in the magazine *Gravitas* he quotes that sad Marxist hulk Robin Mathews, both synapses buzzing, as saying: "Metcalf has always supported the reactionary forces in Canada at the level of 'the barking dog.'" What this means I'm not entirely sure. Actually I hold no party political position; I simply find politicians embarrassing. When it comes to literary editing, however, I suspect that I've been the very reverse of reactionary.

In the foreword to *82: Best Canadian Stories* Leon Rooke wrote, "This is winsome stuff, gladdening to the heart, necessary to life and limb. The 'best' writer—our position of faith—is always the stranger, the writer not heard from yet."

I wrote an essay about Keath Fraser for *The New Quarterly* which describes the central joy of editing, the joy of finding, in Leon's words, "the writer not heard from yet."

I first encountered Keath's writing in 1981 when I was editing Oberon's *Best Canadian Stories* with Leon Rooke. I remember I was sitting in the kitchen with a moody cup of coffee eyeing the morning's pile of manila envelopes. I ripped one open and glanced over the opening sentence. The story was entitled "Le Mal de l'Air." This is what I read:

"Suppose he had a three-day-old festering on the elbow, ate pork at his mother's on Sunday and got sick: his wife would rather blame his illness on bee-stings than on worms in a good woman's meat."

Huh?

The second sentence:

"Bees she believed just as likely to cause nausea and the shakes as they were a slowly puffed-up arm."

By now I was intrigued.

By the time I'd finished the first paragraph I realized I'd found a writer of strange power and accomplishment. I read the entire story sitting there in the kitchen in a state of mounting excitement.

Here's the paragraph in full:

> Suppose he had a three-day-old festering on the elbow, ate pork at his mother's on Sunday and got sick: his wife would rather blame his illness on bee-stings than on worms in a good woman's meat. Bees she believed just as likely to cause nausea and the shakes as they were a slowly puffed-up arm. Her responses were intemperate and increasingly persistent. She had been to the doctor who could find nothing wrong inside her long, splendid body. Once she took her cello to the Gulf Islands and played on the beach for a pair of misplaced whimbrels. She wasn't happy. You had to conclude that something had infected their marriage. "Or am I just getting bitter," wondered the discomfited Miles, "as the two of us grow alike?"

What a *mysterious* paragraph this was. What could I make of it? It was alive with differing cadences, tones, and levels of diction. It was full of movement. It was busy. The first sentence changed pace at the colon, changed from a colloquial tone to something more formal. Then followed the playful buzz of "bees she believed." Then in the third sentence the diction changed again becoming Latinate, echoing perhaps the words of a doctor or psychiatrist.

But why did he use the words "a good woman's meat"? Why was she good? The word seemed to come from the unnamed wife rather than from Miles. Was it perhaps in defence of the mother whom Miles has accused of bad housewifery? In the word "good" were we hearing an incredibly compressed version of their quarrel?

The simple inversion of "Bees she believed" stressed the irrationality of her belief. The strong stresses falling one after the other prepared us for the "intemperate" responses in the next sentence. And I wonder if Keath intended us to be thinking of the phrase "bees in her bonnet."

But what on earth were "misplaced whimbrels"? According to the *Shorter Oxford*, "Applied to various small species of curlew." According to *Webster's New World Dictionary*, "any of a group of European shore birds resembling the curlew, but smaller, with a pale stripe along the crown: they breed on the islands north of England."

So did that mean the whimbrels were "misplaced"—put in the wrong place—because they're supposed to be in Europe and not on the Gulf Islands? That made no sense whatever, so I consulted W. Earl Godfrey's *Birds of Canada* and discovered that *Webster's New World Dictionary* had let me down. Whimbrels were not confined to Europe. There is a North American whimbrel also known as the Hudsonian curlew. One population of whimbrels winters in California and nests in northwest Alaska and Canada. It is a spring and autumn transient in British Columbia and common on the coast.

So a reasonable reading of "misplaced" would be that this particular pair of whimbrels hadn't migrated at the right time. But "misplace" also means "to bestow (one's love, trust, affection, etc.) on an unsuitable or undeserving object." So the whimbrels, by playful extension, are also "misplaced" because they are receiving the misplaced attention of Miles's wife.

(I was later to learn that Keath's work bulges with puns, play, complexities; it is best approached with humility and an array of dictionaries.)

The whimbrel sentence captured the wife's "intemperate" quality perfectly. The slightly sad vision of a woman on a beach playing the cello to an audience of two birds suggested about the wife hysteria, drama, theatricality of emotion. Yet at the same time the sentence was comic, of course, and the brief sentence "She wasn't happy" reinforced the comic tone.

But the comic tone also had the effect of making me wonder about Miles. What sort of husband would react in that way to his wife's distress?

And worrying at the paragraph again—*why* "whimbrels"? Did he just like the sound of it? Did he choose it for comic effect?

Did he swell the sentence up with ornithological exactitude so that he could deflate it the more comically with: "She wasn't happy"?

(In 1986 at the Kingston Conference, Keath was to say: "For me pleasure is the ability to bury a reader in the story even if we don't understand it at all. Have respect for the mystery. A fiction is more than understanding; it's perception and delight." So his advice to me would probably be to relax and re-read.)

Miles is "discomfited." I suspect that some readers might have read that as "discomforted" meaning essentially "made uncomfortable" but "discomfited" means something much stronger: "1. Originally, to defeat; overthrow; put to flight; hence 2. To overthrow the plans or expectations of; thwart; frustrate."

And this harsher word fits perfectly with the picture the paragraph paints of marital discord.

(In Keath's choices of words secondary meanings often seem to obliquely thicken the story's stew. The verbal noun "festering," for example, has a secondary meaning of "rankling" meaning "embittering" which accords with the word "discomfited.")

Another aspect of this busy paragraph is the sounding of the story's emotional notes: "festering," "sick," "illness," "nausea," "infected."

I read recently a book of art criticism by Robert Hughes called *Nothing If Not Critical* and was struck by the following passage on Manet. Hughes is referring to a painting from 1866 called *The Fifer*.

Manet's sense of touch was extraordinary but its bravura passages are in the details: how the generalized bagginess of a trouser leg, for instance, rendered in flat, thin paint and firmed up with swift daubs of darker tone in the folds, contrasts with the thick creamy white directional brush strokes that model the curve of a spat. The creaseless intelligent play of flat and round, thick and thin, "slow" and "fast" passages of paint is what gives Manet's surface its probing liveliness. There is nothing "miraculous" about it, but it was not the result of a mechanically acquired technique either.

It is there because, in his best work, Manet's inquisitiveness never failed him; every inch of surface records an active desire to see and then find the proper translation of sight into mark.

Although it is always dangerous to compare painting and writing, I thought the paragraph a useful way to think about how writing works. "The ceaseless intelligent play of flat and round, thick and thin, 'slow' and 'fast' passages of paint"; those words are surely pregnant with suggestion for a way of approaching Keath Fraser's writing.

I was so impressed by Keath's work that I offered to help him get a collection published. What could I do but love the man who wrote this sentence: "His dinner lay in him like hooves."

Hooves!

There's a simile to savour.

WINNING THE WAR

IN THE ACADEMIC YEAR 1983–84 Mavis
Gallant was writer-in-residence at the University of Toronto and was
awarded the Canada-Australia Literary Prize, an alternating award
designed to deepen the two countries' knowledge of each other's
literature. The Australian High Commission in Ottawa arranged
a luncheon in her honour in a private room in the National Arts
Centre. Mavis had apparently requested my presence.

I strolled up to the NAC and found the room. I was alone
except for a man fighting starched napery on a makeshift bar. Then
Mavis arrived, escorted by a subdued suit from External Affairs. Mavis
inspected the table and went around reading all the name cards.
Grumbling pugnaciously about his politics, she switched the name
card of a Canada Council functionary, seating him at a distance and
placing me beside her.

Lunch proceeded with a litany of complaint from Mavis about
the interminable line-ups at the Ontario Health Insurance office, the
architectural brutality of the Robarts Library, the tardiness of Professor
Solecki in providing her with a typewriter, the appalling manners of
that very bearded man, you know—flapping a hand—in Alberta . . .

Until, after dessert, waiters filled the glasses again and the High
Commissioner rose and made a deft and graceful little speech ending
with the words:

"And now let us drink a toast to Mavis Gallant and to the day she
sets foot on our shores."

In a loud Lady Bracknell voice she said, "GO to Australia! I have no intention of GOING to Australia! Why would anyone think . . . I'm writing a book. Who *in their right mind* . . ."

When the clamour died down and the High Commissioner and his entourage had departed and the man from External had simply decamped, I offered to walk Mavis back to her hotel. We strolled along Sparks Street in the sunshine and she said, "I really don't know why you keep on doing these anthologies. No one will ever thank you for them. In fact, they'll hate you. You should just get on with your own work."

Because I was rather in awe of her as a writer I said something or other bland in reply but I've often thought of that conversation and all these years later still wish I'd explained myself. I wish I'd said, "You chose to leave and at the time you did it was doubtless the smartest thing to do. You went into a kind of exile and as things turned out you live your daily life in the pleasures of Paris but your work goes first to *The New Yorker* and then, in the USA, to Random House. What I'm getting at is that you're not dependent on Paris or on France itself for your career. My case is a bit different. I chose to come here—quite possibly a mistake—but choose I did and then I reinforced that choice by becoming a citizen. I make very little money from my writing, so have to work at other things. My daily life is enmeshed in Canadian literary matters in a way that yours probably isn't in French literary matters.

"And as a writer, citizen, and teacher I feel I have responsibilities to the literature. But there's nothing particularly *virtuous* in all this. I'm just very much involved with this society, locked in mortal combat with the bloody place. I feel I have to attempt to shape taste, to encourage younger writers, to edit, to criticize—and anthologies are an expression of that."

A touch pompous but I still wish I'd said something of the kind.

In 1980 it had occurred to me to try to revive the idea of *New Canadian Writing*, that is, the idea of putting three writers together in a book, each writer being given room for a handful of stories. I decided on the title *First Impressions* because the book would, I hoped, be making a good first impression and first *impressions* are what book collectors collect, the first printing of the first edition. I took the idea to Macklem who was agreeable. I had wanted the books all to be called *First Impressions* and designated 2 and 3 and so on. But in 1981 Macklem overrode me and called the second volume *Second Impressions*. And then *Third Impressions* rendering the title meaningless. He was equally stubborn over my story collection, insisting right up to his defeat that the book should be entitled not *The Teeth of My Father* but *My Father's Teeth*. A strange deafness on his part. After I left Oberon, the series was continued as *Coming Attractions*.

Although Michael Macklem has published dozens of important books and laboured mightily on behalf of Canadian writing, no one would describe him as a fount of sweetness and light. He is one of the most abrasive men I've ever met. His idea of a conversation is to talk louder whenever his interlocutor attempts to say anything. He seems to have little grasp of social niceties. When Myrna and I first moved to Ottawa I suggested that it might be the polite thing to invite Michael and his wife, Anne, to dinner. Michael stood in the entrance hall and looked about and then said, "Well, there's some money here and I know *you* haven't got any so it must be hers."

Myrna was less than charmed.

The introduction to *Third Impressions* in 1982 is worth reproducing as I outlined a rationale for the series:

It is increasingly difficult for short story writers to make the great leap from publication in the literary magazines to publication in book form. There are the obvious primary reasons for this difficulty, which are economic, and then there are the obvious secondary reasons, which are cultural and economic—the lack of any literary infrastructure in Canada, the decay of traditional faith in the idea of investing in a literary career rather than solely in discrete books that offer the hope of immediate financial return, the deep-seated feeling in publishers and readers that short stories, while admirable, are *really*, though one wouldn't shout it, merely limbering-up exercises.

There is another, usually adverse, factor, however, which is not often discussed and that is the part played in the story writer's fortunes by chance. When I was thinking about putting this book together, I wrote to several young writers whose names were familiar to me through their work in the literary magazines. I also solicited names from such literary colleagues as Geoff Hancock of *Canadian Fiction Magazine* and Robert Weaver of CBC's *Anthology*. One of the first names on my list was Guy Vanderhaeghe, whose work over the last two years has been gaining in strength and authority and one of whose stories I had earlier selected for inclusion in *Best Canadian Stories*.

I wrote to Vanderhaeghe but I was about a week too late. A collection of his stories had just been accepted by another publisher. I was delighted for him, of course, but, given the literary climate, surprised; I found myself thinking about the vagaries of publishing. I found myself thinking how quality is sometimes only perceived by someone's directing attention to it; how such "directing" is so often at whim and attention paid to it by chance.

My own work was first published in book form simply because somebody at Clarke, Irwin had decided to take an altruistic risk on an annual volume called *New Canadian Writing*. These books, featuring the work of three writers per volume, survived for two years. *Aurora*, which published a story by Vanderhaeghe, lasted for three years before succumbing to the public's indifference. What, I wonder, might have happened to Vanderhaeghe had he been writing and publishing the *same* stories at a period when *Aurora* hadn't existed, when *Best Canadian Stories* hadn't been born. Would he have remained known only to those who read the literary magazines?

I'm afraid it's very possible.

Many people assert that if a thing is good, it will be recognized and rewarded as such, that quality, as it were, will out. The implication of this idea for us is that stuff that remains in the literary magazines *deserves* to remain there. I wish I could wholeheartedly believe that.

After more than 15 years of involvement in Canada's literary world, I don't have an exactly Panglossian view of its workings; chance seems more firmly seated in its halls of judgement than taste. I remember taking upon myself years ago the role of honorary agent for Clark Blaise; I wrote a letter of support to McClelland and Stewart urging them to publish *A North American Education*. My letter to Anna Porter, then editor-in-chief, was written in words of fire. To no avail. The manuscript was returned to Blaise pretty much by return mail; Anna Porter had thought the stories "boring." And this from the editor-in-chief of Canada's most prestigious publisher about what is, unarguably, one of the most brilliant story collections ever published in Canada.

Third Impressions itself and the earlier books in this series exist, too, by chance. They exist because I happened to be worried about diminishing opportunities for younger writers, because Michael Macklem, Oberon's publisher, happened to be prepared to listen to me that day and happened, perhaps, to have had a good breakfast. I happened to care about younger writers because I care about writing in general and because chance had so arranged things that I was *taught* to care by the great kindness shown to me when I was young by Margaret Laurence and Mordecai Richler.

The choice of writers in this book is also, to an extent, the result of chance. They are writers who have taken my eye. But I am not, God knows, without blind spots. Is there someone as brilliant as Blaise who is cursing *my* stupidity and shortsightedness? Are there brilliant stories in the literary magazines that my glazed eyes have failed to recognize?

I hope not.

But expect so.

My own beginnings were a long time ago and now I feel rather like the narrator in Norman Levine's story "We All Begin in a Little Magazine," but I can remember how wildly excited I was when I was first published in a magazine. I told everyone I met as casually as my delight allowed.

"Congratulations!" they said. "*Prism?*"

And I was forced to admit that, no, it *wasn't* available on newsstands. Or at libraries. Or anywhere really. And the years passed with my friends asking how you spelled *Wascana Review* and was *Tamarack* as in the tree—until that day arrived when five stories were published in *New Canadian Writing 1969*. The fact that the book wasn't widely available in grocery stores, nor, truth be told, in bookstores didn't bother me a bit. It was a *book*—or at least, a third of a book—and the effect on me was tonic. With that publication, I started to allow myself to think of myself as a writer; I was, in my own eyes, no longer a high-school teacher with delusions of grandeur but a published author whose book was, if you went to a hell of a lot of trouble, available.

The rewards were immediate. They were not, needless to say, financial. The most immediate reward was that I started writing even harder than before and soon had a book that was wholly mine—*The Lady Who Sold Furniture*.

Writers whose work appeared in the first two issues of *Impressions* have, apparently, been similarly galvanized. Martin Avery is publishing a novel. Ernest Hekkanen has just completed a novel. Mike Mason has published a novella and is writing with great urgency. Linda Svendsen's work has appeared again in *Atlantic Monthly* and she seems to be nearing her first collection.

The value of publication in such a book as *Impressions* is, then, for the writers, obvious. But what of readers? Are readers having foisted on them what is, if one hopes these writers are to have a long career, juvenilia? This point was fairly raised in a condescending review of *Second Impressions* written by an unhappy lady in Toronto. My heart always sinks when I glance at the foot of a review and see: *X is a freelance writer living in Y.* This tends to mean that the reviewer is either a part-time journalist in search of $75 or, worse, an unpublished writer into whose soul the iron has entered.

This reviewer of *Second Impressions* said snottily of the writing that it was "at least as competent as the writing one finds in little literary publications," which is not surprising in that most of it was *from* "little literary publications." But perhaps this reviewer is unaware that the work of Margaret Laurence, Alice Munro, Clark Blaise, Norman Levine, Jack Hodgins, Leon Rooke, Hugh Hood, and Margaret Atwood—not to mention Hemingway, Pound, Waugh—appeared or appears regularly in the little magazines.

"Little literary publications," forsooth!

Are these volumes the literary equivalent of Amateur Night with fumbling conjurors and singers excruciatingly off-key? Obviously, *I* don't believe so. Nor do the dedicated editors of the literary magazines who first published most of these stories. And obviously the editors of *Atlantic Monthly* don't think so.

On the other hand, I do believe that the writers in this book and in the earlier ones are capable of producing still better work, work that is more deeply imaginative, more complicated, more demanding. But whether they *will* go on from strength to strength depends. It depends on talent—which they obviously have—and it depends on many variables that could be lumped together under chance—money, time, tranquillity, understanding wives or husbands, health, fair winds. But perhaps more than anything else it depends on the interest and support and criticism they receive from readers.

The highlights of the three volumes were, for me, Linda Svendsen, Don Dickinson, and Isabel Huggan, who with much coaxing and prompting added to the three stories in *First Impressions* to gain international acclaim with *The Elizabeth Stories*.

Nineteen eighty-two turned out to be my last year with Oberon. There were touchy quarrels with Macklem but more serious, perhaps, was the sense that Oberon was not becoming the press we'd hoped for. Its energy was failing. The press did no advertising, organized no readings, failed to launch its new titles. Far too many of the books it was publishing were undistinguished. There were too many books of insipid poetry, too many books of merely competent stories. There were too many seasons featuring yet another volume by Raymond Souster, yet another anaemic gathering by the indefatigable Elizabeth Brewster. There was no commanding artistic vision. The books seemed random.

Oberon had published a few singular books by Hugh Hood, Leon Rooke, Norman Levine, Keath Fraser, and David Helwig but their sharpness was somehow blunted by the blandness of the company they kept. The energy and virtuosity of the writing in *Best Canadian Stories* was not reflected in Oberon's list. The press seemed to be fading.

When the breakup came with Macklem I arranged to publish with Jack David and Robert Lecker at ECW Press. I also arranged for Leon Rooke and Hugh Hood to move there. Jack and Robert were dedicated to Canadian literature but were financially unstable. In taking us on they bit off more than they could chew and Jack told me later that with the flow of books and with a coast-to-coast tour we called the ECW Roadshow we brought the press to the brink of ruin. Hugh published *None Genuine Without This Signature* and *Black and White Keys*, Leon published *Death Suite* and *The Birth Control King of the Upper Volta*, while I published *Kicking Against the Pricks*.

Leon and I were still hankering after putting our mark on the Canadian story and we persuaded Ed Carson at General Publishing to start an annual anthology which would be the flagship title for his New Press Canadian Classics series. The book was to be called *The New Press Anthology: Best Canadian Short Fiction*. I remember with pleasure the unnecessarily frequent martini-drenched planning sessions held with Ed Carson and Leon at the Courtyard Café at the Windsor Arms in Toronto.

The first volume appeared in 1984 in mass market format and from the very beginning we realized that we were dealing with a literary world that had undergone a sea change. Possibly we had ourselves effected a change. Possibly Canada was simply struggling out of its weird time warp. Alongside Alice Munro, Ray Smith, Carol Shields, Clark Blaise, Margaret Atwood, and Norman Levine, we were drawing in new names and new sensibilities which were sophisticated and innovative.

In eight short years we had moved from Joan Harcourt's "simple, sturdy constructions" and Mavis Gallant's "pallid little 'I' stories" to the joy of discovering a new writer whose opening two sentences were: "May, Minnie, Maud for God's sake, or Myrna—even worse. Names she might have worn like a crown of link sausages."

How complex, how plump, how rich.

(The opening sentences of an early Terry Griggs story called "India.")

Ed Carson had given us $1,500 to award to the best story in each volume. The prize was, of course, intended to create publicity. In that first volume we gave the prize to Mavis Gallant for "Luc and His

Father." The second New Press Fiction Prize was awarded to Ray Smith for his novella "The Continental" and Rohinton Mistry achieved his first publication in book form with his story "Auspicious Occasion." After this second volume there were palace revolutions at General Publishing, defections, financial reversals, changing priorities, and the series was cancelled. Ed Carson moved to Random House.

Leon and I started talking about a new venture, an annual book which would be closer in feel to a magazine, a big magazine that featured new fiction but also included poetry, memoirs, profiles, and a review article about the year's best books. I took the idea to Macmillan and in 1988 *The Macmillan Anthology (1)* appeared with fiction by, among others, Keath Fraser, Mavis Gallant, Terry Griggs, Norman Levine, and Diane Schoemperlen. The book also featured poetry by Lorna Crozier and John Newlove. Sam Tata photographed the writers for us. Sinclair Ross wrote a memoir about life with his mother entitled "Just Wind and Horses" and John Mills wrote a comic memoir about owning a steam laundry in Montreal and his attempts to seduce Aviva Layton away from Irving. Janice Kulyk Keefer wrote a profile of Mavis Gallant and Mavis Gallant gave us "Leaving the Party," one of her comic stories about life in Paris. Michael Darling wrote "The Year in Review," a castigation of varieties of bad writing.

It was a rich book and lavishly produced.

With *The Macmillan Anthology (2)* disaster struck. Leon and I had a falling-out which we could not resolve. Leon, without much consultation, had put together a seventy-eight-page section of the book and written an introduction to it which began:

Over the summer of 1988 and on into fall, over 80 poets, novelists, short-story writers, and dramatists were invited to contribute what I shamelessly insisted on calling Position Papers: brief documents that would lay out the writers' literary aesthetic, define major operating principles, encapsulate aims and objectives, describe the philosophical lodestone that steered the individual writer's work—and in the bargain consider, generally, the way of literature in the world. Is the humanist tradition, I asked these writers, ragged and crippled and largely defunct in these postmodernist times, or can literature still shoot, as Cynthia Ozick and others insist it must, "for a corona, subtle or otherwise, of moral grandeur"? Can it prop up humanity's flagging spirit, somehow make easier the sleep of the innocent, vanquished dead?

Leon Rooke has written some of the finest stories published in Canada yet when he edges towards his Southern-Baptist-Preacher Mode he can be capable of writing blather. Language and rhetoric grip him and the result tends to be sloppy and imprecise. Can one "prop up" spirit? What does "the innocent, vanquished dead" *mean?*

The responses Leon gathered made me cringe. Give writers a chance to be windy and pompous and they'll grab it every time. The responses made much of Love, Death, Posterity, the Human Condition, and reiterated: Only Connect.

All this was bad enough but Leon concluded this introduction with what I felt amounted to a personal attack. He wrote: "A cadre of good citizens felt kinship with the project, and gratitude for the opportunity, but refused out of firm disagreement with John Metcalf for his variety of stands on assorted issues related to art and society."

Silence would have sufficed. I felt that this was a betrayal.

I did not doubt that what Leon was reporting was accurate. As Connie Rooke said to me at about this time, "You have *no idea* how many enemies you've got out there." I was busy in 1987 and 1988 with the Tanks Campaign, Bill Hoffer's guerrilla-theatre offensive against the Canada Council. I had on all possible occasions attacked Margaret Atwood's critical book *Survival*, describing it as not only silly but dangerous; this was widely considered *lèse-majesté*. I'd also in 1987 published the pamphlet "Freedom from Culture," an attack on subsidy culture, which caused froth to appear at the corners of mouths.

One paragraph can stand for the tone of the whole.

The purpose of the Book Purchase Programme was to give added subsidy to the publishers and to get Canadian books into the hands of Canadian readers. Year after year of purchase passed until the news leaked out that the Council had been unable to give many of the Book Kits away: even such truly captive audiences as the inmates of prisons spurned them. Kits composed of Canadian fiction were met with particular opprobrium. By 1985, in a rented warehouse on Richmond Road in Toronto, the Canada Council had accumulated 70,000 volumes of unwanted CanLit.

I'd also edited in 1987 and 1988 *The Bumper Book* and *Carry on Bumping*, volumes of squibs, jibes, vulgarities, and literary scurrility, books which drew out the enemy delightfully in their reviews: "bedevilled by spite, resentment, and jealousy," "gratuitous bitchiness," "bile," "anti-Canadian."

I was becoming a hammer of the Canadian cultural nationalists and Leon wanted to distance himself.

I edited *The Third Macmillan Anthology* with Kent Thompson. Regrettably it was to be the last. It was particularly rich with fiction by Mary Borsky, Douglas Glover, Terry Griggs, Hugh Hood, Leon Rooke, Diane Schoemperlen, and Linda Svendsen. "The Year in Review" by Kevin Connolly, Michael Darling, and Fraser Sutherland was deliciously tart. But the books were large and lavish and not selling well and Macmillan decided not to lose more money.

The coolness between Leon and me lasted for some time but Leon's a difficult man to remain angry with. So now our quarrel is water (and Scotch) under the bridge. In 1991 I republished with Porcupine's Quill some of his out-of-print stories in a volume called *The Happiness of Others* and we're soon to republish more. Myrna always proffers Scotch when Leon visits for the pleasure of hearing him say in that beguiling accent, "Well, just a touch."

In 1985 I guest edited a polemical issue of *The Literary Review*, an American quarterly published by Fairleigh Dickinson University in Rutherford, New Jersey. The title of the issue was *On the Edge: Canadian Short Stories.* Barry Cameron wrote an introduction describing for American readers the battle we were engaged in.

Try to swallow *this* academic horse pill.

When one studies *Canadian* literature, one is not studying literature as such but the literature written in Canada or by Canadians in a nationalist context. In such a situation, a writer who has less merit on other ideological grounds—aesthetic, for instance, which is conventionally privileged by students of literature—may be more important in a social or historical sense. Thus a self-consciously Canadian writer like Hugh MacLennan may be given precedence on the curriculum over, say, Leon Rooke (who would, incidentally, probably be discriminated against unjustly and solely because of his post-modernist tendencies), Margaret Laurence over Mavis Gallant on the grounds of Canadian setting, or W. P. Kinsella over John Metcalf because Kinsella writes about Canadian Indians.

This sort of tension between so-called nationalist (social and historical) values, on the one hand, and the apparent absence of those values despite other merits, on the other, exists of course whenever literature is situated nationally; but that tension is exacerbated when one is dealing with a nascent literature like Canada's. This is not to say that all those writers who are attractive to the nationalists lack literary merit or that the Canadian social formation and history are not inscribed in the texts of these writers collected here, but it is to say that because they do not deal overtly with acceptable ideological themes . . . most of those in this anthology have resided in or on the margins of Canadian literary discourse until very recently.

Clark Blaise, Leon Rooke, and I were editing not as scholars or academics but as writers, front-line troops in a battle to set in place the next generation of writers, hand-picked by us as gifted and as likely to stand for the positions we'd been asserting and defending. Academic critics such as David Jackel in the *Literary History of Canada, Volume Four* (1990) continue to raise their thin bleat against "rootless cosmopolitanism" but who's listening? The war is largely over. Only a few feeble pockets of resistance to clean up. A Valgardson here. A Kinsella there. Skirmishes on the lower slopes of Maude Barlow.

In 1992 I put together an anthology called *The New Story Writers*. I chose to include Don Dickinson, Keath Fraser, Douglas Glover, Terry Griggs, Steven Heighton, Dayv James-French, Rohinton Mistry, Diane Schoemperlen, and Linda Svendsen.

Anthologizing is necessary but inexact. It is easy to recognize talent but impossible to predict the shape of careers. A couple of the writers on this list may fall away from the short story but I remain satisfied with the book.

In the fall of 2001 Kim Jernigan, Peter Hinchcliffe and I put on a short story conference as part of the Stratford Festival. It was organized by *The New Quarterly* and the Porcupine's Quill, though most of the tedious organization fell on Kim's shoulders as she was in Stratford. Kim has exquisite taste and *The New Quarterly* unerringly recognizes important new talent. Both Kim and I felt that there was a flowering going on in the story form that was extraordinary and we both felt we should examine and celebrate this efflorescence.

The conference lasted for three days and featured panel discussions, readings, and lectures. Alice Quinn, Alice Munro's editor at *The New Yorker*, came to talk about Alice's work. The central idea of the conference was that older writers would give talks on the work of younger ones. Academics were not wanted.

I found that the writers I'd celebrated in 1992 in *The New Story Writers* were suddenly not so new and mysteriously not as young as they'd been. In fact, they were now the mid-career writers lecturing on the work of writers far younger. These younger writers represent what will soon be a *third* generation.

The conference was called "Wild Writers We Have Known: A Celebration of the Canadian Short Story in English." The writers present were a roll-call: Caroline Adderson, Mike Barnes, David Bergen, Libby Creelman, Michael Crummey, Keath Fraser, Douglas Glover, Terry Griggs, Steven Heighton, Mark Anthony Jarman, Elise Levine, Annabel Lyon, K. D. Miller, Andrew Pyper, Veronica Ross, Sandra Sabatini, Robyn Sarah, Diane Schoemperlen, Russell Smith, and Michael Winter. Leon Rooke attended as reader and godfather.

They gave us a feast of language unimaginable in 1976.

On the first evening of the conference there was a reception in a Stratford restaurant and to walk into that bar and see all those friends and acquaintances gathered, that array of very sophisticated talent, warmed the cockles and astonished me anew at what we'd done.

Kim Jernigan said to me, "Do you realize that there are twenty-one writers here and that you've edited and published sixteen of them?"

Writing about the conference in the *National Post* Jeet Heer said:

A teacher can never fully know what impact he or she has, since students go on to have lives of their own. After many years of tireless service to Canadian literature, for which he's received little money and much abuse, Metcalf occasionally feels beleaguered and tired.

Yet at the Stratford conference he will see the fruits of his pedagogical labours: an entire generation of Canadian writers committed to the deeply Metcalfian goods of cosmopolitanism and aestheticism.

ACTS OF KINDNESS AND LOVE

MYRNA AND I lived in Delta from 1976 to 1981. Myrna's son, Ronnie, adapted to the life astonishingly. In Côte St. Luc we could hardly pry him away from the TV. He shrank in urban nervousness even from a passing poodle. Within weeks in Delta he'd made friends with our neighbour, Wayne Woods, whose farm was half a mile away up the dirt road, and went there every day after school to help with milking and chores. He metamorphosed into a dung-stained urchin who barged his way fearlessly through herds of pressing heifers and slapped a flank with the best of them.

When Elizabeth came up for the holidays she, too, took to this country life with ease, astonishing us all one day by finding and casually picking up a black rat snake that was at least six feet long. Ronnie and she established a sideline of catching leopard frogs which they sold to American tourists who used them as live bait for bass fishing on Beverley Lake.

We were doing reasonably well financially in those years, which was just as well as this was a rocky country. Many wives had to work "out" in Hershey's chocolate factory on the line in Smith's Falls or as cleaners in Brockville's psychiatric empire. I was awarded Canada Council grants in 1976, 1978, and 1980. Royalties were coming in from a variety of publishers. In this period I earned over $16,000 from McGraw-Hill Ryerson alone, and most of that royalties on *Sixteen by Twelve*. I wrote a large number of reports on manuscripts for the Canada Council. I was also reviewing for newspapers, reading manuscripts for Oberon Press, writing CBC commissions, and giving public readings.

The texture of our day-to-day life can best be suggested by reproducing here a memoir I wrote for Elizabeth. It is tinged a little with guilt and sadness but captures, I hope, a time and place. The memoir is entitled *Acts of Kindness and of Love* which is, of course, a quotation from Wordsworth's "Tintern Abbey."

The "beauteous forms" Wordsworth refers to are the farms, the cottages, the woods, hedges, and orchards.

> These beauteous forms,
> Through a long absence, have not been to me
> As is a landscape to a blind man's eye:
> But oft, in lonely rooms, and 'mid the din
> Of towns and cities, I have owed to them,
> In hours of weariness, sensations sweet,
> Felt in the blood and felt along the heart;
> And passing even into my purer mind,
> With tranquil restoration:—feelings too
> Of unremembered pleasure: such, perhaps,
> As have no slight or trivial influence
> On that best portion of a good man's life,
> His little, nameless, unremembered, acts
> Of kindness and of love.

In George Tetford's yard, leaning against the green-and-silver Ford pickup, sitting on the tractor, crowding at the picnic table, we're all awaiting the arrival of George's uncle Willard with his flat black box of knives. Maureen, George's wife, stays on the porch; the business of the afternoon is not for women. Down behind the barn, greasy black smoke is piling into the sky from the old tires that are heating the water in the oil drum.

Two of Maureen's kids and my daughter, Liz, are whispering with the pasty-faced and treacherous Howland kids from the next farm up the road. Their mother doses them every Saturday with molasses and sulphur but they remain chronically loathsome with sties, snot, boils, and impetigo. Nothing will purify their rotten blood. They leave Liz tied to fence posts with binder twine. They take the ladder away. They abandon her to geese.

Where the road curves we see the travelling dust of Uncle Willard's truck. One of George's dogs runs out to the gate and stands there with its bow legs quivering. Another starts yapping hysterically at the trunk of the maple tree and yaps and yaps until someone scores on its ribs with a stone. Behind Maureen on the porch, the kitchen curtains are pulled aside as George's malignant mother cranes for a better view.

Half the house and farm are hers. She has suffered from a weak heart for more than forty years. Convenient palpitations strike whenever she is crossed or thwarted. She lives to rule poor George and undermine Maureen. Her only other consolation is religion. Nominally she's a Baptist, but she watches all the TV evangelists of whatever stripe and writes away to Tennessee box numbers for strange pamphlets which she presses on visitors. Sometimes she makes doughnuts for the local children—"fried cakes" she calls them— but Liz won't eat them because she's repelled by Mrs. Tetford's upper arms, by the wobble of the sausage-mottled flab.

Uncle Willard in his truck leads the procession down to the barn. The hogs are already in the calf box in the back of George's pickup. George lowers the tailgate and fixes some old boards to form a ramp. He lifts out the battered .22 rifle that's usually kept in the barn and jiggles a single cartridge into the breech. Then reaching into the cab, he fetches out four bottles of Pepsi, a column of Styrofoam cups, and a bottle of Golden Wedding. Shots of rye are poured for all the men. Uncle Willard opens his box of knives on the hood of his truck and selects one that's been honed away over the years to a thin and wicked arc. He drinks the rye down neat and sighs.

"Well, George," he says.

George nods.

"Well, George," says Uncle Willard, "tell me this, then. Why's Labatt's Blue like making love in a rowboat?"

Uncle Willard's repertoire is inexhaustible. He's a fixture at Grinley's Feed and Seed and at White's Garage in the village. He often entertains in the back of the hardware store and is frequently to be found with his cronies at the township dump where the dump's custodian has built a crazy lean-to with scrap board and tin on which he's nailed a large sign saying: Office.

While the men are still laughing at the answer to the Labatt's riddle, George slides up the door on the calf box. The three hogs inside stare up and press back against the box's rear wall. One of Maureen's brothers hands up the .22. George shoots one of the hogs between the eyes. Maureen's brothers get a hook into its mouth and down its throat and rush the body down the ramp and onto the ground where it thrashes and works itself about. Uncle Willard sticks it in the throat and joggles the knife about in the hole so that the still-pumping heart splashes out thick blood. In the November air, steam rises from the pools of it. The hog lies on its side, its legs scoring brown tracks in the turf.

Liz takes hold of my hand and tugs at me to bend down.

I put my arm around her.

"It's OK," I say. "The pig's dead. It isn't feeling anything. That's just its nerves. There's nothing to be frightened of."

"I'm not," she says. Her eyes are alive with pleasure. "Did you hear?" she whispers. "Mr. Tetford? Say the F-word?"

George secures chains round the hocks and the carcass is hoisted up to hang head-down from the front-end loader. Maureen's brothers are trying to force another bald tire further into the fire's centre. The heat is so intense, it's difficult to get near. The tractor lurches towards the oil drum, the carcass swaying and clanking. After the hog is scalded, George and Uncle Willard select knives and start scraping off the bristles with the concentration and delicacy of barbers wielding cut-throat razors. George works with his mouth open, Uncle Willard hisses through his teeth like an ostler. Some twenty minutes later the hog hangs oddly white in the afternoon light exactly the colour of a peeled mushroom.

Uncle Willard rests against the pickup and swills Golden Wedding around his teeth.

"Well, George," he says. "There were two bulls up on a hill. An old bull and a young bull. And down below," he says, "there's a herd of heifers. So the young bull says to the old bull . . ."

Uncle Willard nods as the others laugh; he keeps his face professionally straight. He seems almost disapproving of their laughter.

"What's the difference," he says, testing the edge of a new knife on the ball of his thumb, "what's the difference between a recruit into the army and a constipated owl?"

He makes the first cut.

After excising what he now calls—because all the children have crowded back—the hog's jimmy-riddler, he knots binder twine around what he calls the waterworks to prevent leaks and dripping. Then he starts to open up the body. As he cuts, the guts start to pile and slobber out against his stomach. He braces up their weight on his forearm so that nothing ruptures, so that the gall bladder or matter in the intestines does not spoil the meat. He cuts the liver free and drops it into a plastic margarine pail. The dogs are watching intently. Rex whines and shuffles nearer on his behind as if he's suffering from worms. The tricky part over, Uncle Willard lets the guts slop down into the nettles where they shine and subside and spread and settle.

"What?" he says.

"Where's its speaker?" repeats the smallest Howland kid.

"It's got eyelashes," says Liz. "Look, you can touch them. Orange eyelashes."

The small Howland scowls.

"I wanna see it. I wanna see its speaker."

"*Stereos* have speakers," says Liz. "*Microphones* have speakers."

It is getting colder. The afternoon is drawing in. Liz wanders off and starts to help Maureen's brothers feed the fire. The second hog is shot and bled. George pulls the pickup closer to where they're scraping off the bristles and turns the radio to the country music station in Watertown, New York. Lugubrious twanging love songs fill the air, songs of confession and maudlin remorse. The level in the bottle of Golden Wedding is dropping. The carcass slips from the front-end loader and the crumbs of dirt and smudges are wiped off its stiffening whiteness with filthy rags from the milk house.

I can see that Liz is getting bored. Maureen's brothers don't want to roast corn from the crib. They don't want to cook windfalls on sticks. George has cut the first pig's head off with a chainsaw but the smallest Howland has got it and is feeding it and won't share. George's kids have gone back to the house to watch TV. The other two Howlands are playing a game with offal and a stick.

I suggest to Liz that it's getting cold and that we walk home to make hot chocolate. We wave to Maureen's brothers and say goodbyes to George and Uncle Willard who pauses in his butchering to say, "Now this here's a golden oldie, John. There was this fellah, his wife had the house painted and as he was getting into bed that night . . ."

We walked up past the corn crib and Maureen's garden and the machine shed and into the yard. George's mother rapped on the kitchen window and beckoned. She'd prepared for Liz a plastic bag of fried cakes.

"Have you got a kiss for an old woman? That's it. *Isn't* she a little angel?"

I frown at Liz who is scrubbing at her lips with the back of her hand.

"Are you good at your books? Oh, I knew it! I just knew it! What a lovely ribbon! A little scholar, is she? Well, then, here's a nice book for you to read in bed for after you've said your prayers."

And so we set off along the dirt road to walk the mile or more home.

In one hand Liz is holding the plastic bag of fried cakes and in the other she is holding a pamphlet entitled:

WHERE ARE THE DEAD?

The house towards which we were walking that November afternoon was a stone farmhouse built in the 1840s. In 1900 or thereabouts someone had built on a frame addition. The stone part of the house had a vaguely Georgian look about it though it did not aspire to the limestone elegance of the houses in Kingston. This house was cruder, dumpier, the style debased, a house for farmers, not for gentlemen. The way it sat squat into the land reminded me of stone farmhouses in Wales. Many of the stone houses in the Rideau Lakes area have this sort of look and feel and I've heard it said that they were built by masons who'd sought local employment when the building of the locks on the Rideau Canal was finished.

The locks nearest to us were at Jones Falls. We used to take the children there to watch the boats going through and to feed the fish in the fish sanctuary. The children used to sprawl on the low footbridge and plop frothy spit into the water, attracting a frenzy of minnows, and, waggling ponderously up out of the darkness into green and sunlit view, the huge catfish with a white growth on its head like a beret.

In the evenings, the locks were often deserted and silver under the green gloom of the trees. The thick scrub and bush on the far bank would be turning black in the gathering twilight and I was always moved by thinking of the immensity of effort involved in building this canal and by the grandeur of the engineering. The great dressed blocks of stone, the massiveness of the gates, the lines of defence falling back to the lockmaster's fortified house—all this classical military architecture conjured up Colonel By and his engineers and sappers and beyond them the shade of the Marquis de Vauban and Europe in its days of might and glory.

WHERE ARE THE DEAD?

Visiting the United States and Canada in 1913, writing travel pieces for the *Westminster Gazette*, Rupert Brooke said of North American landscape:

It is an empty land. A European can find nothing to satisfy the hunger of his heart. The air is too thin to breathe. He requires haunted woods, and the friendly presence of ghosts . . . The maple and the birch conceal no dryads, and Pan has never been heard amongst these reed-beds. Look as long as you like upon a cataract of the New World, you shall not see a white arm in the foam. A godless place. And the dead do not return. That is why there is nothing lurking in the heart of the shadows, and no human mystery in the colours, and neither the same joy nor the kind of peace in dawn and sunset that older lands know. It is, indeed, a new world.

Certainly the land is not as thickly haunted as the English countryside and probably never will be. Canada is too vast to become so minutely groomed and annotated. But Rupert Brooke was certainly wrong about *this* countryside. Here the dead are all around us. They are part of us and we of them. We walk a land they shaped.

Across the road from my house, up on the edge of the rocky pasture, ancient cars sit in the scrub and bush. Bees nest in the rotted upholstery. The magnificent ruin of a combine harvester seems to melt and settle with each passing year. Low juniper bushes are growing through sheets of tin rusted to the thinness of leaf. My daughter thinks of this as an archaeological site.

In my own back field she unearths from an old domestic garbage dump patent medicine bottles which must date from the eighties and nineties of the last century. These she washes and ranges on a bench in the garage along with particularly valuable stones.

In the woods there are indications even older. Foundations of cut blocks. Lilac bushes. Apple trees grown wild. This is a hard country to farm and these abandoned sites mark discouragements, debts called in, drought, the death of a wife.

The land reveals itself slowly to the newcomer. Our ghosts are in its shapes. Rocks are never far from the surface here. Fields are simply soil in pockets. This field before us is shaped in this particular way with a protruding promontory of trees making ploughing difficult because under those trees the rock has surfaced in a sheet. Over *there*, water sits well into summer because it cannot drain away. Pasture, plough, swamp, and sugar bush—these were the shapes and uses forced by soil and rock upon the settlers. I've walked the land about here for miles in all directions mapping it with my muscles. I've come to understand it. I've come to understand the fearsome effort that went into its clearing and shaping. And I've come to love it.

And this small child with whom I'm walking, this much-loved daughter, what does *she* make of this place, this people, this daughter who is only a summer and occasional visitor?

Her maps are more intense than mine. Her maps are summer maps and magical. They show the course of the stream and where the banks of wild mint grow you can walk through up to your waist and the crushed smell of it. Her maps show where the felled and rotting elms lie and where under the fungus-smelling bark the salamanders live. Her maps show the old dry manure pile at Mr. Tetford's where a pair of milk snakes live and the wooden veranda at the side of the Howland house where the great black rat snake basks in the morning sun.

Noted on her maps are ponds of leopard frogs, the platform of twigs where the red-tailed hawk is nesting, the patches in the vast cathedral sugar bush where wild garlic grows, the dead swamp trees where great blue herons sit pretending to be branches.

Her maps record the sites of panic terror.

That place along the dappled path where the partridges explode from beneath the elderberry bushes and stop your heart in your mouth.

That clearing in the birch trees where there's the footprint of a building, tumbled masonry, raspberry canes gone wild, and the shrilling of the cicadas building to an electric whine and then in the still heat and sudden silence the leaves on the birches turn and tremble though there's not a breath of wind.

All this, the smells and shapes of it, its textures and its lovely endless detail—this mushroom-coloured pig, those three scabbed and yellow apples high in the November branches of a roadside tree as we walk homewards on this cold afternoon—all this will haunt her. This country has possessed her. When she is grown and living in some distant city, she will walk this countryside again in dreams. These "beauteous forms," as Wordsworth calls them, will be the bedrock of her life.

When the children were on holiday we spent most of the time going for walks, catching leopard frogs, exploring surrounding villages, fishing in Upper Beverley Lake for sunfish, swimming, sitting empurpled in the tree in front of the house gobbling mulberries.

When the children were in school I was working on a book that was published by Oberon in 1978. The book contained two novellas, "Private Parts: A Memoir" and "Girl in Gingham." The book was published as *Girl in Gingham*. I had been working on the title novella in Montreal in 1975 and finished it in a rented cabin in a neighbour's sugar bush in 1976.

While I'd been working on "The Lady Who Sold Furniture" and teaching myself how to write dialogue I'd also come to revel in the *theatricality* of what I was about. In the setting-up of scenes, their juxtapositions, their starting *in medias res* with their implications emerging from dialogue and action—I was playing with all the lessons I'd absorbed from the *auteur* film directors and from Degas' paintings. The novella form fascinated me because it could be tightly controlled—page by page—as a short story could, yet at the same time was expansive enough to allow for theatrical effects. Individual scenes could be built with lyric intensity and then juxtaposed with broad comedy. Broad comedy could be tempered to become intensely moving. Writing novellas was a particularly joyful kind of playing.

Novellas, the poetic kind I was interested in, were as dense and rich as Christmas puddings. And as time went on I beat more and more candied fruits and angelica into the mix. These novellas make concentrated demands on readers but I believe the pleasures are commensurate. I used dialogue to set scenes and reveal character. The dialogue was edgy, nervous, demanding the reader's committed attention. I was not unaware of Beckett, Pinter, and the absurdist verbal pratfalls of N. F. Simpson. My dialogue was intended as pure theatre.

As an example, here's the opening of a section from "Polly Ongle."

> "*Tabourouette!*" said the waitress, depositing on their table a bowl of potato chips. "Me, I'm scared of lightning!" Turning the glass vase-thing upside down, she lighted the candle inside.
>
> "Cider?" she repeated.
>
> "No?" said Paul.
>
> "Oh, well," said Norma. "I'll have what-do-you-call-it that goes cloudy."
>
> "Pernod," said Paul. "And a Scotch, please."
>
> "Ice?"
>
> "They feel squishy," said Norma, stretching out her leg.
>
> "Umm?"
>
> "My sandals."
>
> He looked down at her foot.

What is so pleasing to me about a passage like this is that the lines of non-speech are really a continuation of the dialogue though unspoken, pleasing also that the dialogue between them while seemingly about drinks and sandals is really both character description and a silent dialogue of eroticism, seemingly entirely innocent but not. And all driving forward crisply.

As the English music-hall comedian Max Miller used to say to the audience after telling one of his more salacious jokes, "Yes, that's right. Oh, yes, it's continental stuff I'm giving you."

I ended "Polly Ongle" with its protagonist pursuing an intimate, elegiac "conversation" with a statue of General José de San Martin in a public park. It's a scene that would translate without the slightest distortion into gorgeous film. And was conceived in exactly those terms.

I have never been troubled by critics, academic or otherwise, who regard stories and novellas as a minor form. I pursued this argument with Professors Sam Solecki and W. J. Keith in our book *Volleys*. I simply cite as iron-clad refutation of their position *Death in Venice* and V. S. Naipaul's *In a Free State*, another book which flared out over my literary landscape illuminating much and filling me with delight and awe. *In a Free State* appeared in 1971 and was described as a novel but its compression and its lyrical method of movement mark it clearly in my opinion as a novella. V. S. Naipaul is also a wonderful story writer, a genre in which he's been undervalued. I always recommend *A Flag on the Island* and claim the story "The Nightwatchman's Occurrence Book" as one of the funniest stories in English.

"Girl in Gingham" was madly theatrical and I much enjoyed staging the scenes and pacing them effectively. It was interesting to move from fast to slow, from action to meditation, working the emotional weights of sections against each other until it all flowed into the final scene in the restaurant. The other novella, "Private Parts: A Memoir," was by its pseudo-memoir form inherently less given to dramatic scenes. I concentrated more on achieving a *tone* for the novella. I remain pleased with both pieces.

———————

While we certainly enjoyed the peace of the country and its beauty we both found that a little peace could go a long way. It was alarming to find ourselves discussing as a topic of some fascination the passage of the snowplough and we often longed for conversation that Delta could not supply.

Paul Theroux published a novel in 1974 called *The Black House* about a recently retired man called Munday who buys an old house in a Devonshire village. He and his wife are staying at the village pub, kept by Mr. Flack, until their furniture is delivered. Here is a scene in the pub one evening.

> The men grew audible again, they coughed with force, one inhaled snuff deeply from the knuckles on the back of his hand, another smoked a rolled twisted cigarette, and the drawling was renewed: the price of apples, the cost of living, a lunatic in the next village, reckless drivers, a pair of vicious dogs Hosmer said should be put down. ("And I know how to do it.")
>
> "You could write a book about this place," said Mr. Flack, who took Munday's silence for attention.
>
> "Me?" said Munday.
>
> "Anyone who knew how," said Mr. Flack.
>
> Munday's laughter was harsh; the four men stared at him. He waited until they began another private conversation—this one about a dead badger—before he went up to his room.

I laughed out loud when I first read this. Whether Devon or Delta, it catches exactly and mordantly the scope and tenor of village conversation.

—this one about a dead badger—

To counter dead badgerdom we had throngs of visitors who came to stay for weekends, John Mills, Jack David, Ray Smith, Leon and Connie Rooke, Harry Hill, Douglas Rollins, Jim Gaite, Kent Thompson, Robert Lecker—and Hugh Hood would drop over from nearby Charleston Lake and Matt Cohen from his retreat in Verona.

Whenever Geoff Hancock, editor of *Canadian Fiction Magazine*, came to stay we spent boozy afternoons listening to the lesser Chicago luminaries. It was our own King Biscuit Time show listening to records by Magic Sam, Johnny Shines, Son House, Jimmy Rodgers, Roosevelt Sykes, Elmore James, Robert Nighthawk, Otis Rush, and Shakey Walter Horton.

On one occasion, the living room seemed to be becoming hazy with smoke.

"The ducks!" yelled Myrna.

She ran into the kitchen.

"It's not too bad," she called. "I'll baste the burned bits with orange juice. It's only Geoff Hancock."

After the fall of Saigon in 1975 we were following newspaper reports of the plight of refugees. By 1977 we were reading increasingly of boats full of refugees being attacked on the high seas by pirates and fired upon by government vessels. All this heartlessness reminded Myrna vividly of the Jews in the thirties being rejected by port after port, country after country, Canada among them, and sailing on to their deaths. She resolved that we must help.

Myrna has family connections to Naomi Bronstein who was working with orphans in Saigon in 1975. Through her we knew of Sandra Simpson, the founder of Families for Children, who was running orphanages in Vietnam and Cambodia. She also ran orphanages in Bangladesh, India, and, later, Somalia. Myrna phoned Sandra in Toronto and offered help. This was at the precise moment that Ontario was dithering about initiating the Unaccompanied Indo-Chinese Minor Refugee Program. With Sandra's help we agreed to sponsor and became the guardians of two children who were in a Malaysian refugee camp at Pilau Bidong.

The bureaucratic foot-dragging and obfuscation were bewildering. Myrna wrote to all levels of government up to and including Flora MacDonald and Pierre Trudeau. She wrote to Employment and Immigration Canada, the Ontario Ministry of Community and Social Services, the Secretary of State for External Affairs, the Ministry of the Attorney General, the Office of the Official Guardian . . . Eventually we ended up with a brother and sister, Duong Le Binh, a girl of sixteen, and Duong Gia Phu, a boy of ten.

We had explained to Ron why we were doing this but he was difficult to win over. He said, "But I *like* being an only child." The whole situation was difficult for both him and Elizabeth.

Le Binh and Gia Phu spoke Vietnamese and Cantonese. They spoke no English. Communication was difficult. They did not seem to understand why they were with us. We decided that we needed someone who spoke English and Cantonese to explain matters to them. Fortunately we had a friend, Jack Chiang, originally from Taiwan, who was the photography editor at the Kingston *Whig-Standard*. Jack drove up from Kingston and took the two of them out in his car. They were gone for about two hours.

"Well," said Jack, "I'd get rid of them if I were you. I've never met such weird kids in my life."

He explained that they were Chinese and had lived in the Cholon sector of Saigon. The extended family had lived together in a compound almost entirely cut off from the world. Their father was a weaver. Number One Uncle was the one who "go outside," who dealt with the outside world. Jack was groping to explain exactly what we were dealing with.

"It's like they came from China two or three hundred years ago and they still think and speak like people did then. Yes, that's it. They're like, you know, those German guys that wear black suits in the States, Mennonites. They're like Amish. *That's* what they're like. Weird."

Both children were obviously unhappy and obviously missing their parents painfully. They learned English slowly. We had decided that the essence of the matter was that, for their own sakes and for their future, we had to integrate them as soon as we could. We started with names. Le Binh we decided to call Lee, Gia Phu, we changed to Jim.

We sent them to school hoping that they'd pick up some English there and we persevered at home with looking through magazines and naming objects in photographs, with endless repetitions of words and phrases. Progress was painful. Lee referred to the fridge as the *wish-wish* and after an outing to Ottawa called the Parliament Buildings the *bi how* meaning "big house."

Attempts to interest them in matters Canadian fell flat. The entire household ate with chopsticks and Myrna bought the Chinese ingredients that Lee wanted—ingredients for kou-tien, lopchong, bok choy, mustard greens, light and dark soy, fish sauce, noodles. If Myrna made a Western dish, Lee would push it around with chopsticks exclaiming in disgust, "What *this!*"

Lee and Jim gradually learned some halting English and we tried all the time to engage them in conversation. Sitting with Lee one evening looking at magazine photos and attempting to build vocabulary I came upon a photo of a model.

"Isn't she beautiful, Lee?"

"I no like it," said Lee, "round eye."

It was difficult to understand how they saw us and how they understood Canada. It was fairly obvious that they thought the Chinese way of conducting oneself was the only way. The word *ethnocentrism* only hints at how rigid they were. They behaved towards us as though they were house guests and made little attempt to join in any family activities. They sometimes said things so revealing that they were, so to speak, a glimpse into the abyss. One day in 1979 Lee came home from school and said, "Trudeau, he gone."

"That's right, Lee."

"What happen he now?"

"Well," I said, about to launch into the idea of political parties, but she interrupted me with an expression of inquiry and drew a finger across her throat in a slitting gesture.

So much for civics.

Our neighbour gave Jim a green John Deere tractor cap. Lee snatched it from his head, saying, "Chinese boy no wear green hat." Furore developed. More floods of tears.

"Jack," I said on the phone, "what should I know about green hats?"

He listened and then explained that wearing a green hat was in ancient Chinese tradition the mark of a cuckold.

"What did I tell you?" said Jack. "Sincerely weird."

We were somewhat discouraged by the lack of progress but we took part in another campaign to bring five young men to Canada from the Southeast Asian camps. This organization was called the Rideau Committee to Save the Boat People. Five area families volunteered homes for them but we had to raise $10,000 to be held in trust to satisfy government sponsorship requirements.

In 1980 we also arranged for St. Xavier's Church in Brockville to sponsor our children's two uncles and two aunts still in Pilau Bidong Camp. Lee and Jim were much cheered to be able to spend time with them. The four of them, tiny people, lived in an apartment the church provided which they provisioned with huge sacks of rice.

Jim was of particular concern to us. He was passive and sat about the house staring into space with his mouth open. Myrna came into the kitchen one night after getting the two boys bathed and into bed and she said, "You know, that Jim . . ."

"Ummh?"

"Well, he's the first ten-year-old I've met with B.O. And," she added, "a moustache."

We grilled Lee on the matter and she confessed that everyone had lied about Jim's age because the fee to escape Vietnam was less for younger children. It was also believed in the camps that the younger children were the easier it was for them to be accepted into Canadian and American families. Jim, it turned out, was thirteen. He became something of a project for Myrna. She does tend to get the bit between her teeth. And Jim's teeth became an obsession. All his teeth were pitted with black holes and were rotten. His upper teeth were splintered into spikes and fangs. Nothing was salvable. Myrna took him to our local dentist who said he needed complete top dentures. Myrna took him at the appointed time but the dentist said she couldn't do the work that day because her assistant was off sick. Myrna, not to be baulked, said, "Show me what to do and I'll be your assistant." And, fearsome woman that she is, she indeed operated the water and the suction while the wreckage of Jim's teeth was removed.

During these months Myrna and I had been talking about adopting a child. Myrna was becoming increasingly interested in Families for Children and increasingly interested in Sandra Simpson. Sandra and her husband, Lloyd, were unlikely do-gooders. Sandra is a woman of great compassion and little sentimentality. She has a raucous sense of humour. Her own family is vast, being made up of all the adoption breakdowns and of children difficult to place. At one time she had well over twenty children in the house, including the crippled, the autistic, and the blind. While looking after this alarming brood Sandra was running orphanages, raising money constantly, and dealing with the bureaucracies of three and four governments at a time as she arranged international adoptions. It all seemed to an outside eye to be endless chaos—but it somehow worked.

Sandra's main aim was not international adoption but in-country care in the orphanages. It was amazing to watch this woman bend people to her will. When she opened an orphanage in Mogadishu, Myrna helped to gather supplies in Ottawa which were shipped to join everything being stored at Sandra's Montreal house. Myrna drove a forklift truck in Cohen's Demolition warehouse gathering up military cots. Sandra had secured a Canadian Forces Hercules by sweet-talking the minister of defence at a social function. When it came time to ship everything to Trenton, a truck of soldiers showed up at the house ordered there by the commander of a local army base who was enjoying the attentions of another Families for Children volunteer.

"Mrs. Simpson!" said the officer in charge of loading at Trenton, a testy man who obviously disapproved of civilian meddling, "You've subverted the Canadian Air Force to your ends and now I see you've turned your attention to the Army."

We phoned Sandra and she told us that she had two children in India that she wanted to place. The children were in the Families for Children orphanage in Coimbatore in Tamil Nadu State. The grim address was: Behind the Blind Institute on Chemical Road.

Sandra sent us photographs of a boy, Manikem, aged nine, and Rangidam, a girl aged seven.

I showed the photographs to Lee and Jim.

"What for they come?" said Jim.

Lee frowned at the photographs.

"India people same thing monkey," she said.

So in 1980 there were six children in the house. Rangi spoke Tamil. Manikem, whose name we changed to Daniel, spoke Malayalam. And then my mother and her friend arrived from England to add to this menagerie. My mother and I have had a relationship which might be described as "troubled." Now in her hundredth year, she recently told me that the happiest day of her entire life was when I was accepted into a pre-kindergarten group at the age of three.

"The relief," she said, "at getting rid of you, you can't imagine." The state between us ever since might best be described as a state of truce. I have written a version of this relationship in my novella "Private Parts." The underlying tensions reveal themselves in oblique emotional outbursts. One day in this summer visit I noticed she was getting moody and suggested we go for a walk. Tears started running down her cheeks. She burst out with a pronouncement I've been trying to think of a response to for twenty years.

"I could die happily," she said, "if only you had some decent furniture."

Rangidam stayed close to the house and close to Myrna and told us later when she had learned some English that she was frightened of the monkeys catching her. Rangi also spoke of running away from home in India and of a mother who had put her feet in the cooking fire. She had been living on the street before someone had taken her to the orphanage. Danny's situation had been more stable. His father had died in an accident and his mother had remarried. Her new husband did not accept Danny and his mother had taken him to the orphanage to protect him. Because he'd had some experience of a family he was better able to adjust than Rangi.

In 1980 ECW Press published my novel *General Ludd*. I had had a difficult time writing it and the book fell into two parts. I had intended it to be a lighthearted comedy; there was a hiatus in the writing of it and the last half became increasingly bleak. It is not a good novel. It isn't even an adequate one. I seriously considered withdrawing it before publication but then, in weakness, let it go forward. It received glowing reviews. John Moss in his *A Reader's Guide to the Canadian Novel* wrote: "*General Ludd* is probably the finest comic novel ever published in Canada. *Going Down Slow* earned Metcalf fair consideration as a writer in the tradition of Richler, Davies, Leacock, and Haliburton. With *General Ludd*, he follows comfortably in the wake of Cervantes, or Fielding, or Trollope, or Waugh at his very best."

Such preposterous bombast over such an obviously botched attempt at a novel is why I despair of criticism in Canada. Keath Fraser got closer to the mark when he said to me that the book founders under its freight of ideas.

Lee and Jim were making it increasingly clear that they were happy only when they were with their aunts and uncles. They began to spend more time in Brockville. Myrna and I were also feeling considerable stress as Lee was falling to bits emotionally. These tensions were not Lee and Jim's fault. They were worried about their parents and wanted only to be reunited. It was probably misguided of us to expect any emotional return from them but it is difficult to live with people who refuse to connect with you.

Lee and Jim decided that they wanted to live in Brockville with their aunts and uncles. They made this move and subsequently managed to get their parents and two younger siblings out of Vietnam. The whole family was reunited and they all live in Toronto now. Both Lee and Jim are married and with children of their own.

Myrna and I and Ron, Rangi, and Dan moved to Ottawa to begin the Long Sentence.

AN EAGER EYE

PROFESSOR HENRY BEISSEL, head of the Creative Writing Department at Concordia, phoned me in 1981 inviting me to Montreal as writer-in-residence. I came to an arrangement with the department whereby I would stay in Montreal a couple of nights a week. At the time of my arrival Henry was away on tour in Germany reading his poetry. Sitting in my office one afternoon I heard his familiar accent in the corridor. I went to say hello and there he stood positively effulgent in a white linen suit and a swishy silk-lined cape.

"How went your tour?"

He considered the question and then said quite unselfconsciously, "They loved me."

I was pleased to be in Montreal, not only for the income and as a respite from my children but because I was able to spend a lot of time with Elizabeth Lang at her store on Greene Avenue in Westmount. Elizabeth let me examine and handle all her African masks and figures and made me free of her stockroom, pleased to teach me in the way Bernard Halliday had been.

Grey bun and Birkenstocks but with an almost girlish enthusiasm for art and commerce. I can see the two of us now in the intricate dance of purchase.

"Look at the lines," she'd murmur, as I ran my hands hopelessly over the horns of a *chi wara*, the antelope mask worn caplike by the Bambara tribe, the dancer's face and body hidden under cascades of raffia.

"So powerful," she'd murmur.

"Yes, *but*, Elizabeth, I've read that they were last danced—in the fields, I mean—in 1934. So there's no way . . ."

"But who's to say exactly," she'd say, "what 'genuine' means? What's genuine is what *it* says to *you*."

"But if it wasn't used for their own ritual purposes . . ."

"You've been reading books again by Americans. Rules! Rules! Who approaches Art with rules?"

"Well, that's all very well, but . . ."

"Now if we were dealing with a mask of the Guro . . ."

A tiny shrug.

The suggestion of a moue.

"But *this* . . ."

Not long afterwards, Elizabeth was tragically killed in a traffic accident. As she was stepping between two parked cars, one reversed and she was crushed to death. The Elizabeth and Justin Lang African collection, more than six hundred items, was donated to the Agnes Etherington Art Centre at Queen's, where a paltry selection is now indifferently displayed.

I had become interested in African art in the sixties and can remember the exact moment that I was drawn to it. I was walking along Sherbrooke Street and paused to look in the window of Le Petit Musée. There among Chinese bowls and flintlock pistols and a Georgian silver coffee pot stood a wooden *thing*. It had a large disc-like face with delicately suggested features and a column as a body. Tiny breasts stood out. It made me look at it harder than anything had for years. I went into the store and asked the owner, Max Klein, what that thing in the window *was*.

He explained that it was a kind of doll from the Ashanti tribe in Ghana. But not exactly a doll. Women who were pregnant or wished to become pregnant carried these "dolls" tucked in their robes at the back. The face embodied the Ashanti ideal of good looks and the doll was thought to confer these attractive features on the child-to-be-born. The object was known as an *akua ba*.

I was so moved aesthetically by this thing that I bought it on the spot, having with me, by chance, its exact price as I was on my way to pay the rent.

Over the years since then I taught myself a great deal about African carving, reading the journal *African Art* and gathering together a useful library of reference. I also read the fieldwork of ethnologists and anthropologists. I sometimes thought the inside of my head was coming to resemble the higgledy-piggledy cabinets of Oxford's Pitt-Rivers Museum. Push this button and the cabinet lights up to reveal the varied tribal concepts of the human figure: Dogon, Fanti, Luba, Fang, and Pende; push that button for cross-cultural arcana. My mind was chock-a-block with information.

There are funerary masks of the Igbo and Ibibio people of southern Nigerian—Cross River masks, too—which are decorated in white, the colour widely associated with death. The very earliest masks used a white clay as pigment but quite early on the carvers decided that a British shoe polish for white leather and sneakers called Meltonia was just the job. It amuses me to imagine scientists in the war against fake and fraud testing not for the fingerprint trace elements of Nigerian clay but for the correct formula for Meltonia Shoe Cream. Similarly, the Yoruba colour of choice was obtained from Reckitt's Blue Dye laundry bags. Beads were fashioned from the thick glass of Pond's Cold Cream jars. In Benin, they continue to cast plaques and figures of the Oba with his mud-fish legs using spent cartridge cases from the Biafran war.

But information is no substitute for having handled so many pieces that the eye goes immediately to the piece that is "right." It is a fusion of knowledge, taste, and experience. The feeling is exactly like that of Jonathan Gash's Lovejoy character, an antiques "divvie," for whom bells ring when he comes across a genuine artifact.

At exactly the moment that I became near-expert, the prices skyrocketed and I had to revert to sad gazing in museums.

Le Petit Musée soon became one of my favourite shops. It carried a vast stock of antiquities and pottery and silver, glass, edged weapons, firearms, African carvings, furniture, jade, ivory, Japanese prints, Arabic bowls, calligraphy . . . This wonderful emporium was presided over by Max Klein, a tall and elegant Viennese Jew, grave of mien and manner but charged with the invigorating larcenous instincts common to all in the antiques business.

Mr. Klein's always grave demeanour and his pronouncements afforded me rich amusement. Once while gazing in abstracted manner at a vitrine, he said, "I have always understood an interest in pottery in a Canadian-born man as an infallible indicator."

On another occasion he was trying to sell me a bronze adze.

"It is," he said, "fairly obviously Celtic."

I had been boning up on the subject.

"Or possibly," I said, "Luristan."

He inclined his head.

"Or possibly," the lovely old operator conceded, "Luristan."

Over the years, I've bought many a small antiquity from Max Klein, Han jade, Luristan bronzes, amber, Greek wine cups, Kufic calligraphy from the Abbasid dynasty. I've always liked to have a few antiquities about me; apart from their beauty, they give life a context and solidity. If I can work one of these artifacts into the texture of daily life I'm doubly delighted. Rootling about one day in a coin shop in Ottawa I found two identical examples of what is known as "spade" money. These Chinese coins are rectangular in shape and bifurcate. In the upper part, the "body" as it were, there is a hole cast through. They bear a design which I've always taken to be a lotus. They date from the reign of Wang Mang (A.D. 6–23). Myrna and I use them as key rings—much to my brother's anguish—and there is a daily pleasure in touching and using something two thousand years old.

I suppose this love of ancient things dates back in part to my brother's museum in the pantry and to my almost psychotic rage and jealousy and desire at his being given by a retired missionary when he was thirteen or so a beautiful bronze Chinese bell and a pair of black figure *lekythoi*.

When young, I wanted to be a painter so intensely that the fact that I had an *anti-talent* for the activity seemed irrelevant. During my two sixth-form years I devoured Skira art books and mucked about in the art room labouring on sludgy landscapes. There was a new teacher at the school in his first year out of the Slade. We admired each other's suede shoes. Using a brush or his thumb, he'd turn an inch or two of my turgid determination into something full of life and sparkle.

"Do you think it's getting any better?" I'd ask him.

"Christ, no!" he'd say. "It's worse than shit-sausage but keep daubing away. It'll help develop your eye a bit and keep you from playing with yourself."

(Needless to say, he lasted only two terms.)

He once took me to London to visit the studio of *his* teacher, John Minton. With the brushes, the clutter, the painty smells, and the cooking sherry we drank from teacups, I felt I was at the source. There's a haunting portrait of Minton by Lucian Freud in the National Portrait Gallery in London. He committed suicide in 1967, anguished, apparently, by his homosexuality.

While I was at Bristol University I was keenly interested in the painting of William Scott and haunted the Arnolfini Gallery where he showed. At the Bristol Guild of Applied Art I used to stroke and lust after the Bernard Leach pottery. But it was not until I came to Canada that I actually bought a painting.

I'd been one evening to Sir George Williams University, now Concordia, to listen to some wretched poet. Who it was I can't remember now but he was reading in front of an exhibition of paintings by Roy Kiyooka who was painter-in-residence that year. All next day, teaching, I saw those green egg shapes swimming before my eyes. The paintings were in the Pop-Op style but had far more *presence* than such work usually did. I phoned Kiyooka and asked him if he'd sell me the painting and let me pay for it over a period of time. He seemed perfectly agreeable and I arranged to go to his house in NDG the next evening.

He opened the door and stared at me in silence. He shuffled to one side which I took as an invitation to enter. We walked into a front room entirely bare except for a kitchen chair. Leaning against one wall was a package done up in corrugated cardboard and tape. Kiyooka still had not spoken. He stood staring intently into the empty fireplace. I had put $500 into an envelope in a vestigial notion of bourgeois manners and now handed it to him. He still just stared at me in silence. The cliché "inscrutable" flashed into my mind. Had I unknowingly breached some matter of etiquette in picture buying? Had I unknowingly flouted some intricacy of Japanese courtesy?

Feeling quite sweaty, I began to babble inanities about the weather. But something about his face . . . Slowly, very slowly, it dawned on me. He wasn't inscrutable. He was stoned. He was massively, monumentally stoned, stoned beyond even the *possibility* of speech. I picked up the painting, bade him a cheery farewell, and left him staring, rapt, into the grate.

I'm telling the story about Roy Kiyooka as a way into saying that buying a painting is essential in beginning self-education in visual art. It concentrates one's eye and aesthetic faculties as nothing else can to know that imminently you are going to part with the price of four refrigerators and a high-end dishwasher.

It's not really possible to understand a painting without living with it. Dailiness is important in revealing the painting that is flashy or meretricious, the painting where awkwardness bleeds through. Posters and reproductions of any kind are a delusion, because they always betray the original by masking texture and flattening the paint's true life. The Irish painter Jack Yeats even stipulated in his will that no reproductions of his work be made, so sure was he that reproductions betrayed.

I've been familiar for many years, through photographs, with Picasso's great painting *Night Fishing in Antibes*. I can still feel the intensity of shock at seeing the painting at MOMA in New York. No photograph had prepared me for the complexity and gorgeousness of its colour. This was a Picasso I had never known.

Lucian Freud said something simple yet profound when he said, "Learning to paint is literally learning to use paint."

Many people seem to feel intimidated by the hush of commercial galleries and the seeming disdain of their often bitchy staff but they are, after all, only *shops*. And for the most part crammed, as my painter friend Tony Calzetta says, with Stuff.

The Canadian art world should intimidate no one. It is easy to grasp. Just glance through a couple of Joyner's Canadian Art auction catalogues and you'll get the picture. What the audience, such as it is, is willing to pay for is second- and third-rate landscape paintings. Old barn, cedar rail fence, trees.

Especially trees.

Abstract work tends to cause titters of unease.

Joyner has been quoted as saying that he would not hold an auction of abstract work as the results would entirely destroy what market there is.

David Milne (1882–1953) is beginning to be recognized by the more daring.

Even in the realm of paint one cannot escape the contamination of nationalism. The Group of Seven (1920) remain Canada's pin-up boys. See "Trees" above. Canada's pin-up *girl* is Emily Carr, who trumped the deal by painting autochthonous totem poles *amidst* trees. Hugh Hood and I shared a profound loathing for her work. Hugh always claimed that it was patently obvious that these muddily coloured exercises were all versions of her vulva. I miss conversations with Hugh; they were always bracing.

Since the Group of Seven and Emily Carr, popular taste has celebrated Ken Danby, Robert Bateman, Toller Cranston, Charles Pachter, and the like. "Woodland" artists like Norval Morrisseau and Daphne Odjig blossomed. This "Woodland School" paints decorative myths and legends badly. Morrisseau first showed at the Pollock Gallery in 1962. He is often described as a shaman. I've never been sure about what it is that shamans *do* but I've rather doubted the sincerity of the man's calling since hearing Jack Pollock's comic accounts of Morrisseau's epic matings with a life-size rubber doll.

Also widely revered are the paintings of Alex Colville, weirdly frozen frames from an untold narrative, enabling the viewer to invent the implied story. What happened to the running girl? Why is she running so fast? What might she be screaming? Who is she waving at? Why should we be asking stupid questions like this?

The actual *paint* is devoid of interest.

Popular with many are Inuit carvings, dismissed by all experts in tribal sculpture as "airport art."

I like to furnish my fiction with Inuit sculpture.

"On the glass table in front of the couch lay a gigantic soapstone seal with a bulbous Eskimo trying to do something to it."

"Bulbous" was good.

". . . trying to do something to it," obviously derives from Kingsley Amis. As does, "It was nice in the bathroom," from the same novella.)

Canada has had and still has superbly gifted painters but usually doesn't seem able to recognize them. *The Canadian Encyclopedia* describes painting as "an essentially reactionary form." If I were wealthy and had acres of wall space I'd chuckle to see the National

Gallery silting itself up with conceptual profundities and feeble-minded videos while for absurdly low prices I'd be buying the reactionary canvases of Guido Molinari, Yves Gaucher, Charles Gagnon, William Ronald, Alexandra Luke, Ray Mead, Kazuo Nakamura, Tom Hodgson, Harold Klunder . . .

And Tony Calzetta.

Tony Calzetta was born in 1945 in Windsor, Ontario, to a Croatian mother and Italian father. He attended Catholic schools in Windsor and went to the University of Detroit, from which he graduated in 1968 with the degree of Bachelor of Science. Most of the courses he took were, however, in math, business studies, and accounting, and his degree might more properly be described as being in commerce.

On leaving the university, he immediately secured a job in Windsor with Price-Waterhouse, where he remained in increasing misery for two years. At the beginning of 1970, he gave notice and went to Toronto to look for work. For the next nine months he worked as a labourer for a construction company. Up in the morning dark, the crew's boss passing round brandy to numb them against the day. Following this, he drifted back to Windsor and worked in a desultory manner as a drapery installer.

During this period of drift, he somehow arrived at the idea that what he really wanted to do was to study art. Drawing and painting had always fascinated him. When a child, he had badgered his parents into buying oil paints for him, but the murky results were not wildly encouraging as he'd been unaware that turpentine was supposed to be mixed with the oil. On the slender basis of this childhood interest and in the what-the-hell climate of the time, he phoned the art department of the University of Windsor in September 1971 and was instructed to appear with his portfolio.

"You talk about embarrassment! My portfolio was a ratty piece of cardboard in which I'd got sandwiched some little drawings I'd done when I was about ten years old, a few watercolours, and a copy of a brassiere commercial from a magazine. And when I got to the interview room there were all these black portfolios open to show work that was professionally matted and I thought, Oh, my God! What have you *done* to yourself, you fool!"

He graduated with a BFA in 1975 and went to York, from which he graduated in 1977 with an MFA. His first three shows after York were at the Pollock Gallery. I first encountered the work at his third show at the Pollock Gallery in 1980. I was in Toronto on some kind of publishing business and wandered into the gallery on a whim. What hit me was one of those rare art experiences where one feels one's life suddenly illuminated, enlarged, enriched. Over the years since then Tony has become my closest friend.

It is extremely difficult to write about paintings but I will attempt to describe what I saw and first felt at that Pollock Gallery show. These were the *Cloud* paintings, the elements of landscape drawn in a cartoon-like style to make landscapes or seascapes afresh by combining the conventional "signs" for rain, clouds, waves. These paintings were at the same time very sophisticated and elegant and yet childlike. There are suggestions in them of Paterson Ewen and Philip Guston. I have one of these huge canvases in Ottawa and its charcoal-drawn centre shape has been variously referred to by visitors as a cauliflower, a mop, a brain, and an engorged sexual organ; this may say more about the visitors than about the painting.

The central problem is that the "clouds" have charcoal-drawn stems on them which attach them to the side or top of the paintings.

"*Is* it a cloud?" I say.

"Well," he says, "it *could* be. It is and it isn't."

John Newlove claims to hate all painters because, he says, at the drop of a hat they're always ready to impart to you their philosophy of life. Which derives from the one book they've ever read. Which is inevitably a work of science fiction.

One knows, rather guiltily, what he *means*, of course, but of Tony Calzetta this isn't true at all. Tony is reticent and ambiguous to the point of being shifty. He spouts no philosophy. I think he wants the paintings to remain undefined and mysterious. Talking about them makes him uncomfortable. I think he has the feeling that if we can't define the painting then we're unable to turn it off. We'll keep looking, keep wondering, "*Is* it a cloud?"

The shocking part of the third *Cloud* exhibition at the Pollock Gallery was the energy of the line. This show broke through into what has now become the essence of his work—the combining of drawing with painting, the use of charcoal to produce a line of marvellous sensitivity. Paul Klee spoke famously of "taking a line for a walk"; Tony takes them for a hundred-metre sprint.

He said to me once, "The energy that's conveyed in a line is so exciting. The line defines the image. The line *is* the energy. Colour supplies the mood."

On another occasion, he said, "Charcoal's a sensual pleasure. There's a film on Alechinsky working and there's one part where he has a huge sheet of paper and he's putting down a line in charcoal and—oh, God!—the excitement just of the *sound*."

Tony works in series and his images—his iconography, as the art historians love to say—evolve from series to series. You couldn't possibly predict the next series but when it arrives it has an inevitability about it. Clouds move to the sides of the paintings and become curtains. Dramatic skies become pelmets. The waves turn into a stage. What were once strange floating objects in the sea now become boulders on the stage, flatirons, possibly ruined buildings. Sometimes huge slabs of rock are furnished with wheels. The paintings are somewhat surreal and nearly always cheerful if not funny.

Philip Ottenbrite, when he was working at the Mira Godard Gallery, said, "The history of Tony's work has a real logic to it and a sense of progression. He has a very personal sense of style, and elegance is the essence of that style. He makes everything he does look very easy but that ease has been *worked* for. He's bringing something new to painting. I don't want to inflate things but his work has a certain . . . majesty. He's unique. His work fits into no category and of course he's suffered because of that.

"I can tell you one important thing from personal experience. The work of many painters—it dies on the wall after two months. That never happens with Tony. Energy emanates from a Calzetta canvas and keeps on emanating. He's poured so much energy into the canvas, you see, that we keep on receiving it, the picture keeps growing and expanding for us."

Tony has always insisted on his own direction and usually, of course, to his detriment. Being funny in Canada probably isn't a good idea; being funny in Canadian painting is probably unforgivable.

Above: The launch of the New Story Writers at the National Library in 1992. Steve Heighton, Linda Svendsen, Blair Sharpe, Myrna, Don Dickinson, and Douglas Glover. Steve is good-humouredly accepting advice on letting the photographer see the book cover.

Right: Tim Inkster at the Eden Mills Writers' Festival in the late 1990s.

Below: Tim and Elke selling books at Eden Mills. Tim is giving an uncommitted browser possibly homicidal consideration. (AUTHOR)

Above: With Tony Calzetta, Lise Giroux, and Yoni Freeman at the 1995 Toronto launch of *Acts of Kindness and of Love*, a *livre d'artist*. Tony based his hand-coloured prints on Delta's sturdiest crop—Scotch thistles.

Right: Kim Jernigan at Eden Mills. For more than fifteen years she has been the editor and guiding force behind the *New Quarterly* exhibiting exemplary taste and heartbreaking faith.

Below: With Sharon and Jack David of ECW Press. Jack David and Robert Lecker are two of Canadian literature's unsung heroes.

Members of the Burning Rock Writers' Group on tour in 1995: Stephanie Squires, Claire Wilkshire, Lisa Moore. Along with Michael Winter, we made a meal of technique and burgers in the Elgin Street Diner. (MICHAEL WINTER)

Left: Magnum Readings: Yann Martel, 1993. The first reading Yann had ever given. Unsure of the ropes, he learned his lengthy story "The Facts Behind the Helsinki Roccamatios" off by heart and recited it. (MICHELLINE ROCHETTE)

Right: Magnum Readings: Rohinton Mistry, 1991. Rohinton and I had much the same sort of British education, the main difference being that I got Latin and he got Gujarati. (MICHELLINE ROCHETTE)

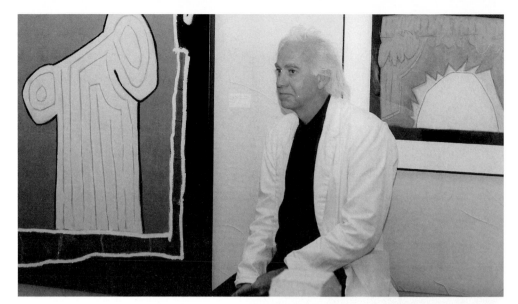

Above: Magnum Readings: Leon Rooke, 1991. A pensive Leon sitting between an exuberant Tony Calzetta canvas and a quieter, lyrical drawing of a strange something on a stage. (AUTHOR)

Right: Terry Griggs at a reading in the mid-1990s in Ottawa. Keath Fraser said of her: "It's interesting to read a writer who more or less forsakes narrative for metaphor." (AUTHOR)

Below: Bharati Mukherjee and Clark Blaise reading in Ottawa, 1997. After half a lifetime of knowing Clark I'm still in awe of his mastery. (AUTHOR)

Mary Borsky with Steve Heighton at the 1995 Ottawa launch of *Influence of the Moon*. Mary Borsky's stories remain one of Canada's best-kept literary secrets, though I whisper the secret almost daily. (AUTHOR)

Left: Russell Smith, elegance personified, at the National Arts Centre, 1999. His mother said to me she'd prefer him to have a job with a dental plan. (AUTHOR)
Right: Michael Winter in St. John's, 1997. Bravura technique, which leaves many of his contemporaries thoughtful and uneasy, except for Russell Smith, who revels in the pyrotechnics. (AUTHOR)

Leon Rooke at Food for Thought Bookstore in Ottawa, 1993. Whatever the moment dictates gets thrown in, a soft-shoe shuffle, a limping war-wound, cries to make the welkin ring. (AUTHOR)

Clark Blaise and Philip Marchand, the Franco-American mafia, at the Elgin Street Diner after the Ottawa launch of *Ripostes* in 1998. (AUTHOR)

With Myrna and Irving Layton, 1993, at his eightieth birthday party at Magnum Books and the launch of *Dance with Desire*. Myrna has adored him since her high school days. (MICHELLINE ROCHETTE)

In my study in front of Tony Calzetta's *Fountainheady*, a picture of a lovely, well, *thing* with wheels on, now donated to the University of Toronto Art Centre. (BLAIR SHARPE)

Left: Norman Levine at Laurence Sterne's house, Shandy Hall, 2001. Bernard Levin in the *Sunday Times* wrote: "Mr. Levine is a true artist who grinds his bones—and anything else he can lay his hands on—to make his bread." (AUTHOR)

Right: Tony Calzetta in the cloisters of the Maison de Santé St. Paul in Provence. It was founded in AD 982. Myrna found a mad woman under the altar. (AUTHOR)

With Eric Ormsby at Eden Mills Writers' Festival 2002. Even in wilting heat, standards were maintained. (IRENA MURRAY)

He gives his paintings such titles as *Jive Ass Atomic Art Queen*, *Lester's Love Wagon Leaves Late* and *The Queen Realizing the Court Was Starving Lets Out a Scream and Orders the Crew to Their Boats in Search of Herring*. And, of course, he arrived upon the scene just when the mindlessness of "conceptual" art had begun to dominate. He finds paintings with writing on them dreary beyond bearing. When he comes to stay with us he always says, "Let's go down to the National Gallery for a good read."

Tony often refers to the Theory of Stuff. The world, he says, is crammed with Stuff. Most Stuff is awful. Therefore when looking at an exhibition, hurry round and find the best painting. This saves time and effort because, the best painting found, the rest becomes Stuff. And there's no point in squandering time on Stuff. Especially when that time could be spent quaffing martinis.

It's more than possible, though, that Tony's vision and dedication to purpose will be vindicated. Who knows which of us time will treat well? I felt a sudden warning shift in the world when I went with Myrna, Tony, and his companion, Gabrielle de Montmollin, to see a Philip Guston exhibition at the National Gallery. In the first room there were examples of his work as an abstract expressionist. These were well done but there was a faded feeling about them; they were a minor part of a movement now history. When one moved on into the *Guston* Gustons—violent, crude, uncouth, almost barbaric—it was easy to see the *necessity* of his breaking out of a past which was becoming too pretty, vitiated.

I think Tony felt that warning shift in the world many, many years ago; that he did so is a measure of his originality and talent and steadfastness.

Tony's art and his day-to-day life are inseparable. His concerns are always aesthetic and he reveals himself as much in making toast as in painting. He has, typically, a professional restaurant gas stove, a Garland, and makes toast in a medieval-looking utensil, a thing exactly like a wok but with holes in it like a colander. This he sets on the gas; the toast when done is pimpled with black spots. He refuses to discuss this practice.

Not only have I had the profound pleasure of watching his work evolve over a twenty-year period but I've also had the pleasure of his friendship and learned from him so many good things: Japanese papers, Asiago cheese, tarte Tatin, the importance of Chaim Soutine, *rascasse* in bouillabaisse, the existence of the Musée Dapper in Paris, Sienna cake, martinis with a drop of fino sherry, Tio Pepe, say, instead of vermouth.

Tony's ease and charm inevitably attract a wide acquaintance, some of them quite mad. One acquaintance seriously cherishes the vision of opening a restaurant serving nothing but liver and Geneva gin. Another collects Jaguar cars. Another photographs Chinese herbal remedies. Orbiting Tony is exhausting. Days spent with him usually evolve into celebration, a key perhaps to both his life and his art. He shapes his life into ritual and ceremony. There is even a certain majesty to his hangovers. I treasure the memory of Tony, much hung over, tottering along the Danforth in search of a beef heart to roast, a sovereign cure, he claims.

A couple of years ago Tony and Gabrielle spent the winter and spring in Provence at Gabrielle's house, La Garance, in the village of Les Bouilladoires. Myrna and I visited in March and they took us to Gordes and Gabrielle showed us the tiny house Jack Pollock writes about in *Letters to M* where she had nursed him during his long decline into cocaine and AIDS. Then to Les Baux-de-Provence and a visit to the mental hospital Maison de Santé St. Paul which started as a monastery in 982. Here Vincent Van Gogh committed himself in May 1889 and stayed until May 1890. During this year he painted 150 pictures and executed 100 drawings. There was an exhibition on of sad daubs by current inmates and Tony said they exhibited better taste and attack than anything he'd seen in Toronto for a decade. Myrna went into the ancient chapel and found under the altar a mad-woman lying on the floor.

We filled Tony's *bidon* with Lubéron wine and then back to Bouilladoire for Henri Bardouin pastis and the inevitable talk: what had we been working on?

A relative of Gabrielle's who lives in Villefranche had a walled garden. In one of the walls there was a niche, perhaps constructed to house an urn or a statue of the Virgin Mary. Tony had been commissioned to make something beautiful to fill the space, something, as David Bolduc would say, to rest the eye on.

Tony had typically hurled himself into this work. He first had a pair of doors cut from steel plate. Then he welded onto the flat surface further rectangles and strips of plate to give depth and variety to the surface. Then—quintessentially Calzetta—with a grinding wheel he chased into the skin of the metal lyrical whorls, abstract arabesques.

As the garden was close to the sea Tony decided on a seascape. He fired sheets of ceramic, making shapes which fitted together to suggest a ship. He then made rows of waves for the ship to sail on. The back and sides of the niche he tiled with blue-green mosaic chips with here and there the glitter of a gold tile. I could imagine the owner opening the doors of the niche as one might open the ark of the covenant or an elaborate reliquary and gazing upon this almost Byzantine splendour.

But he wouldn't quite grasp that he was looking at the Calzetta signature, looking at a completely new expression of what Tony has been labouring on for years, the playful, elegant combination of conventional signs into new worlds of line and colour. A comparison with the conventions of Japanese prints would not be inappropriate in explaining this aspect of Tony's work.

John Bentley Mays got it about right when he said of Tony's works: "They document no recognizable reality, but simply commend *themselves*, with elegance and masculine beauty, as objects of creative work worthy of our attention."

———————

Not long after my Kiyooka encounter, I met, through Hugh Hood, the photographer Sam Tata. Again it was happy coincidence that I'd bumped into someone eager to teach me both theoretically and by allowing me to watch him on so many occasions at work. In 1991 I edited and published with the Porcupine's Quill his *Portraits of Canadian Writers*.

Prior to meeting Sam I had not given photography much thought. In my snotty teens I probably professed to admire Man Ray but really didn't. "Art" photography seemed to be thought of as shapes that looked like breasts or buttocks but turned out to be disappointing boulders. What appreciation of photography I had was probably reserved for a nudist magazine called *Health and Efficiency* which was printed on yellowish coated stock whose smell I can recall to this day. *Health and Efficiency* featured flabby nudists whose interesting bits were hidden behind coy Ping-Pong bats or beachballs. They were about as arousing as a bulk bin of crunchy granola but in my distant youth one grasped whatever titillation was on offer, which was never, sadly, much.

Sam was born in 1911 in Shanghai. He came to Canada in 1956. He was a Parsi but brought up in Shanghai where his father managed cotton mills for the Tata industrial empire. When we first met and I found out about his background Sam was flabbergasted when I started to ask him questions about Ch'i Pai-shih, one of the painters I most admire. I don't recall now how I'd found out about the painters of the Shanghai School—most probably a scroll seen in a museum—but I had developed a passionate admiration for Ch'i Pai-shih, Ch'ên shih-tsêng, Hsü Pei-hung, and Lin Feng-mien.

In 1988 the Canadian Museum of Contemporary Photography organized a retrospective exhibition of Sam's work and Pierre Dessureault edited a catalogue entitled *The Tata Era/L'Époque Tata* to which I contributed a piece about Sam's portraits entitled "Conversations without Words." I tried to pay tribute to Sam's endless charm and humanity and tried to suggest ways of looking at the richness of his craft. What follows is culled from that tribute.

I am neither photographer nor art critic. My only credentials for writing about Sam Tata are that we have been friends for many years and that I am a seasoned sitter; Sam has been taking my picture regularly since about 1970, photographs that have been reproduced on the jackets of a variety of books and on posters.

The title of this very personal tribute attempts to suggest what is happening when Sam is taking someone's picture. There is between Sam and the sitter a conversation; it is a conversation without words.

This is not to suggest that Sam is taciturn or laconic. While this silent conversation is going on between photographer and subject, Sam will be talking. He rarely stops. Sam is a Vesuvius of conversation, a walking compendium of quotation and reference, a cornucopia of anecdote. His reminiscences of life on three continents flow from him unstoppably.

Sam's stories are of his childhood in Shanghai, of his eccentric expatriate British schoolmasters, of his gilded youth in Shanghai's international society, of Eurasian beauties lost and won. He tells stories of exploits and adventures in Hong King, Japan, and India and though he claims to speak nothing but a word or two of foreign languages I've heard him chatter in Shanghai dialect, Japanese, and Gujarati.

Sam's conversation on any given day might typically range over incidents in the Parsi community, the scurvy behaviour of Bombay taxi drivers, the wisdom of Akbar the Great, the novels of P. G. Wodehouse, the intricate language of Chinese courtesy and insult, the work of Atget or Cartier-Bresson, the life and paintings of Lin Feng-mien, who used to give lessons to Sam's ex-wife Rita, art forgeries in Hong Kong's Nathan Road. A newspaper headline catching his eye—the capture of a mass murderer in British Columbia—will prompt him to recall the line from a Saki story: "Waldo is one of those people who would be enormously improved by death." This in turn will lead to forthright pugnacity on the subject of capital punishment, which will in turn remind him of executions he witnessed in Shanghai before the Maoist troops rode in—a time when he wandered the dangerous streets nonchalantly taking the brilliant photographs that arrest and hold us to this day.

But however convoluted the arabesques of anecdote he always returns to his emotional centre; he always returns to stories of Toni, the daughter he so adores; to stories of his sometimes irascible Gujarati-speaking mother who in fits of exasperation used to hurl at him her tortoiseshell-backed hairbrushes; to stories of his father who by day sternly managed the Tata mills but who by night unbuttoned and sat tall in the saddle with the westerns of Zane Grey.

Sam's conversations with me are not much different from the conversations he has with the people he is photographing. He has said of portraiture: "The sitter must be willing to be photographed. The photographer must be sensitive to the sitter. And a rapport between the two has to be established."

At the beginning of a photographic session, people are wary. The task of the photographer is to get them to relax, to remove the mask. Sam works at establishing the necessary rapport through conversation. He chats with people for twenty minutes or so until they are convinced that he is not a threat. "At some point," says Sam, "both know that they're ready to go." He usually takes a full roll of twenty-four to thirty-six exposures and his experience is that the better pictures start to arrive in the middle—that is, when the sitter has moved from acquiescing in the process to actively embracing the idea of being photographed.

It's important to stress here, however, that creating that necessary rapport isn't a trick or part of some well-rehearsed schtick; Sam's conversation and the rapport it builds are an expression of his personality and nature.

If one looks at a range of Sam's portraits, most of the subjects will be found to be in eye contact or near eye contact with the photographer. Many of the photographs are intense, almost fierce. The people in these photographs are deeply involved, indeed *absorbed*, in the process of being photographed. Sam has said of the experience, "The confrontation is like a conversation—a conversation without words."

Note the words "confrontation" and "conversation"; there is no hint of self-effacement here. Sam has also said: "I cannot avoid myself in every portrait I do."

When he gathered together a selection of his portraits of artists in 1983 he chose to call the book *A Certain Identity*; he derived this title from something written by his friend and mentor Henri Cartier-Bresson: "It is true, too, that a certain identity is manifest in all the portraits taken by one photographer. The photographer is searching for the identity of his sitter, and also trying to fulfil an expression of himself."

"I have to be on my toes," says Sam. "There's a stress and tension in all this and when it's over I enjoy the relaxation; it's a pleasant kind of tiredness."

No one can be entirely unselfconscious when being photographed, of course, but paradoxically someone sitting for Sam is *least* self-conscious when most *consciously* engaged in the process of the wordless conversation.

What I've written so far with its talk of confrontation and of people fulfilling themselves and expressing themselves and attending to "inner lines of force" perhaps gives the impression that a portrait session with Sam is a deeply emotional experience akin to therapy or a group encounter. Nothing could be further from the truth. The photographer Geoffrey James got close to the nature of the experience when he wrote: "I have been photographed by Sam several times, and always experience the mild euphoria of having just discovered a painless dentist."

Because the sitter must be relaxed, Sam always prefers to work with available light and in the familiar surroundings of the subject's home; he sees the studio and the paraphernalia of tripods, flashes, and reflectors as inhibiting. Many of Sam's portraits, then, offer us the almost voyeuristic pleasure of observing domestic interiors, for there are usually *things* in Sam's pictures—ornaments, paintings, books, plants, pianos, sculpture, dogs, furniture. These furnishings and possessions further express and suggest the sitter's personality; Sam has actually called these photographs "environmental portraits."

These background details are rarely, however, merely descriptive. Sam is an artist and a considerable one. His pictures are carefully composed. He is, of course, concerned with capturing the "inner lines of force in the being of his subject" but he is equally concerned with the making of a picture, with composition, with shapes, with blackness and whiteness. In successful portraits, psychological and artistic concerns fuse.

In a word, then, Sam's concerns are painterly.

When he comes into someone's home for the first time to make a portrait, he is naturally more aware than anyone else of the quality of the light. In *this* room, the light is flat, rather dead. But *here* it's very full, very alive. And what a handsome armoire that is! From Quebec? Could he see it with the doors open? Are those chisel marks? Or an adze, perhaps? He may well be listening to the history of your armoire or telling you a story about Akbar the Great or a White Russian nightclub hostess in Shanghai—and enjoying the listening or the telling—but because he rarely crops a picture or enlarges detail, his seemingly innocent eye will be framing and composing, seeking textures as he talks.

In the long months of 1991 when Myrna's mother was in the Jewish General Hospital in Montreal dying of cancer, Myrna and I drove down every weekend from Ottawa. On those visits I'd usually walk down to Kensington Street in NDG to visit Sam and we'd pore over his prints and contact sheets. We put together a collection of one hundred photographs that Sam thought represented his best work over the years. I took the pictures away with me, promising to find a publisher. Later I wrote a biographical essay to introduce the collection.

Eleven years later that box of photographs is still sitting in my study, having been considered by publisher after publisher who delivered such verdicts as "too expensive to produce," "It's all a bit liberal-humanist, isn't it?" "Who's ever heard of him?" and "Well, they're just *pictures*—what's the hook?" Dismaying reactions to the work of a man who according to the Canadian Museum of Contemporary Photography defined an epoch.

Perhaps Sam's work will come into its own when the National Portrait Gallery opens and they're searching for exhibits. They already sound desperate for stock. An Ottawa functionary was interviewed last year by the *Ottawa Citizen* and was asked what *sort* of famous Canadians would be honoured in the proposed Gallery. He prevaricated for a while and then said, "Canadians like . . . like Northern Dancer."

Sam himself is now frail and largely lost to us. He suffered a stroke and his memory was impaired. When it happened, I went down to Montreal on the bus and went straight to the Royal Victoria Hospital. Sam saw me come into the room and said, "Why, John! What are *you* doing here?" He seemed bright and voluble and we chatted for a while and then I needed to visit a washroom. I was away a few minutes. When I went back into the room, his face lit up and he said, "John!" reaching out his hands to me. "What are *you* doing here?"

THE TANKS CAMPAIGN

I FIRST ENCOUNTERED William Hoffer through his catalogues. When I started many years ago to collect and document the short story in Canada it was inevitable I would meet Bill, though we first got to know each other through letters. He gradually became interested in what I was trying to do and helped me to narrow the focus. He was particularly helpful when I was putting together a collection of Contact Press and he eventually supervised its sale to the National Library.

"I *had* to help you sell it," he said when I again thanked him. "You owed the shop over $4,000."

We soon discovered shared convictions. Bill had very few serious customers outside the universities—he often said seventeen, worldwide—and we were both convinced that all the celebratory razzle-dazzle on the surface of things masked a deeply alarming reality. That reality was that the audience was tiny, that it had not prepared itself to be able to distinguish significant work, and that there was a blank ignorance of our literary past. We both felt there was an almost total confusion of literature with nationalism.

Literature, we both felt, had been co-opted by the state. Money, we believed, masked the truth of this reality. The large sums shovelled out through the Canada Council were cloyingly referred to as "watering the young shoots of Canadian literature" or "nurturing Canadian literature's fragile blooms."

Bill's retort: *The only plant that can't be killed by overwatering is seaweed.*

He decided that he would launch a campaign against the Canada Council and against the idea of state subsidy to protest all the toxic sludge the money had generated. His first line of attack was through his catalogues. Most dealers in antiquarian books and first editions are discreet and circumspect. It was, therefore, astonishing and liberating to read Bill's increasingly vitriolic annotations:

Lane (Patrick) *Beware the Months of Fire.* Toronto: Anansi, 1974. Cloth in dust jacket. Of the eight "previous books by the same author," five are broadsides or leaflets. This is the CanLit equivalent of wearing elevator shoes.

or

Davey (Frank) *Griffon.* np. (Toronto) Massasauga Editions, 1972. Small stapled wrappers. The edition limited to 200 numbered copies. A review copy, with the slip laid in. Davey produced two booklets under this imprint, both of which disfigure List 70.

or

Davies (Robertson) *The Rebel Angels.* New York: The Viking Press, 1982. Cloth and boards in dust jacket. The first American edition of the senile civil servant's late pant around the track. When young he almost mattered, but now stands more revealed (in Charles Olson's brilliant observation of how it is in life). Catalogued in weary acceptance of the obligation, only for the money.

Bill's campaign against the idea of subsidy to the arts began in 1985. He wanted to call the campaign "Tanks Are Mighty Fine Things" after the title of a book published by the Chrysler Corporation in 1946. Permission was denied and so Bill called the campaign, simply, Tanks.

The campaign was both farcical and intensely serious. He wrote: "For more than 15 years I have used every avenue available to object to the false culture we promote in Canada, not because I have grudges, but because it is impossible for me to be a serious bookseller in a society that takes nothing seriously."

Again, he wrote: "For many years I have ridiculed the absurd spectacle of apparently grown men and women pretending to have succeeded at the very difficult tasks of art."

When questioned about what would happen when, Samson-like, he'd pulled down the pillar and the Temple of Subsidy had collapsed about him, he'd quote a Yiddish saying: *The worst truth is better than the best lie.*

What he meant by this was that even if we reduced literature to *samizdat*, to Xeroxes passed from hand to hand, that would be preferable to the lie that official CanLit had become.

Because no one would engage in debate on this topic, Bill employed a comic-book language to gain attention and to prosecute the campaign. He styled himself Commander of Tanks. Marius Kociejowski, a Canadian poet who lives in London, was given England, while I was designated Commander for Ontario and Toronto. The poet and teacher Peter Sanger was installed as District Commissioner for the Maritimes. Allies in the American book trade were also commissioned and issued titles and insignia. This small group along with a handful of delighted and appalled readers of Bill's catalogues constituted what he called his "slapstick army."

Certain writers, academics, and bureaucrats were designated "War Criminals." Bill defined as War Criminals "those who are more enthusiastic about getting grants than they are about the things they get the grants to do." He went on to say, "The fictional absolutism of the *Tanks* vocabulary . . . had the virtue of being hugely entertaining to those who were not offended by it, and incredibly offensive to those who were."

Bowering (George), editor *Great Canadian Sports Stories*. Ottawa: Oberon Press, 1979. Cloth in dust jacket. Various tedious contributors. Offered as a scarce Bowering C item, and an out of the way anthology. Oberon Press is "owned" by Michael Macklem, one of the more ugly of the meek members of the resurrection in Canada. Macklem has attempted to be the James Laughlin of

Canadian publishing, but has managed little more than strict compliance with the Official Languages Act through the publication of endless translations of bad French-Canadian novels all of which remain in print in their first printings of fewer than 200 copies in cloth. Anyone who has suffered the misfortune of actually speaking to him has discovered how offensive a man he is, how unjustified in his high opinion of himself. I take this opportunity to dispose of him; I have dispatched a war criminal indictment under separate cover.

$35.00

The Tanks vocabulary began to creep even into his private correspondence. In a letter to me he wrote: "All I want to do is to roll my 11 armoured divisions into town, destroy everything without pity, burn down the unsanitary shanty towns (weird regional magazines, creative writing departments, etc., etc.) and set the Canadian people free. God, in the form of George Patton, casting man out of a Garden of Eden in which every piece of fruit is poisoned . . ."

Bill's opening shot of the campaign was by way of pamphlet. He wrote: "In London, Marius Kociejowski, a Canadian poet in exile, showed me his essay *The Machine Minders*. It was so perfectly suitable to what I was trying to do with *Tanks* that I brought it back and made it the first *Tanks* imprint, using it as an example of criticism, and as a way of walking point with my metaphorical army of ideas against subsidies to the arts."

The second shot fired was my own pamphlet "Freedom from Culture." This appeared in 1987 and over the following year was printed in four editions. One of these editions was printed in large numbers by the Fraser Institute, a "strange bedfellows" deal that Bill had struck.

The pamphlet's intention was to be funny about Subsidy, Government, Bureaucracy, and the Administration of Culture but utterly serious in pointing out that:

It is not only individual writers who are softened and subverted by grants; the method by which grants are awarded has further emasculated our literary world. The Canada Council prides itself on its jury system. Grants are given to writers by juries of their peers. Officers of the Council do not interfere or attempt to influence decisions. Everyone prides themselves on this exemplary arm's length relationship with government. But this very jury system which protects writers from direct government influence is responsible for a totally servile literary climate in the country.

Canadian writers do not brawl in the country's newspaper columns. We lack the pleasures of literary brouhaha and imbroglio. We don't have honest reviewing, we don't have pungent criticism, we don't have open faction. Reviews written by Canadian writers are usually ecstatic—or cautious, circumspect, tepid. Spades tend to get described not as spades but as agricultural implements. CanLit suffers from terminal politeness.

Very few writers in Canada care to express publicly their honest opinions about the work of other writers and of the literature in general. Every writer in Canada knows that the writer he criticizes today may be sitting on a jury tomorrow and handing out grants—or not, as the case might be. Self-interest dictates lies. Or, at best, silence.

Even the academic critics are in a similar situation since their commentaries on and discussion of the texts are similarly juried by the Canada Council. Fatuous flatulence or costive noodling, it all gets the professorial nod. Backs are scratched and logs are rolled. There are conferences to attend. Readings to deliver. Subsidized seminars in Tahiti.

We're all in this together.

. . .

And what of audience?

From 1957 onwards, million upon million has been spent in Canada to provide us with a literature. We have, in effect, tried to buy a literature much as a parvenu might hire a decorator to create for him instant antiquity—and with much the same embarrassing results.

The policies and activities of the Council and other granting agencies have flooded the country with unwanted and unreadable books; alienated readers in public libraries offer up silent thanks for the maple leaf stickers on spines which identify books as Canadian. Worse than this flood of inadequacy, the Council has put into place a parody of the entire machinery of a literary culture; for the benefit of no readership, subsidized books are reviewed in subsidized journals by subsidized writers. It all fills one with the slightly uneasy amusement one feels in watching a chimpanzees' tea party.

Nor can we rely on our academics to comment on the Emperor's New Clothes and destroy this machinery gone mad because they themselves are a paid part of it; they are subsidized to inflate, conflate, huff and puff. We can't expect the monkey to berate the organ-grinder.

It's fairly obvious by now that the Canada Council has failed. In failing to build an audience it has failed entirely. Indeed, the Council's existence absolves any possible audience from responsibility. "Art and suchlike," we might imagine people saying, "it's nothing to do with me. The State takes care of that sort of thing."

The perpetuation of its own bureaucratic routines and the expansion of its "programmes" have become the Council's *raison d'être*.

Writing in Canada became CanLit.

CanLit is fast petrifying into Culture.

The values of artists are necessarily elitist. The values of a bureaucracy are necessarily bureaucratic. The Canada Council in its administration of Culture is quite understandably concerned with regional representation, with aboriginal representation, with proportional language representation, and with equality of sexual representation on juries and in awards. Such a concern with "fairness" is laudable in a political context; in artistic terms it is risible.

What the Council *really* wants—though it would claim otherwise—is to use its funding as an equivalent of the federal equalization payments to the provinces. Fund more women in Saskatchewan. More painters needed in New Brunswick. Too many anglophone writers in Toronto. A dearth of francophone drama in Manitoba.

And if applicants with vaguely artistic aspirations couldn't qualify as any conceivable variety of artist, they could always

apply for the popularist Explorations Grant—the type of programme described by Charles Osborne [of the Arts Council of
Great Britain] as "that perversion of the aesthetic urge invented
by bored arts administrators yearning to become social workers."

What has all this to do with art?

With literature?

These and other such observations brought down on my head
more vituperation and seething hatred than I could have imagined.
The go-back-to-where-you-came-from brigade frothed and splut-
tered in apoplectic rage tossing about words like *traitor*, *fascist*, and
Brit. Even today, sixteen years later, these dumbores are still hooting
their outrage like chimps who've had their peanuts pinched.

The Canada Council itself was sufficiently worried by "Freedom
from Culture" that it hired Professor Tom Henighan of Carleton
University to write an article refuting it. This he sat himself down to
do but found halfway through that I'd converted him.

The Tanks campaign's main offensive was the publication of six
volumes Bill intended to be exemplary—exemplary both as literature and as book design. He was setting out to prove that exceptional
literature, beautifully designed, could be produced without subsidy
and could make a profit.

The books were *Eight Poems*, by Norm Sibum; *The Voyeur and the
Countess Wielpolska*, by George McWhirter; *The Topography of Typog-
raphy* by El Lissitzky; *Five Stories*, by W. P. Kinsella; *Corpses, Brats and
Cricket Music*, by George Faludy, translated from the Hungarian by
Robin Skelton; and *Autobiographies*, by Elizabeth Smart (edited by
Christina Burridge).

What to say of these books?

Norm Sibum's poems are, as always, interesting and involving.
George McWhirter's two-page poem is competent; laid into the
folder are two lithographs of trees by Diane Ostoich, lithographs
which stand in no relation whatsoever to the poem.

Marius Kociejowski's essay *The Machine Minders* is disfigured by
Maureen Sugrue's awful illustrations.

I'm not able to say how well Robin Skelton translated George
Faludy's poetry as I cannot read Hungarian. The verse *sounds* as if he's

got it right but I must admit that Skelton makes me uneasy. His own poetry is correct and competent but somehow bloodless. His claims to have been a "witch" must surely give any sane person pause. My ex-wife worked for years for a New York publisher of books concerning the occult—a natural, if not inevitable, place for her to end up. She once phoned me to ask if I knew a Robin Skelton because they'd just received from him the typescript of a book of "spells." One spell, she said, caused levitation.

The Topography of Typography is four sheets printed beautifully by Glenn Goluska at his Imprimerie Dromadaire. It is, like all such exercises, precious.

I have profound problems with Elizabeth Smart. I *loathe* her writing and consider *By Grand Central Station I Sat Down and Wept* an abomination, a foul gush of emotional incontinence. I considered her relationship with George Barker sad and shabby; when I met her in Toronto she had become an utterly hopeless drunk. George Barker sticks in my mind less for his poetry than for his remark in a London pub to the young Norman Levine: "Sorry chum, nothing personal. But coming from Canada, you haven't got a chance."

I begged Bill not to publish W. P. Kinsella's crudities. Back came contempt, condescension, accusation, paranoia—to all of which I paid little attention. Bill's hostilities were reflex.

The Tanks books were frankly a hodge-podge. They weren't beautiful. The artwork did not marry the texts and in some cases was simply inept. The format of the books (eleven by about seven inches) seemed to emphasize their awkwardness.

Although the books were the campaign's loudest salvo, there was a constant chatter of small arms fire which never seemed to quiet— letters, conversations in the shop and on the phone, harangues at book fairs, reissues of "Freedom from Culture," and, of course, the increasingly vituperative catalogues.

Even though Bill was positively bleeding money on the project and was deeply depressed about the failure of the books to sell, he soon managed to turn defeat into victory. In the sometimes strange way his mind worked he now started to propose that the fact that he had produced the books with his own money and not with "funny money" was a victorious protest in itself against the system and a standing rebuke to it. The failure of the books to sell he put down to media hostility or indifference, apathetic bookstore owners, and a Canadian literary sensibility numbed by thirty years of subsidized inanity.

Had his books been good books, I could have agreed with him more wholeheartedly.

During the National Book Festival in April 1987, there was a debate in Vancouver between the forces of Tanks and the forces of the Canada Council: Bill and I defending our objections, and Andreas Schroeder and David Godfrey defending subsidy. The debate was chaired by Eleanor Wachtel. The question was, Have government subsidies benefited Canadian literature?

Bill had commissioned a striking poster from Carol Moiseiwitsch and these were widely displayed in Vancouver. The debate took place on a Monday evening and on the preceding Saturday in the *Globe and Mail* William French announced that there was no point in going since all the tickets were sold out. There were no tickets as the event was free of charge. Despite this confusion, about 150 people turned up and the evening was filmed by the local community TV channel.

Everyone seemed mildly hysterical and paranoid. More heat than light was shed; books were brandished; statistics bandied about. A local crazy had to be escorted out in full rant denouncing logging, the persecution of beluga whales, and harmful rays emitted by the CBC. Other hecklers took his place.

There are over 350 wonderful presses in this country! shouted one.

Shame! cried another. *Shame!*

Eleanor Wachtel tried to impose order.

The level of debate was infantile. David Godfrey held up a book of poems by Dorothy Livesay and demanded to know whether she was a worthy poet. It was conceded that she had *some* value. Then, declared Godfrey, the argument was won as the book in question, this very book, had been published by a subsidized small press. *His* press. And so on. Bill Hoffer said suddenly that Dave Godfrey had no moral right to be speaking in this debate as he owned a company that wrote software for the Chinese military. Dave Godfrey threatened to sue Bill Hoffer if Hoffer ever repeated that remark. Hoffer repeated it.

It was a ridiculous evening. According to subsequent newspaper accounts the pro-subsidy forces were victorious; to us it seemed simply a cacophony.

Dave Godfrey behaved with concentrated viciousness and after the debate jostled his way out without speaking to anyone. I insisted on stopping him and shaking his hand; he snarled at me about the company I kept. I had not gone to Vancouver for a fight; I had gone there for what was to me an important intellectual discussion. The discussion didn't really take place; it's essential for Canada's future that it does.

It seems to me now, looking back, that the Great Vancouver Debate marked the beginning of an emotional disintegration in Bill. He wrote of that night: "I didn't do well at the debate, and John had to carry most of the weight. Everything had simply become too terrible to endure."

But he was later to write—and I think with some justice: "It was a peculiar event in many ways. But it happened, and that was the victory. For the first time the dreaded language of objection achieved enough legitimacy to require response."

Much of Bill's life was lived in a mess and an uproar. He was tall and almost emaciated and moved with awkward vigour. He looked rabbinical and not Reform either. His suits and flapping jackets were far from clean and his body odour was sometimes so fearsome that after his visits Myrna threw wide every window and bundled his sheets into the washing machine with dispatch. His control of his diabetes was intermittent and he was often soaked in diabetic and alcoholic sweats. He drank too much at home and was profligate in bars. He became infatuated easily, amours which always seemed to involve theatrical scenes with husbands or boyfriends and sudden international travel.

And Bill talked. Words poured out of him. His energy was exhausting. He was a complex and cranky man and essentially contentious by nature. Enemies abounded; plots against him were always afoot. His rhetoric could easily spiral into incoherence. Even his friends and those who agreed with his basic ideas could sometimes be left wondering if they were in the company of a genius or a madman.

I remember him sitting in our kitchen launching some complicated flight, words tumbling out of him, when Myrna suddenly interrupted. She said, "But that doesn't follow. That doesn't make sense."

He turned upon her and snapped, "There is nothing wrong with the transmission. Check the set."

When he was drinking in the afternoons he often conducted his business from a strip joint near his Gastown shop called, I seem to remember, No. 5. It was loud and smelled like a lion's cage that had been hastily sluiced out with Old Dutch. I remember once listening to Bill's explication of whatever he was explicating that day while alleged sisters on the stage inside a glass-sided shower soaped each other with interminable suds. He seemed known to most of the customers and was addressed by waiters and bouncers as "Professor."

All was not earnest lecture or exhortation, however. Bill was often bubbling with wit and stratagems, provocations he found amusing. An event. A Party. A Black-Tie Party. A Social Event. *The* Black-Tie Social Event of the Vancouver Season. On and on it swelled in his mind.

He'd hold a Book Burning!

In the parking lot beside his store he'd have waiters circulating with champagne while from the stock in the warehouse he'd burn . . . whatever was that day's rage and contempt, all the bill bissett books, all grOnk pamphlets, all bpNichol's endless verbiage, all productions of blewointment press, crates of Fred Cogswell's Fiddlehead Poetry Books . . .

Nichol (B.P.) *Still.* Vancouver: Pulp Press, 1983. Original wrappers. Author's signed presentation to Bill Bissett, who has scrawled a number of notes relating to grant opportunities on the first and last leaves. Winner of the Three-Day Novel-Writing Contest. Steve Osborne and I made this contest up as a joke in 1976, never thinking that literature could fall so low as to take it seriously.

But this sketch of Bill leaves out of the picture that flamboyant, eccentric, slightly crazy as he may have been, he was at the same time probably the most gifted bookman Canada has ever seen. He had a bloodhound nose for books. From other bookstores, from Goodwills, from junk furniture stores, from dumpsters, Bill would conjure rarities.

I remember walking along Wellington Street in Ottawa with him and his sudden wheeling into a junk furniture store and unearthing from under a wind-up gramophone a July 1956 *Esquire* containing a Mavis Gallant story and two copies of *Chatelaine* dated March 1956 and July 1956 carrying two Alice Munro stories: "How Could I Do That?" (uncollected) and "Good-by Myra." Bill bought these for pennies and said to me outside, "I *could* give you these but I'm going to charge you $20 to teach you a lesson."

Bill's catalogues, or lists, as he modestly insisted on calling them, were an education in themselves but visits to the store and to the warehouse entirely rearranged one's understanding of such words as *scarce* or *rare* as one gazed, pop-eyed, on a dozen copies of John Newlove's *Grave Sirs* or on a stack of Gwendolyn MacEwen's *The Drunken Clock*. Or looked at the boxes in the basement which contained the entire remaindering of Mavis Gallant's *The Pegnitz Junction*.

In the early days of Oberon Press, Michael Macklem had a marketing arrangement with a small London publisher called Dobson. Oberon books in England were distributed under Dobson's imprint. Bill had the idea of going to see Dobson and cornering Oberon books whose print runs would have been tiny. This scheme fell through because Dobson was too lethargic to locate boxes and open them but it illustrates Bill's piratical gusto.

And then in the catalogues came the great discoveries . . . When Frederick Philip Grove was revealed as Felix Paul Greve, it was Bill who unearthed all the work in German, helped in this, in part, by Professor Dr. Walter Pache, then at Trier and subsequently at the University of Augsberg. It was Bill who was instrumental in revealing, through research in the University of Calgary archives, that Brian Moore had written four paperback thrillers under the names Michael Brian and Bernard Mara, all of them preceding his "first" book, *The Lonely Passion of Judith Hearne*.

Peter Howard of Serendipity Books in California has written of these and similar feats: "These acts no other Canadian bookseller could emulate."

When I was looking through the collection of papers and documents Bill and I had intended publishing as "The Tanks Diary" I came across a letter to Bill from John Newlove. It concerned buying a set of the Tanks books and the last few lines seem prescient now.

"I did see you at the Antiquarian Book Fair. I said hello to you. But you were fulminating and sailed on by like some rusty, derelict freighter careering madly towards the rocks."

Not long after the failure of the Tanks campaign Bill told me that as W. H. Auden had said of Yeats that Ireland had "hurt him into poetry" so he felt that Canada had hurt him into redefining himself. He said he felt Canada was too primitive to allow him to be the person he wanted to be. He closed the shop, shipped his books to Peter Howard in California, and moved to live in Moscow, where he learned Russian every day from a tutor and had visions of opening a store which would deal not in modern first editions but in the antiquarian books of Europe. In 1997 he developed cancer of the brain and returned to Victoria to die in his father's care.

Let me, sadly and affectionately, give him the last word.

Ringwood (Gwen Pharis) *The Courting of Marie Jenvrin*. Toronto: Samuel French (Canada) Limited, 1951. On the copyright page appears a brief plug by the publisher that ought to warm the hearts of our new nationalists.

"Printed in Canada on Canadian paper by Monetary Times Printing Co. of Canada, Ltd., Toronto, Canada."

Original printed wrappers. A bright copy, but the text is occasionally marked in pen.

LEGO

DOUBT should always nag the anthologist. It is a necessary anxiety. Surely posterity . . . This is one of my horrors. One of the 4 a.m. rehearsals when sleep won't come. Is it possible—surely not?—that posterity might view me much as I view such silly old buggers as Sir Arthur Quiller-Couch, A. L. Rowse, and Arthur Bryant?

It is entirely possible.

But, for me, the die is cast.

How, then, do I set about making choices?

In the year I was born, 1938, Cyril Connolly published a book about literary style called *Enemies of Promise*. When I read this book years later it changed and deepened my understanding of literature to such an extent that I can say absolutely seriously that the book changed my life. Connolly's career as writer, reviewer, editor, publisher, book collector, cultural impresario, and *arbiter elegantiae* also suggested to me the possibility of a literary life lived passionately. Here from the book's opening chapter is the passage which had such a profound impact on me so many years ago:

> What kills a literary reputation is inflation. The advertising, publicity and enthusiasm which a book generates—in a word its success—imply a reaction against it. The element of inflation in a writer's success, the extent to which it has been forced, is something that has to be written off. One can fool the public about a

book but the public will store up resentment in proportion to its folly. The public can be fooled deliberately by advertising and publicity or it can be fooled by accident, by the writer fooling himself. If we look at the boom pages of the Sunday papers we can see the fooling of the public going on, inflation at work. A word like genius is used so many times that eventually the sentence "Jenkins has genius. *Cauliflower Ear* is immense!" becomes true because he has as much genius and is as immense as are the other writers who have been praised there. It is the words that suffer for in the inflation they have lost their meaning. The public at first suffers too but in the end it ceases to care and so new words have to be dragged out of retirement and forced to suggest merit. Often the public is taken in by a book because, although bad, it is topical, its up-to-dateness passes as originality, its ideas seem important because they are "in the air." *The Bridge of San Luis Rey, Dusty Answer, Decline and Fall, Brave New World, The Postman Always Rings Twice, The Fountain, Good-bye Mr. Chips* are examples of books which had a success quite out of proportion to their undoubted merit and which now reacts unfavourably on their authors, because the overexcitable public who read those books have been fooled. None of the authors expected their books to become best-sellers but, without knowing it, they had hit upon the contemporary chemical combination of illusion with disillusion which makes books sell.

But it is also possible to write a good book and for it to be imitated and for those imitations to have more success than the original so that when the vogue which they have created and surfeited is past, they drag the good book down with them. This is what happened to Hemingway who made certain pointillist discoveries in style which have led almost to his undoing. So much depends on style, this factor of which we are growing more and more suspicious, that although the tendency of criticism is to explain a writer either in terms of his sexual experience or his economic background, I still believe his technique remains the soundest base for a diagnosis, that it should be possible to learn as much about an author's income and sex-life from one paragraph of his writing as from his cheque stubs and his love-letters and that one should also be able to learn how well he writes, and who are his influences. Critics who ignore style are liable to lump good and bad writers together in support of pre-conceived theories.

An expert should be able to tell a carpet by one skein of it; a vintage by rinsing a glassful round his mouth. Applied to prose there is one advantage attached to this method—a passage taken from its context is isolated from the rest of a book, and cannot depend on the goodwill which the author has cleverly established with his reader. This is important, for in all the books which become best-sellers and then flop, this salesmanship exists. The author has fooled the reader by winning him over at the beginning, and so establishing a favourable atmosphere for putting across his inferior article—for making him accept false sentiment, bad writing, or unreal situations. To write a best-seller is to set oneself a problem in seduction. A book of this kind is a confidence trick. The reader is given a cigar and a glass of brandy and asked to put his feet up and listen. The author then tells him the tale. The most favourable atmosphere is a stall at a theatre, and consequently of all things which enjoy contemporary success that which obtains it with least merit is the average play.

One sentence from these paragraphs was the Damascus Road experience for me.

"An expert should be able to tell a carpet by one skein of it; a vintage by rinsing a glassful round his mouth."

This sentence changed the way I thought and felt about prose. As the sentence grew in my mind, the implications and ramifications continued to amaze me. The sentence forced me first of all to stop thinking about plot or context. It forced me to think about verbs and nouns, adjectives and adverbs, the nature and level of diction, the placement of words, the rhythms of sentences, the functions of punctuation. In brief, it forced me to consider writing as *technical performance*, as rhetoric organized to achieve certain emotional effects.

The sentence also implies, of course, that the entire story, the entire book, must be written with an intensity that will live up to and survive the sort of scrutiny given to the one paragraph. Connolly is implying a prose written with the deliberation usually given to poetry.

The sentence further implies that form and content are indivisible, that the *way* something is being said *is* what is being said.

The sentence also suggests that a piece of writing should be a refined pleasure—as is wine, as are the old Persian carpets made before the introduction of aniline dyes. This in turn implies that good prose is not something we read through for comprehension, for information, as a medium for getting us from A to B. Connolly suggests we *taste* the prose, fondle it, explore and experience it. What a radical way of looking at prose this is! For when we have explored it, we have not finished with it; we cannot then dismiss it as "understood." We can come back to it again and again as we do with paintings or music. "Understanding" in the utilitarian high-school or university sense is a barrier to understanding. If we have read properly, we have not "understood" the prose—an intellectual activity—rather, we have *experienced* the prose by entering into a relationship with it. Prose which is brilliantly performed offers inexhaustible pleasures.

So much conventional writing is close to being automatic writing. Without formal innovation—which is a breaking through crusted convention to emotion and significance—writing becomes portly and arteriosclerotic. It is salutary for a young writer to watch the comfortably middlebrow, authors once internationally acclaimed, parading to oblivion . . .

When I look back down the vista of books that have come and gone, when I idly pick up this one or that to read a paragraph or two—as I happened to glance last week at John Buchan's *The House of the Four Winds* and at J. B. Priestley's *The Good Companions*—I'm always struck now by the flabby, imprecise language, by the sheer padding and hackery, by the use of words and phrases as mere verbal counters which, shuffled together, clack out conventional sentences.

Here, for example, is the first paragraph of the first chapter of *The House of the Four Winds*. I have italicized the clichés, the verbal counters, and the deliberately archaic usages which stand for "rusticity."

The inn at Kremisch, the Stag with the Two Heads, has an upper room *so bowed with age* that it *leans drunkenly* over the village street. It is a bare place, which must be chilly in winter, for the old *casement* has many chinks in it, and the china stove does not look efficient, and the *rough beechen table*, marked by many beer mugs, and the seats of beechwood and hide *are scarcely luxurious*. But on this summer night to one who had been tramping all day on roads deep in white dust under *a merciless sun*, it seemed a *haven of ease*. Jaikie had eaten *an admirable supper* on a corner of the table, a supper of cold ham, an omelet, hot toasted rye-cakes and *a seductive cheese*. He had drunk wine tapped from a barrel and *cold as water from a mountain spring*, and had concluded with coffee and cream in a blue cup as large as a basin. Now he could light his pipe and watch the green dusk deepen behind the onion spire of the village church.

This was never writing; it is the equivalent with words of joining together bits of Lego.

Innovative shapes must be forged in language which is precise and quick to the touch. Touching that language must be like touching skin or an animal's pelt. Nothing else will do; nothing else will last. This is not to say that the writing must be "poetic" or fancy in any way; rather, it must be precise, concentrated, and above all, appropriate.

Let us look at a more contentious example.

Rohinton Mistry's first book of stories, *Tales from Firozsha Baag*, was reviewed by Michael Darling in *The Macmillan Anthology (1)*. He wrote in part:

> Mistry is not deceived that story-writing is an academic game of narrative hide-and-seek; he has a moral vision and a desire to impart it through carefully structured language. The fact that the language often fails him does not negate the sincerity of the attempt . . .
>
> Mistry's weakness is his diction, which occasionally seems to evoke the legacy of the Raj; phrases like "high dudgeon," "unbeknownst to," and "cherubic features" don't really fit the contexts into which they're placed. Also, the Indian words are often strung together in what seems like an unnecessary striving for "local colour": "*Bawaji* got *paan pichkari* right on his white *dugli* . . ." A little of this goes a long way, which Mistry

seems to be aware of, as by the end of the book the non-English words are few and far between.

Darling has, as usual, put his finger exactly on the problem. Consider the following quotations:

> The first light of morning barely illumined the sky as Gustad Noble faced eastward to offer his orisons to Ahura Mazda. The hour was approaching six, and up in the compound's solitary tree the sparrows began to call.

and

> Erie had been listening all that week to thaw, a trickle of melt tickling her inner ear, the sound of water dripping off the eaves, *drip* into that handful of bare stones by the corner of the barn, *drop* off the branches of the forsythia out front.

The first quotation is the opening sentences of Rohinton Mistry's *Such a Long Journey*, the second the opening of Terry Griggs's "Man with the Axe."

It is immediately obvious that the writers approach language in an entirely different spirit. Terry Griggs is specific, concentrated, *wired*, one might say, alive to every nuance. Listen to the pretty run of *i*-sounds in "a trickle of melt tickling her inner ear." One can hear the sounds and see the nest of gleaming pebbles the drips have excavated.

The problem with Mistry's opening sentences is more complicated than the use of such almost archaic words as *illumined* and *orisons*. The very rhythms of the sentences are flat and conventional and such constructions as "the first light of morning" and "barely illumined the sky" are little more than formulas, counters shuffled into place.

The use of the word *orisons* is injudicious. *Orisons* is not as neutral as *prayers* because it suggests prayers within the Christian tradition, suggests Catholic Europe. The only uses of the word I can remember in literature are in Wilfred Owen's "Dulce et Decorum

Est" and Hamlet to Ophelia: "Nymph, in thy orisons/Be all my sins remembered." The scene is traditionally played with Ophelia reading from a missal.

The use of the word *call* is inappropriate, *call* being associated with the distinctive cry of larger birds, rooks, say, or loons. Sparrows chirp. Or at least do something with an *i* in it.

Consider now the following paragraph from *Such a Long Journey*:

> Besides, Crawford Market was a place he despised at the best of times. Unlike his father before him, who used to relish the trip and looked on it as a challenge: to venture boldly into the den of scoundrels, as he called it; then to badger and bargain with the shopkeepers, tease and mock them, their produce, their habits, but always preserving the correct tone that trod the narrow line between badinage and belligerence; and finally, to emerge unscathed and triumphant, banner held high, having got the better of the rogues. Unlike his father, who enjoyed this game, Gustad felt intimidated by Crawford Market.

While there is probably an intention to suggest something of the father's zest and vocabulary in this paragraph, we should not overlook the formulaic writing. Here now is the same paragraph with phrases and clauses which are formulas or close to it italicized and with the particularly British stylistic tic of pairing words indicated with brackets.

> Besides, Crawford Market was a place he despised *at the best of times*. Unlike *his father before him*, who used to relish the trip and *looked on it as a challenge*: *to venture boldly* into the *den of scoundrels*, as he called it: then to (badger and bargain) with the shopkeepers, (tease and mock) them, their produce, their habits, *but always preserving the correct tone that trod the narrow line* between (badinage and belligerence); and finally, *to emerge (unscathed* and triumphant), *banner held high, having got the better of the rogues.* Unlike his father, who enjoyed this game, Gustad felt intimidated by Crawford Market.

I wish that this were a caricature of the father, deliberately employing a string of formulas and deliberately employing a faded diction to capture him, but what I suspect is Lego.

Choosing stories, then, and editing.

I am likely to enter a story in an arbitrary manner. I might read the first sentence first but am just as likely to read a paragraph at random. All that concerns me is to get a feel for the quality of the language—the Connolly prescription. When I start reading, I'm waiting for the writing to plug me into its current. I am more excited by a single spark of language than I am by reams of solid competence. A hash of a story, a veritable dog's dinner, can interest me more than quires of competence if it's touched by the fire of language.

I was reading a story the other day by a beginning writer,* perhaps the second story she has published. Within four sentences I knew she was a writer I wanted to read and keep an eye on.

They call it a state of emergency. White dervishes scour Stephenville, the blue arm of the plough impotently slashes through the snow. In St. John's where my mother is, the wires are frozen with sleet and the electricity is out. She's in the plaid chair, I know, one emergency candle and a flashing drink of rye.

The spark?
Well, yes, of course—*flashing*.

---

* I first published the sentence about that "beginner" in *Quarry* magazine in 1992. The writer is Lisa Moore, and she has now published two collections of stories and was shortlisted in 2002 for the Giller Prize.

A LONG SENTENCE:
THE OTTAWA YEARS

WHILE TRUDGING ALONG BANK STREET
in December one year in solidly frozen snow that would be there until
April I heard rapping on a window and glanced up to see Richard
Simmins sitting at a café table. I joined him for a coffee and we sat
talking about books and writing. Richard, now dead too early, was
important in what cultural life Ottawa affords.

His first career was as a curator and he was responsible, among
much else, for mounting the Regina Five exhibition at the National
Gallery of Canada in 1961 and then sending the show on its travels,
giving many Canadians their first glimpse of abstract painting. One
of the Regina Five was Ronald Bloore, a painter of great elegance and
austerity. I regret to this day not buying a painting of Bloore's called
Byzantine Doors, a white-on-white painting from his *Byzantine Light*
series, a painting I still sometimes see as I'm drifting off to sleep.

Richard's success in his curatorial career was accompanied, however, by increasingly self-destructive drinking which caused him to
crash, losing his job and his marriage. Later he joined Alcoholics
Anonymous and reconstituted himself as a bookseller. His shops,
first on Bank, subsequently on Sparks, and finally on Dalhousie, were
social centres for young writers, painters, and musicians. Richard had
a great interest in my collecting and took pleasure in finding for me
stubborn volumes.

The teaching aspect of bookselling, the fathering and fostering,
has been to an extent destroyed by the sale of books on the Internet.

As Janet Inksetter of Annex Books in Toronto said to me recently, "I didn't enter into this way of life to spend my days sitting in front of a screen."

I greatly enjoyed Richard and always dropped into his store to chat, to buy books, to listen to his elegant anecdotes. If he'd accumulated a clutch of my books, he'd say, "Would you mind signing these for stock?" And I used to write in all of them *For Al Stock—with best wishes . . .*

Richard, perhaps because of his curatorial past, was keenly interested in archives and urged me to start keeping a diary. He used to say, "Although you can't think this yet, can't see yourself in that way, you're already a figure of historical importance. I can see that. Others can already see that. So what you must do is archive yourself."

I pass on this advice to writers younger than myself with whom I work. Most feel the attitude pretentious or immodest. I counter with an anecdote about sitting on a session of the National Archival Appraisal Board under the chairmanship of David Russell, ex-archivist for the Province of Ontario. We were evaluating that day the papers of John McCrae, author of "In Flanders Fields."

David, a man of vast erudition and geniality, said of the papers that there was a diary McCrae had kept (probably illegally) in the trenches and eight hundred letters, starting with letters McCrae had written at the age of seven and ending with letters written from the front in 1915. David said that in his many years of experience the mere existence of eight hundred letters was such a rare occurrence that he had few other instances against which to compare and measure.

My younger writer friends—especially those editing magazines—must be accumulating correspondence which would put the McCrae numbers in the shade. It's a pity to think that false modesty on the part of some is squandering the wholeness of our literary past.

I was persuaded by Richard's arguments and started keeping a diary; currently I'm writing in volume 33.

One of Richard's typically wry anecdotes was about receiving a phone call from a woman with books to sell. She lived some way out in the country and Richard probed a bit in order to decide if the trip was worth his while.

What *sort* of books were they? Textbooks? *National Geographic* magazines? *Readers' Digest* Condensed Books? No, no, none of them. No, just books. All kinds. Then the clinching question.

"How many," asked Richard, "would you say there are?"

A long considering silence.

"Oh," said the woman, "about a cord."

When we'd finished talking books that December morning we sat in companionable silence watching the plodpast of the scabbed and skanky panhandlers and derelicts making their way from Big Buds (Where Your Dollar Makes More Cents) to Tim Hortons Donuts. I was fidgeting with packets of Sweet'n'Low. It was too cold to snow. The coloured lights in the window of Radio Shack looked almost alluring.

"Ottawa, John," suddenly intoned Richard. "Ottawa lacks magic."

———————

Trips to hospitals, dentists, grocery shopping, the cinema in Kingston, the ferrying of visitors to and from Brockville railway station —after five years Myrna felt she was turning into a chauffeur. She wanted to move back to a city where the children could walk to activities or take buses. She was also becoming bored with Delta. I, of course, retreated every day to write and edit, leaving her long days to fill after the children had clambered into the school bus.

I had never learned to drive. In England for years after the war cars were not readily available. My father as a clergyman was allowed to own one for his pastoral visiting but the thought of letting a boy near it would never have entered his mind. A girlfriend at Bristol tried to teach me. There was but one lesson. The whole business I knew to be utterly beyond me. I drove into the back of a parked car. Myrna *claims* that I am so oblivious to cars that when someone asked what make of car we had I said, "It's grey."

We decided that we were pretty much forced to remain in Ontario. Montreal would have been our first choice. Myrna was born there and spoke French from an early age. I had lived there for many years and thought it Canada's most civilized city. But we did not want to place Danny and Rangidam in a situation where they would have to learn yet another language when their grip on English was uncertain. And Myrna was simmering with rage that the Parti Québécois had defined her as an allophone. PQ linguistic mumbo jumbo meaning that she wasn't *pure laine* and wasn't welcome.

Toronto was impossible for both of us. Myrna has that old Montreal contempt for the place which stems from the days when Toronto was white-sliced and irredeemably hick. For me Toronto was impossible because it offered too many distractions, jazz, other writers, painters, bookstores. I had a need to be out of the swim.

We pondered Kingston. I liked Sydenham Ward with its stylish limestone houses, felt refreshed by their age. But the rest of Kingston was slummy and then degenerated further into strips and malls. We also felt dubious about a city which lived on institutions—a university, the army, hospitals, prisons.

"Imagine the parties!" said Myrna.

And so we began to think about Ottawa. I had been to Ottawa in the winter of 1962 and found it frozenly hideous; it put me in mind of John Betjeman's aesthetic plea, "Come, friendly bombs, and rain on Slough!"

We made several forays in 1981 and on one of these found ourselves driving along the edge of a small park. I saw a For Sale sign outside a reasonably elegant three-storey Victorian house and said, "That's the one for us!" We secured an appointment to look inside and the inside was very elegant indeed, having been refurbished by its owner whose profession was building and restoration.

Myrna said that one couldn't just . . . and forced us to look at a dreary succession of doomed structures. We returned to that first house and bought it, though Myrna was aghast at the price and predicted a future, not distant either, of ruin and penury. We sold the farm and fields in Delta, Myrna's mother, Annie Mendelson, contributed generously, and I sold my manuscripts and correspondence to the Special Collections at the University of Calgary and contributed my mite.

With three children in the house we had to decide how we were to live. I've found that most memoirs skate rather airily over such matters:

. . . so we gathered the children and took ship the next week for Istanbul . . .

Only people like actors and painters who live desperately seem to remember early struggles. Montreal lives for me in memories of Brunswick sardines and day-old kaiser rolls marked down at Cantor's Bakery. Annabel Lyon told me recently that she does like real food but eats tofu "for economic reasons."

I was brought up to believe that in marriages men supported women. I felt that any other arrangement was unmanly. How, then, Myrna wanted to know, was I going to proceed? We could scarcely rely on grants. We could scarcely uproot three children every year as I travelled to take up writer-in-residence posts in the Yukon or Winnipeg. Royalties on fiction would barely buy the children shoes. Getting a job teaching would stop me from writing.

Myrna proposed that I carried on doing what I did best, contributing where I could, while she would get a job to support us. After much angst and travail we fell into the pattern she proposed. Myrna proposed this because it was a practical solution to a problem but she also believes passionately in the importance of literature and has a luminous spirit. Everything I've been able to achieve in literary life is her gift to me—and to writing in Canada in general—and I am grateful to her daily.

John Mills, in biblical mode, describes such an arrangement as living "in the sweat of one's frau," referring to God's words to Adam on expelling him from Eden, "In the sweat of thy face shalt thou eat bread."

The Ottawa years stretched ahead. How right Richard Simmins was when he said Ottawa lacked magic. It is clean. It is green. It is the country's capital and contains such national institutions as the Archives, the hideous, ever-leaking National Library, and the National Gallery, yet it remains little more than a small Victorian town, the integrity of its architecture desecrated by brutal highrises and apartment buildings. The residents seem blind to this vandalism and to the telephone poles that line the streets and the wires festooned above; I almost reeled one day when Councillor Diane Holmes said to me that she thought Elgin Street one of the most beautiful streets in the world. Elgin Street! One of Ottawa's few virtues for me is that while I'm locked away for hours every day I know I'm not missing a thing. I regard the place as a backwater backdrop.

It is difficult for an autobiographer to make writing sound interesting. There is only so much any reader can take of "so the next day he again got up at 6 a.m., shovelled in the cornflakes, and then sat at his desk for another seven hours writing with his Pilot Fineliner on yellow pads of ruled paper." I'm going to let the reader assume that this is precisely what happened most days and I'll talk of other things.

Dull as Ottawa was our personal lives were far from dull and we were soon to be placed under almost unbearable stress. Rangidam, free of the fear of attack by monkeys, began to behave with increasing abandon. She wandered off and offered herself up to strangers for adoption. She stole bicycles. She shoplifted. She stole other children's lunches. She stole and sold her older brother's clothes. She stole money from the parents of playmates, on one occasion plundering a single father's considerable savings towards Christmas. She turned into an implacable liar and showed no remorse.

Myrna and I were endlessly worried about her but all the lies and larceny were but the hors d'oeuvres. As puberty set in she started claiming that men had exposed themselves or attacked her in parking lots, in a cinema, in a public park. The police were a little puzzled because the people she described were so vividly distinguished—red hair and massive facial scars, for example—that they'd have been found or identified quickly. But weren't.

Then came a call from the police. Rangi had told other children at school that her brothers had raped her. Myrna and I knew that this was arrant nonsense, such nonsense, indeed, that before the arrival of the police Myrna laughed it off, saying that it was nice to think of *something* the three of them did together.

The police team arrived at the house with their carrying-case of articulated sex dolls and began an interrogation of the children—a decidedly uncomical evening. They concluded eventually that the story was not true.

These troubles did not end and we became adept at dealing with social workers and Children's Aid, though Myrna learned the language far more quickly than I did. I would argue and remonstrate and achieve nothing; Myrna, smarter than I, simply adopted a dopey expression and said, "I don't think I'm comfortable with that."

"Comfortable!"

Rangidam remained incorrigible and was eventually sent by Children's Aid to a group home which attempted to treat her. The two rather strange ladies who ran the home tried to inculcate discipline, restraint, and affection by making each child responsible for the care of a pet. In Rangi's case no results were discernible. Long before this—utterly desperate—I had had her examined by a psychologist who had concluded that she had been so badly damaged in her years in India that she was simply not capable of many ordinary human emotions.

All this was grindingly sad and the grief did not subside for years. One night three or four years after these events we received a call from the Major Crimes Squad in Vancouver asking if we had a daughter of East Indian descent. Could we fax a photo? They had a corpse.

The corpse turned out not to be Rangidam and she continued to wander lost in a world of petty crime, prostitution, drug-dealing and addiction, a world she inhabits still.

But life had to go on. Otherwise we'd all have been driven broodingly mad. Between 1981 and 1990 I wrote and edited more than twenty books. The first book I wrote in the new house was *Kicking Against the Pricks*, a collection of essays about literary life in Canada. This book was important not for its sales or popularity but because it cemented my reputation amongst media hacks as being a "curmudgeon" or a "gadfly," epithets bestowed on anyone who disagrees with ignorant, tasteless mainstream opinions about literature in Canada. The book also seemed to render me *persona non grata* with universities coast to coast.

I felt increasingly isolated in a critical sense. The adulation of Robertson Davies can serve as a good example. I reviewed his relentlessly bad novel *The Rebel Angels* in 1981, pointing out that *all* the characters, young, old, male, and female, spoke in exactly the same voice. No one else seemed to consider this a flaw. A bleating chorus sounded Davies's genius. Poor benighted Beverley Slopen, then a book columnist for the *Toronto Star*, chided my review for being "churlish," a comment which suggests the gooey depths of media sycophancy. Much was made by the Canadian media of the fact that Anthony Burgess admired Davies; not one among them ever considered the possibility that Burgess as a novelist was possibly worse than Davies.

(Though I remain an admirer of Burgess's *Inside Mr. Enderby*, one of his few books not hobbled by intellect.)

Years later I wrote of Davies: "Like the yokels at a medicine show the audience was awed by the gravity of mien, the silver splendour of the beard, the Edwardian knickerbockers.

"This *had* to be art."

Of course, to describe someone as a curmudgeon or a gadfly is dismissive and a way of rejecting the criticism without addressing it. I felt driven to writing and editing critical work because Canadian literary judgements are usually fatuous. *The Bumper Book, Carry On Bumping, What Is a Canadian Literature?* and *Volleys* all appeared during the eighties, unleashed into a world where David Staines, the buffoonish dean of arts at the University of Ottawa and general editor of the New Canadian Library series, could state in print that Morley Callaghan was a better writer than Ernest Hemingway, a world which institutes its awards and prizes in the names of mediocre writers like Marian Engel and Matt Cohen, a world where increasingly only the winners of prizes are read.

In 1986 Macmillan published *Adult Entertainment*. It contains two novellas, "Polly Ongle" and "Travelling Northward," and three short stories. I felt that I had been writing at full stretch and remain pleased with this book. Reviews were generally good. The book was shortlisted for the Governor General's Award, though only because Norman Levine who was on the jury made himself awkward on its behalf; the other jurors were, he said, entirely dismissive.

I had at this time acquired David Colbert as an agent. David was aggressive, abrasive, rude, and arrogant which as long as I wasn't on the receiving end I considered excellent traits in an agent. He managed to place *Adult Entertainment* with St. Martin's Press in New York. The book was well received in the *Los Angeles Times* and the *Washington Post* and was selected by the *New York Times Book Review* as one of the Notable Books of the Year.

However, the editor I was dealing with at St. Martin's left to join another press about three weeks after the book came out. It was explained to me that in large houses in the States books are sponsored and nurtured by their editors. Without an editor to promote it a book simply withers on the vine. This is precisely what happened to *Adult Entertainment*. Despite being selected as a Notable Book it was remaindered within a year.

The novella "Travelling Northward" will, I hope, be the title novella in a new book of pieces about its protagonist Robert Forde. Forde is a novelist and quite a few people have assumed he's an alter ego. There's a germ of truth in that but these Forde stories are not autobiographical in the usual sense. I've been thinking about the shape of this book for years now and feel pleasantly alarmed that its constituent pieces are so untraditional. Several are concerned with the nature of the rupture that took place in our civilization after about 1950. Forde is puzzled. Something happened and he doesn't know what it was. But it's decidedly nothing good. The stories are composed through archipelagoes, as it were, of brooding imagery. The piece I'm working on now, "Ceazer Salad," is a meditation recording a walk up Elgin Street to the Parliament Buildings. *Travelling Northward* is a book which is both daunting and alluring, daunting because it is unlike anything I've ever attempted before and alluring for exactly the same reason.

During these years that I was writing and editing books I was also collecting them. I was working on press collections—Contact, Oberon, and Anansi—and on the idea that had come to me in Bernard Halliday's musty house in Leicester so many years earlier. Building a collection as opposed to simply haphazardly acquiring books is time-consuming; it is rather like conducting a ceaseless conversation. One is incessantly looking at books in stores, writing letters, talking to dealers, reading catalogues, attending book fairs, learning points and prices, overseeing standing orders, reading reviews, making the rounds—a buzz as of bees hangs over the whole enterprise.

I was buying books locally from Rhys Knott, Patrick McGahern, and David Dorken and from the Toronto dealers Janet Inksetter, David Mason, Steven Temple, Richard Shuh and Linda Woolley, Nelson Ball, and Nicky Drumbolis. I was also buying books from

Ken Lopez in Massachusetts and from dealers in New Jersey and Boston. In England I was buying books from Dalian Books, Ulysses Book Store, David Rees, and Ian McKelvie, among others.

I bought Alice Munro translations from Germany, Finland, Sweden, France, Holland, Spain, and Denmark and chased down her advance proofs and editions in England and the States. When you increase this sort of effort to twelve authors it becomes something of a chore.

Last year Myrna and I and my daughter-in-law Kate Fildes and her mother, Isabel, finished a mammoth cataloguing of all this material which we entitled rather grandiosely, *The Short Story in Canada: Books from the Library of John and Myrna Metcalf.* We catalogued 5,192 items. The Rare Books and Special Collections Division of McGill University Libraries has expressed interest in acquiring the collection.

It was also during the early eighties that live jazz came back into my life. The Château Laurier had a "pub" in its inner depths called the Cock and Lion and some entirely misguided manager decided on a jazz policy for the hotel. This policy held for two years or more. I shudder to think how much money they must have lost. On some nights there were as few as six people in the bar, on other nights the room bulged with noisy mobs from conventions. Every week a new band took the stage, playing louder and louder to drown out the braying of conventioneering proctologists.

I remember an ancient Bud Freeman steadying himself against the side of the piano, giving a slight bow, and introducing himself by saying, "I'm very glad to be here tonight. At my age I'm glad to be anywhere." I remember taking Laurel Massé out for lunch, a brilliant bouncy singer from Chicago who used to sing with the Manhattan Transfer before jazz claimed her utterly. Mose Allison singing "Parchman Farm." Scott Hamilton and Warren Vaché, Chet Baker, Canadian friends P. J. Perry from Winnipeg and Dave Turner from Montreal. Zoot Sims sitting on a kitchen chair playing with a breathy, lyric intensity; we didn't know then that he was dying of cancer. The list of great musicians went on and on and late nights again took their toll.

Zoot Sims—and this anecdote catches the flavour of the man—

was once on a CBC show with Oscar Peterson and Oscar pompously said, "Tell me, Zoot. What is the future of the saxophone?" Zoot studied his battered old horn and said, "Well, I'm thinking of having it replated."

After the first set one night I bought a drink for and was chatting with Robert Rodney Chudnick, better known as Red Rodney, Charlie Parker's trumpet player. He joined Parker in 1949 and stayed with the band until 1952; he told me that when they were travelling he was always ordered to carry Parker's suitcase. He also talked about his heroin addiction, an addiction he'd sought so that he too by "crossing over the line" might play with Parker's endless invention.

I remember thinking at the time: I am talking to a man who played with Bird. As with many things in my life I couldn't get over how strange it was, strange that a little boy who'd grown up using the Elizabethan *thee* and *thou* in a stronghold of clog-wearing primitive Methodists in Yorkshire should be drinking Scotch in what my scholarly brother still refers to as the "New World" with a pioneer bop trumpet player.

Quite unlike life in the manse.

The writing life is necessarily solitary and needs a firm discipline. The occasional day spent working with other people or simply in conversation comes as a treat in itself. I always look forward to days at the Archives evaluating literary material for tax credit. There is something pleasantly collegial about working with David Russell and, say, Peter Harcourt and John Moldenhaur.

There is also the coarse, snoopy pleasure of reading people's letters and diaries. It is a condition of this kind of work, though, that one's lips have to remain sealed, which is a pity because some of the gossip is of high grade. The huge archive of the Colbert Agency was an eye-popper as we studied the royalty statements of about half the writers in Canada. We were all fascinated by the chatty archive of John "Buffy" Glassco, author of *Memoirs of Montparnasse*, and author also of *Contes en Crinoline*, *Fetish Girl*, *The English Governess*, and *The Temple of Pederasty*. His remarks concerning Margaret Atwood were of peculiar interest.

Any appraisal is, in fact, something of a fiction. We collude in saying that ten boxes of paper are "worth," say, $40,000. William

Hoffer wrote in his essay "Cheap Sons of Bitches: Memoirs of the Book Trade":

> As is the case in so many areas of Canadian cultural life, there is no genuine market for most Canadian literature. As a member of the National Archival Appraisal Board, I am constantly forced to consider the "technical" value of collections of manuscripts, while at the same time fully aware that were the material to be auctioned, it would bring nothing. Similarly, the pricing of Canadian first editions has been somewhat technical. Both booksellers and book buyers have eventually "assigned" value to particular books.

It was this hollowness at the centre, this central lie, that drove us to the Tanks campaign.

By 1993 Myrna had had enough of the civil service. The lively people she had worked for earlier, like Pierre de Blois, had left, and people with little, correct minds had risen to positions of power. Poor John Newlove whom they'd earlier been able to protect was now nagged and threatened by a senior manager, exquisitely dim in the manner of CNN's Connie Chung, for such infractions—despite John's explanation of its etymology—as permitting the use of the word *niggardly*. Such was the atmosphere Myrna fled.

Our son Ron had finished high school and had turned his hand to a variety of jobs, settling on the restaurant business and becoming the general manager of Dunn's Famous Smoked Meat restaurant in the Ottawa market. After some time, the owner, Stanley Devine, sent him to Toronto to open a branch of Dunn's on Adelaide Street. He oversaw this with great success and we were very proud of him. After a period of illness in Toronto he returned to Ottawa intent on opening his own restaurant. Myrna and he went into partnership and on November 11, 1993, opened the Elgin Street Diner. Our younger son, Dan, works there as well.

Myrna said that selling hamburgers was *intellectually* more interesting than working in the public service.

The restaurant is open twenty-four hours a day, 365 days a year. Breakfast is served twenty-four hours a day. The restaurant employs thirty-five staff. The food is simple "diner food," club sandwiches, burgers, fries, milkshakes, but is of high quality. The poutine has been voted the best in Ottawa and has been discussed by poutine lovers on the CBC; I have *seen* this dish on numerous occasions, but nothing could tempt me.

During the daytime the Elgin Street Diner, under Myrna's control, or under Ron's wife, Kate Fildes, is a family and neighbourhood hangout. Small children demand Myrna's presence and tell her long tales of their daily doings; she gives her most favoured ones dollops of ice cream. Old people, too, who are lonely and bored confide in her and she makes them feel valued and at home. Even the mildly crazed are cared for; one old lady asked daily for a table for six, the other five, her nonexistent family, being on their way. Myrna solved this by seating her at a table for one and saying, "They always take a little while to get here so I'll put you here for now and move you when they arrive." Myrna at work is a display of natural goodness.

The overnight shift is an entirely different scene and my son Ron rides herd on it. When the bars close, the Diner fills to capacity and pulsates with noisy, inebriated energy and stays that way for hours. People congregate there from all over the city. Over the years, the Diner has become an Ottawa institution.

The Diner's business has increased every year and some part of this is owing to the cheerful service of the staff and the patient talents of Jason Hughes, the Diner's chef.

Myrna, Ron, and Kate are kind enough to let me use the Diner as an unofficial "office" to entertain visiting authors. It is an office distinguished by walls hung with blow-ups of Sam Tata photographs, sadly the only permanent exhibition of his work in Canada.

On the rare days when driblets of money arrived in the mail I'd be tempted to go out for lunch and nearly always went to Chez Jean-Pierre on Somerset Street. The restaurant was owned and run by Jean-Pierre Muller from Strasbourg who had been the chef at the American embassy but had quit, saying he didn't want to spend the rest of his life making hamburgers. I knew whenever I went that Charles Ritchie would likely be there.

I'd read and enjoyed his diaries, particularly *Storm Signals*, which covers the war years in London. I'd first met him when having breakfast and a brood in a café on Elgin Street. I'd finished reading the *Globe and Mail* and as I passed his table said, "Mr. Ritchie. Would you care for the *Globe and Mail*?" He looked up in patrician horror and said, "Good *God*, no!"

We got to know each other quite well and he would sit drinking cognac in Chez Jean-Pierre spinning out anecdotes about Vincent and Alice Massey, Mike Pearson, Elizabeth Bowen, Mackenzie King whom he loathed, and John Diefenbaker, whom he'd loathed even more. He described Diefenbaker as "a congenital liar" and King as "neurasthenic." This increasingly gaunt and frail man who'd been ambassador to Washington and high commissioner to the United Kingdom told me that for twenty years he'd tried to write fiction but couldn't and that that failure had induced in him a permanent melancholy. Aesthetic standards, he used to say, are the only standards worth upholding. Life's most rewarding activities, he claimed, were gossip and sexual intercourse. Family life, he said, made him long for the brothel.

By about 3 p.m. he'd be close to legless, though faultlessly weaving stories still, and Jean-Pierre, who was fond of him, would drive him the short distance home to his apartment.

If I bumped into him on the street I'd always stop to chat and ask whether he was working on a new diary.

"Oh," he'd say, "one needs to scribble away at *something* if only to stop oneself getting into the sherry at 10 a.m."

He stopped me on Elgin Street one January morning in 1987 and told me that someone had given him a copy of *Adult Entertainment* for Christmas.

"What a long, bleak day I'd been expecting," he said, "the insufferable dreariness of festivity, but you saved Christmas for me. What *lovely* writing! I *chortled.*"

Another of the pleasures of Ottawa was escaping from the place and during the eighties I travelled on Canada's behalf and on behalf of PEN International to academic conferences in Germany, France, Italy, and Yugoslavia.

I was sitting at my desk one morning when the phone rang. The caller identified himself as Guy Gervais of the cultural section of External Affairs.

"Would you," he said, "be prepared to go to teach about Canadian literature for two months in Milan?"

I said that I'd be very interested indeed but before I could give him a firm answer I'd have to consult my wife. I said I'd call him back. I called Myrna at Official Languages and she was agreeable and thought she could wangle some time off to join me for part of the stint.

"Mr. Gervais?"

"Yes."

"This is John Metcalf."

There was a silence.

"I'm returning your call of this morning. About Milan."

"Milan?"

"The teaching job. I spoke to my wife and she's agreeable."

The silence stretched and became uncomfortable.

"*Who* did you say that you are?"

"John Metcalf. We spoke earlier. This morning."

Another silence.

"*Oh, my God!*" he said. "I thought you were W. O. Mitchell."

This is how I ended up in Bologna, sent there as a consolation prize.

Mark Twain was once asked on his return from Europe what he had thought of Rome.

"Rome . . ." he said to his wife. "Was that the place we saw the yellow dog?"

I'm afraid I'm a very Twainish tourist and much of what follows is quirky, idiosyncratic, and unreliable. I do make efforts to see the Cathedral, the Gallery, and the Castle but my attention is more usually on the doorlatch than the door.

The first of these travels was in 1984 when I went to Munich and Grainau in Bavaria to give a paper entitled "The Curate's Egg." It was principally an illustration of Morley Callaghan's manifold ineptitudes and a celebration of Hemingway's felicities. As I left the lecture hall I heard a little martinet from Vienna, his Polish-sounding surname a concatenation of consonants, sputtering to his cronies, "He was lecturing us! He *dared* to lecture us!"

Following the lecture I was sitting having a drink with Professor Dr. Walter Pache of the University of Trier when we were approached by my Ottawa neighbour Richard Tait. He asked if he might join us and I said with a cold rage of which I hadn't thought myself capable, "I can't physically prevent you but I'd rather you didn't."

Richard lived four doors away from us. He was an anglophile diplomat very much in the Charles Ritchie mould. He had been Canada's ambassador to the European Union in Brussels and on his return to Ottawa had been placed in charge of cultural matters in External Affairs. He was bitter about this as Culture was a resounding demotion. He claimed the department was simply a dumping ground for the eccentric and mentally ill. He said one of his male employees came to work every day on a tricycle dressed in pieces of what looked like eighteenth-century French military uniform and put in eight solid hours of knitting.

Richard administered a fund used to buy paintings and prints for External Affairs and for Canadian embassies around the world. I interested him in Tony Calzetta's work. Richard had a good eye and owned some lovely bowls (hmmm!) which I always admired when visiting. Tony had left the Pollock Gallery and now was exhibiting at Mira Godard's, probably the most prestigious gallery in Toronto at that time.

I arranged to meet Richard in Toronto and I took him to meet Tony and look at the studio. He was enormously enthusiastic and told Tony that he'd buy some drawings and quite probably three canvases. He also promised Tony, *guaranteed* Tony, a show at the Canadian gallery in New York, the 49th Parallel, a state-owned gallery designed to spotlight Canadian art and artists.

Richard and I arranged to meet the next morning at Mira Godard's and look at Tony's new exhibition together. The canvases were large, vibrant, gorgeous in their colours. Myrna and I recently donated one of the paintings from this series, *Advance Machine Romance*, to the University of Toronto Art Centre.

While Richard and I were looking, I was chatting to him about the difficulties of Tony's life as an artist, the struggle to make ends meet, the wasting of his time in having to do drywall and construction work. I told him about an exhibition at Mira Godard's, a first exhibition for a young painter from New York, where the canvases were priced at $12,000, when a Canadian painter *at mid-career* would be charging $5,000 or less. I told him that Tony, because so original, found it difficult to get support, that he'd just been turned down *again* for a Canada Council grant.

"Turned down!" said Richard. "I wasn't told this. I can't . . ."

He waved his hand about the gallery.

"This is a professional judgement."

He shook his head.

"I'm sorry," he said, "I'm sorry but he's forfeited official credibility."

On the floor above Tony's show there was an exhibition on of watercolour landscapes by Dorothy Knowles of Saskatchewan. The paintings were competent, inoffensive, irrelevant. Richard, I learned subsequently, returned to the gallery and bought the entire show.

In Grainau I was still angry with this paltry man and over the years the incident has not receded. It has become emblematic for me of the danger of the state and its bureaucracy. Its relationship with art is usually capricious and always contagious.

Another German expedition took in Trier, Bonn, and Siegen in Westphalia. In Siegen I was teaching for Professor Dr. Christian Thomson, a most unlikely academic, jovial and with a vast appetite for visual arts. He decided that he would make a film of me to exercise his students and for fun resolved to shoot it in the large house, now a gallery and museum, where Sir Peter Paul Rubens was born in 1577. The "Sir" was conferred by Charles I of England in return for a decorated ceiling. The film is in my archives at the University of Calgary.

Christian took a party of us to the house when it was officially closed and proceeded to set up lights and tripods and all the paraphernalia of film-making. One of his students knocked over a heavy light stand which crashed into the wall near a painting. There were no audible alarms or sounds of sirens but within two minutes the grounds filled with uniformed police in jeeplike vehicles and armed with machine guns. Shouting from a window, Christian negotiated our surrender.

The following year Christian was guest editing an issue of a Swiss magazine which was to explore the scope of Canadian painting and sculpture. He came over to stay with us and I took him to Toronto to meet various painters and look round the galleries. He was quickly drawn to the work of Medrie McPhee. I had also arranged a lunch with John Bentley Mays who was then the *Globe and Mail* art critic. Mays was aggressive and awkward. The first thing he said was, "Why would anyone want to write about Canadian art? There is no Canadian art worth writing about."

He went on to say that he had never owned a painting, that he couldn't understand why anyone would want to. He was rude to the waiter. He was dismissive towards Christian. He was wearing a shiny grey suit, possibly silk, and on his lapel he sported a diamanté brooch which was a portrait of a crowned Queen Elizabeth II. I was faintly embarrassed.

In 1987 I represented Canada, along with Michael Ignatieff, at the PEN International Conference which was held at Lake Bled. In a novella entitled "Forde Abroad" I used this Slovenian excursion as a backdrop but instead of Bled called *my* resort Splad. In the real Bled is the summer palace of ex-King Peter; Cecil Parrott, who translated *The Good Soldier Svejk* for Penguin, was as a young man tutor to the two Crown Princes there. I often think of Svejk explaining to the Lieutenant that the cat died "after inadvertently eating a tin of shoe polish."

The conference was steamy with politics and there were endless hintings about separation and an independent Slovenian state. Wild Macedonians orated. Montenegrins emoted. Han Suyin drifted about conferring. Every word was freighted. There was much talk of the Role of the Artist. I didn't really grasp much of what was going on.

Subsequently I gave lectures in Belgrade, Novi Sad, Sarajevo, and Skopje in Macedonia. Belgrade was hideous with Soviet concrete. I remember thinking during the recent war that if anywhere *had* to be bombed Belgrade wasn't much of a loss.

The Hotel Moskva, in which I stayed, was vast and almost completely empty. The menu in the dining room offered a dish called Butter Tart with Chicken Pluck. I *was* curious but settled for a salad and some Kashkaval cheese, a favourite of Myrna's grandfather. A notice in my room offered to launder my "nightshirst."

In Belgrade I saw a gang of middle-aged women working on road repair with picks and shovels, a sight that made me peculiarly uncomfortable. I dabbled my hand in the Danube. I was filmed by a TV crew walking along the bank of the Sava River and discoursing.

There is nothing like a TV camera for transforming even a sage into an immediate horse's ass.

In Sarajevo I of course went to see the footprint painted on the pavement where the assassin had stood to shoot the Archduke Francis Ferdinand and his wife on June 28, 1914. More interesting than the rather bland architecture of the Austro-Hungarian nineteenth century were the Muslim alleys, markets, and mosques. Visiting dignitaries always bring the gift of a carpet to the main mosque and the carpets are spread on top of each other so that to kneel on them one has to mount the pile on a stepladder.

I stayed at the Holiday Inn in Sarajevo, which was shelled into ruins in the recent war. The university professors of English, all trained in the USA, nearly all seemed to have second jobs to make ends meet. Journals and books were too expensive for them to buy and the university library lagged behind by years. The Holiday Inn had been built for the Winter Olympics some years earlier. Patches of wasteland had been turned into little flower gardens while the Olympics were on but as soon as anything flowered it was picked and was on sale in the market the next morning; the authorities were forced to station soldiers overnight at every garden plot. Nearly everything about Bosnia and Herzegovina struck me as wilted and run-down, an imitation of a Western country, their Westernness merely an inheritance from the Austro-Hungarian imperium and all of it marking time until it relapsed into a more vital Muslim chaos.

Chaos increased the farther south one went. In Skopje in Macedonia my hotel room door had had a hole in it repaired by hammering over the hole a piece of tin. This crude repair seemed to suggest much about the social fabric.

These junkets to foreign countries continued with Greek temples in Agrigento, crusader castles, Roman amphitheatres in Syracuse and Taormina where Leon Rooke and I took to the stage and orated to throat-pulsing lizards warming themselves on the ancient stone.

Rome I remember not for a yellow dog but for a toilet. In a ramshackle hotel near the end of the Via della Croce, a hotel warmly commended by Leon and Connie Rooke, the toilet stood in a tiled room which sloped to a central drain. When flushed, the water circulated in an unsteady oval and, against the laws of nature, rose terrifyingly up the toilet bowl until it reached the rim and hurled turds onto the floor.

Strasbourg I remember chiefly because Carol Shields launched into a feminist harangue claiming that I was a misogynist and deliberately excluded female writers from anthologies and from the list of the Porcupine's Quill. What provoked this harpy act I have no idea; I had to struggle to hold on to the fact that she had written *Various Miracles*. Ray Smith was so appalled that he later wrote her a strong letter of protest.

Ray and Myrna and I months before the conference had made a reservation at Le Crocodil. Ray, I remember, ordered *canard pressé*. I consulted the Jeeves-like sommelier about Alsatian wines and he said in a snooty manner, "What a pleasure it is, monsieur, not to be serving Coca-Cola to Japanese businessmen."

But of all these junkets Bologna was the best. I had initially agreed to go for two months but then decided that that was too long and cut the time to one month. Guy Gervais, bless him, again mismanaged and the cheque I received in Bologna, sent from Rome, was not for four weeks but for eight. I had so much money I literally could not spend it. Cashing the cheque was a vastly comic performance which started with one teller but swelled to a shouting, gesticulating mob of about twenty employees casting doubt on the cheque's authenticity because it had been issued in Rome by, as the manager described them, "southern monkeys."

The department of foreign literary studies was housed in a large and beautiful *palazzo*. One approached along arcaded streets with barrel-vaulted ceilings which were so beautiful that the simple act of walking under them made one feel positively regal.

The department di Lingue e Letterature Straniere itself was another matter. Its Canadian operations doubtless owed their existence to large sums of Canadian government money. I am not saying that its activities were fraudulent but I would say that the department seemed to accept theses in large numbers from students I would have thought not quite prepared for the task at hand.

On my first day there I gave a lecture about Canadian literature to roughly thirty-five students, a lecture which lasted about one and a half hours. Afterwards I asked why the entire class was female.

I was told that literature wasn't important enough to lead to a well-paying job and that therefore it was not a suitable subject for men. I also asked why there had been no questions. The answer to that was twofold; they didn't ask questions, said Professor Giovanna Capone, firstly, because they'd been taught not to and, secondly, because they were probably embarrassed to attempt English in public.

After this first heroic lecture everyone seemed to think I'd performed sterling service and should take the rest of the month to recover; I was urged to travel to Rome, Florence, Milan, and Venice to take in the sights.

Myrna came to join me halfway through and I was achingly lonely for her by then and met her at the railway station with roses and took her back to the Albergo Centrale where our shutters opened onto a sea of waving red roof tiles.

We went to Florence where we did all the touristy things. But more than the Uffizi and the Pitti Palace I remember a twenty-year-old Meursault we were served in the Enoteca Restaurant preceding the *menu dégustation*.

In Venice we ate on the terrace of the Hotel Danieli overlooking the Grand Canal and at its far side the great Palladian church of S. Giorgio Maggiore, a building so perfect, so elegant it moved me nearly to tears. Our waiter at the Danieli was a memorable disgrace, goosing the busboy, and preening intolerably. When I asked him for pepper he brought a mill which ground white pepper. I asked him if he had black and he said, "Oh, eat it up merry christmas!"

My other vivid memory of Venice was of the pavements and squares fouled with spittle, phlegm, and mucus.

Although I loved roaming the streets of the old city of Bologna and visiting its many churches and although I spent time seeking out paintings and prints by the Bolognese painter Giorgio Morandi, our driving interest was in food. The Italians call Bologna "Fat City" because of the wonderful restaurants and because of the rich produce of Emilia Romagna. Myrna and I, gastronomic rubes, were eager to taste everything and we started eating three full meals a day, something we do not ordinarily do.

We had to try genuine mortadella, the original bologna. And the sweet prosciutto from Palma and the salty prosciutto from the

Chianti wine region and the acorn-fed prosciutto of San Daniele. We nibbled on Parmigiano-Reggiano. I discovered mâche. Myrna became a devotee of olive oil.

We applied ourselves to *melanzane al forno*. We put to the test *risotto alla milanese*. We tackled *fagioli in stufa* and *torta di funghi*. We made inroads on *insalata di gamberi alla menta* and *pollo al limoni*. We attacked the *ossobuca alle cipolle*. We gorged on the richness of *polenta con mascarpone e tartufi*.

One evening towards the end of our stay we were sitting in yet another serious restaurant. We were the only customers. The waiter was attentive and charming. We discovered that he had until recently been working in a family restaurant in England. We chatted about Soho and life in London. He ardently supported Tottenham Hotspurs. He brought us an apéritif of Campari and suggested that we start with a very fine, very delicate *quadrucci in brodo*.

We studied the menu. I tried to decide between *quaglie con uva* and *coniglio ripieno*, quail and rabbit. Myrna decided on a shrimp salad with diced cold potatoes and mayonnaise.

The soup was delicious. But filling. The broth, the waiter told us, was made from the dark meat of an entire turkey. It took us some time to finish. My apéritif sat in front of me. I sipped some mineral water. When our waiter returned and set before us rabbit and shrimps I knew that it was the end.

"I can't," I said. "I can't eat this."

"I've been taking senna pods," said Myrna. "It's been five days."

"I'm sorry," I said, "but I just *can't*."

"But we'll hurt his feelings," Myrna said, "and he's been so kind."

"Even a mouthful," I said, "and I know I'd be sick."

We sat for a few minutes and when the waiter went through the bat doors into the kitchen Myrna took the rabbit and the red peppers and the shrimps and potatoes and radicchio and mayonnaise and scraped them into her handbag which she closed with a click.

AN AESTHETIC UNDERGROUND

IN NOVEMBER 1988, Professor J. R. (Tim) Struthers staged a conference at the University of Guelph to celebrate my fiftieth birthday. To my considerable embarrassment he called the conference "Coming of Age: John Metcalf and the Canadian Short Story." Papers were presented. Lectures were delivered. And in the evenings writers read. Among the writers present were Leon Rooke, Keath Fraser, Hugh Hood, Alice Munro, Clark Blaise, Kent Thompson, Ray Smith, Jane Urquhart, Doug Glover, and Dayv James-French.

On the final day of the conference, Myrna and Alice Munro, restive in this academic environment, retreated to the faculty club to absorb dry martinis. Connie Rooke was to drive us out later to her house in Eden Mills for a final party. She had a list of errands to run before we headed to Eden Mills and among them was to pick up some boxes of *empañadas* she was going to serve at the party—*empañadas* being Latin American pasties or turnovers stuffed with ground meats or vegetables and spiced with hot peppers. Connie was rather flustered with all she had to do and kept remarking that whatever we did we mustn't forget to pick up the *empañadas*. She stopped in a shopping mall and walked off out of sight. Into the silence in the car Alice said in a puzzled and slightly querulous voice, "Who *are* the Empañadas?"

But it was not at that splendid party that I first drifted into contact with the Porcupine's Quill. That had happened two evenings earlier at a conference dinner at the Bookshelf Café in Guelph. I found myself seated at the same table as Tim and Elke Inkster, the Porcupine's Quill owners. We were soon discussing the idea of reprinting important Canadian books. What prestigious publishing this would be! As the wine bottles emptied, the vision took on greater clarity. It rose before us, shining. I would select and edit these volumes with John Newlove, whom I would recruit as soon as I returned to Ottawa, and they would sell not only to the General Reader in bookstores but to students in universities and colleges all over Canada, thereby preserving our literary heritage and bringing into the Porcupine's Quill coffers vast sums of money.

It seemed to us foolproof.

We decided to call these reprints the Sherbrooke Street Series. In the fall of 1993, I wrote for the PQ catalogue:

Sherbrooke Street in Montreal has many memories for Tim Inkster, John Newlove, and for me. Tim went to high school at Loyola of Montreal on Sherbrooke Street and I taught at the college for several years. John Newlove and I have both been writers-in-residence there. We all have a vision of Sherbrooke Street as it used to be, the elegant and dignified grey stone houses, the stately trees . . . It was at one time the Champs-Elysées, as it were, of Montreal.

Now the street has fallen prey to developers and has been vandalized by urban planners, the Van Horne mansion wrecked illegally, the heritage streetscape desecrated with brutal concrete, the trees all felled.

Something of the same thing has been happening to our literature. The past is being forgotten; books are slipping out-of-print and out of mind. The outlines of our literary history seem to be blurring; careers seem to be sliding into general oblivion.

The Sherbrooke Street series is our way of attempting to save the vision. We are reprinting and keeping in print important books from our literary past. We cannot have a literature unless the books are available to readers and are being read; we cannot have a future unless we are securely anchored in a past. We are,

St. Augustine reminded us, what we remember. Sherbrooke Street asserts the importance of what we have achieved and is our small gesture of faith in the excellence of what will evolve.

On my return to Ottawa from Guelph in 1988, I talked John Newlove into co-editing the series but he grew bored with the idea and withdrew entirely after about six weeks. We continued to put his name on the books and in the catalogue because I thought it looked more impressive to have two of us, but one day in 1993 I bumped into John in the street and he said that if we didn't stop using his name he'd sue. I didn't really think that he would—but with John you can never be *quite* sure.

I wanted each Sherbrooke Street volume to have an introduction by the author, setting the book in a literary and historical context. In cases where this wasn't possible, I intended commissioning an expert to do the job for me. We thought that these introductions or after-words would also make the books bibliographically significant to libraries and institutions.

In this, we were mistaken.

I attended three annual meeting of the Learned Societies at great expense, manning a Porcupine's Quill booth, attempting to sell Sherbrooke Street books and other PQ titles to Canada's assembled academics. In the three years we sold a total of something like thirteen books.

I recall one shambling scholar at our booth picking up Ray Smith's *Cape Breton Is the Thought-Control Centre of Canada.*

"Is there anything about sailing in this book?"

"Not that I recall, no."

"Ah, well then, it wouldn't interest me *because*, you see," he said triumphantly, "it's *sailing* I'm interested in."

Thinking about the meetings of the Learned Societies reminds me of one attended by ECW Press in Winnipeg. Jack David and Robert Lecker always used to put on wine-and-cheese receptions. They bought wine locally and hired locals to dispense it. An academic surveyed the jumble of bottles on the table and asked of the local, "Where is the Côtes-du-Rhône?"

"Down the corridor," replied the local, "and on your left."

When we started Sherbrooke Street I assumed that we'd keep adding to the series until we arrived at something like the New Canadian Library or the New Press Canadian Classics. This was not to be. When I was setting up a reading tour for Norman Levine to promote and celebrate the 1993 republication of *From a Seaside Town* and *Canada Made Me* I was shocked that McGill, his own university, had no interest whatsoever in hosting a reading. "Nobody teaches him," I was told. My contact in Calgary told me that a few older people might turn out but there wouldn't be any students there because they wouldn't have heard of him as he wasn't on any courses. We were forced to face the brute fact that there really wasn't much of an academic market at all and that the general readership was indifferent. Quietly we let the series lapse.

The reprint books were *Cape Breton Is the Thought-Control Centre of Canada* by Ray Smith (1989); *Lunar Attractions* by Clark Blaise (1990); *The Improved Binoculars* by Irving Layton (1991); *Europe* by Louis Dudek (1991); *The Happiness of Others* by Leon Rooke (1991); *Dance with Desire* by Irving Layton (1992); *From a Seaside Town* and *Canada Made Me* by Norman Levine (1993).

Of these titles perhaps only *Europe* was a mistake. It certainly doesn't stand up as poetry but it's interesting for its ambition. Louis was important more as a teacher and an enthusiast and he is warmly remembered by those he taught such as Michael Darling, David Solway, and Michael Gnarowski.

The Happiness of Others preserves the best of Leon Rooke's stories from *The Love Parlour* and *Cry Evil*, volumes long out of print with Oberon Press. Ray Smith wrote a lengthy and important introduction to *Cape Breton*, essential reading for anyone interested in the short story in Canada.

By the end of 1992 I was beginning to see the shape of the Press in an editorial sense. Between 1974, when they founded the Porcupine's Quill in Erin Village northwest of Toronto, and 1989 when I started working with them, Tim and Elke had published a great deal of poetry but little fiction. I wanted to publish fewer poetry titles and place considerable emphasis on short fiction.

In 1989 I thought that the Press was too slight. Tim and Elke had published some good books but not enough of them. We had to gain mass and weight. Nor was Tim really thinking in national terms. I remember him saying to me in the early days, "Oh, Porcupine's Quill books don't get reviewed."

What I had in mind was building a better press than Contact Press or the House of Anansi had been. I wanted, quite simply, the best literary press in Canada.

This is how I put it in an essay in *The New Quarterly*:

I wanted to counter apathy and blandness. I wanted to shock homogenized minds with the experience of writing at high voltage. I wanted the press to assert relentlessly literature's importance. I wanted the press to be a national press and of national importance. I wanted nothing "small" about this small press. I wanted the press to become something of a "movement." Not a movement committed to a particular "ism," but a gathering together of writers with an aesthetic approach to literature and with a lust for excellence. I wanted our writers to draw strength from community. I wanted each to embolden the next. I wanted writers who loved language and who would swagger and flaunt. I wanted elegance. I wanted sophistication. I wanted a press crackling with energy. I wanted to draw together into one place so many talented writers that we would achieve critical mass and explode upon Canadian society in a dazzling coruscation showering it with unquenchable brilliance.

There was, of course, no money. I was willing to do this job without a salary—which Tim certainly couldn't have afforded—because I was attracted by the extreme romanticism of the task, by the vision of what could be wrought. I was bringing to the Press years of literary experience and a host of literary contacts, contacts not really available to Tim and Elke isolated in Erin Village. I was also bringing to the Press a readiness to talk to people, to listen, to soothe, to cajole.

Tim is very much not a "people person." He is paranoid, belligerent, bloody-minded, and extremely intelligent, all qualities which are probably essential to survival in small press publishing. I sometimes get phone calls from the more emotionally frail among my writers complaining that he has yelled at them or been astonishingly rude. I explain to these ruffled feathers that he has too much on his plate and that he's snarly because harassed.

Hostile and gloomy as he sometimes can be, he is at the same time something of a hero to me. I admire his energy, his devotion to what he does, his obstinate use of Zephyr Antique laid paper, the beautiful end-products of his passion. The fact that Tim still binds his books in the traditional manner and that he binds them with a Smythe book-sewing machine made in 1907 might suggest why I like and admire him and why we've worked together for fifteen years without homicidal incident.

Although I wanted to change the emphasis of the press I certainly wanted to continue publishing poetry but I wanted Selected Poems and Collected Poems rather than slim volumes by tyros. We started in 1990 with George Johnston's collected poems *Endeared by Dark*. Mark Abley wrote about the book and the Press in the Montreal *Gazette*:

> "The way I look at it," Tim Inkster told me the other day, "the printing excellence we're known for is a very sophisticated and understated marketing tool. The authors we publish are important, and we want to make sure their works last."
>
> But there's more to it than that. Just think of the magnificent cover that graces George Johnston's collected poems, *Endeared by Dark*. Since Johnston is a noted translator from Old Norse, Inkster decided that a Viking motif would be appropriate for the book. His unofficial editor-in-chief, John Metcalf, found a photograph of the celebrated Oseberg Ship in Norway but the photo was not good enough to reproduce directly. So Inkster passed it to an artist, Virgil Burnett; and from Burnett's pen-and-ink drawing, Inkster had a magnesium die made. Onto each cover, the die was then foil-stamped by hand.
>
> A complicated process—but the result is a joy to behold. "It's about as nice a production as I've ever had," Johnston says wryly. Against a pale, gray-blue background, the ship's embossed prow soars in gold. "Visually, it's something of a ghost ship," Inkster

explains. "The way you perceive the image changes according to your angle of view. It's designed to sail through your imagination."

And one way or another, that's what a lot of Porcupine's Quill books have been doing of late.

Tim printed five hundred copies of *Endeared by Dark*; total advance trade sales in Canada were forty-five copies.

As the years passed we published Irving Layton, Gael Turnbull, Don Coles, Richard Outram, John Newlove, P. K. Page, and Christopher Wiseman.

Gael Turnbull is an anomaly in this list, being far more "experimental" than any of the others.

Some years ago I became interested in a small literary press called Contact Press which was run in the fifties and sixties by Louis Dudek, Irving Layton, Raymond Souster, and Peter Miller. Myrna and I formed the first complete collection of the books of the press, a collection now in the National Library of Canada.

The Contact Press was perhaps the most centrally important press in the history of Canadian poetry, publisher of the first or very early work of Doug Jones, Alden Nowlen, Eli Mandel, Phyllis Webb, Louis Dudek, Irving Layton, Raymond Souster, Leonard Cohen, W. W. E. Ross, F. R. Scott, Milton Acorn, Gwendolyn MacEwen, John Newlove, Al Purdy, George Bowering, and Margaret Atwood.

One of the early books of the press was entitled *Trio* and it contained the first poems published in book form of three young writers—Eli Mandel, Phyllis Webb, and Gael Turnbull.

Also distributed by the Contact Press were four mimeographed pamphlets of French-Canadian poets translated by Turnbull in 1955 —an early effort at crossing borders and cultures. Gael was living at the time in Iroquois Falls, Ontario, where he practised as a doctor and anaesthetist. He was assisted in the translations by Jean Beaupré, a French teacher in the local high school. Together they presented samples of the work of Paul-Marie Lapointe, Gilles Hénault, Roland Giguère, and Saint-Denys Garneau.

Gael Turnbull was much influenced by Raymond Souster and the Contact Press movement and by Cid Corman and the Black Mountain poets in the States. When he returned to England in 1957, he founded Migrant Press, one of the pioneer small presses for modern poetry in Britain.

I enjoyed the poetry and made efforts to find out about the man. I located him in Edinburgh and went there to see him, bearing with me an offer to publish a Selected Poems in Canada. I spent a couple of nights in my hotel room sitting up into the small hours reading new material and rereading until I was bleary-eyed. The eventual result was *While Breath Persist* which was published by the Porcupine's Quill in 1992.

Whenever I think about Gael Turnbull, I think of his reciting the final lines of "Twenty Words, Twenty Days."

> . . . and I remember an Edinburgh room
> and one saying, when I asked what he'd done that day,
> how much—
>   "I tore it up . . . I wisnae pure enough
> when I wrote . . . I wisnae pure enough . . ."

In 1993 we published Don Coles's *Forests of the Medieval World*. It was the winner of the 1993 Governor General's Award for Poetry. Tim was ecstatic. Then it turned out that Don thought public readings and any sort of public appearance were little short of hucksterism and deeply detrimental to poetry's dignity. He refused to perform. Tim was apoplectic and coarse descriptive invective issued from the telephone for days. There was a gala evening for the winners at the National Library where I had to read in Don Coles's place. Among other of his poems, I read "My Son at the Seashore, Age Two," a pretty little thing.

> He laughs and a breeze
> lifts his hair. His face tilts up
> towards what has happened
> to his hair, that it should lift,
> and his laugh goes. Why
> is this happening, his suddenly
> serious face wants to know, and
> what is happening. But

all it is is a little breeze
lifting his hair for a few seconds,
a little breeze passing by
on its way to oblivion—
as this day is on its way there too,
and as that day, twenty years ago,
was, too.

When I read the last, soft words I heard someone catch their breath. For some reason I was certain it was a woman.

We have also had the honour of publishing the glittering poetry of Richard Outram. Four of his collections are still in print with us: *Man in Love*, *Hiram and Jenny*, *Mogul Recollected*, and *Dove Legend*. Alberto Manguel wrote an essay on Richard Outram in a recent book, *Into the Looking-Glass Wood*. He wrote: "I discovered, in fact, that Outram's entire career had been one of absences. He has never received a national, let alone international award, nor a Canada Council grant; he has never been included in any major anthology of Canadian poetry, rarely been acknowledged in reviews . . ."

Manguel then goes on to claim that Richard Outram is "one of the finest poets in the English language."

Who could resist exploring such a resounding judgement? The answer to *that* rhetorical question is, Nearly every Canadian.

The easiest way into Richard's work is through *Hiram and Jenny*. Hiram and Jenny are two quirky maritime characters and the poems celebrate in playful and gorgeous language their comings and goings, their maunderings and heroics.

Here are just a few lines from "Techne."

Hiram is washing his socks in the creek.
Not far offshore, unseen,
crammed with warheads and comic books
a nuclear submarine

noses about with her cornfed crew,
bored, but ready to cope
at the drop of a ciphered word. . . .

Who could resist reading on? But you will.

By 1991 I had also fully realized what had been nebulous before, that ink and paper were only a part of a literary press. Literary presses which *were* mainly ink and boards and paper—presses like Black Moss, say, or Mosaic—are largely inert. I would never underestimate the importance of Tim's printing and design. He has won awards from the Leipzig Book Fair, the Art Directors' Club of New York, the Alcuin Society and the Society of Graphic Designers of Canada, yet at the same time I believe that a press lives fully only when it creates a personality and mythology.

Faber and Faber had that mythology under T. S. Eliot and continued having it under Charles Monteith; Macmillan in England had it in the late nineteenth and twentieth centuries; Boni and Liveright had it under the hand of Ezra Pound. It comes about, I think, when a certain group of authors, a generation perhaps, come to be associated with a press. In their commingling, the by-product is a glamour, a glitter of talent. The mythology is nurtured by launches, by lunches, by burgeoning friendships and mild rivalries. It grows through editorial soothing and encouragement which is not some insincere schtick but is a genuine interest in the work and its creator. It comes about through a sense of community and shared purpose. It comes about through a shared aesthetic interest in literature. It brings people into a more than commercial association.

The mythology of the press is built by the commingling of the reputations of such brilliant and disparate writers as Caroline Adderson, Michael Winter, Steven Heighton, Libby Creelman, Russell Smith, Andrew Pyper, Mike Barnes, Annabel Lyon, Terry Griggs . . . It is also built by application to endless detail. By phone calls to alert writers to reviews. By letters to celebrate or commiserate. By conversations about books, writing, ideas, reviewing. By the press's ever-expanding Web site.

A good example of that attention to detail is the bookmarks Tim makes, each featuring an author photographed at his or her local bookstore. A simple enough thing to do, but when these bookmarks are distributed all over the country they're just one more reminder of the press's specialness.

The press also builds mythology by turning its principals into a cast of characters. When *The New Quarterly* was about to publish a special issue on my editing work, the editor, Kim Jernigan, wrote in a letter, "You have, as you must know, a reputation for being FORMIDABLE." I have no idea how this slander got abroad but Steve Heighton amplified it in his *New Quarterly* contribution.

How do I know what John is like with the others? I know because whenever I happen to meet other writers he's edited, we always end up huddled together and asking, in hushed tones, "So, what kind of thing does he write on *your* stories?"

I usually answer with a few choice samples of Metcalfian marginalia: "Another EXCREMENTAL metaphor." "Oh Christ, Heighton, are you KIDDING?" And my personal favourite, which appeared, in large caps, between the lines of an unmedicably ailing story, later put down: "YOU CAN ONLY SAY THAT ABOUT HORSES, YOU DINK."

Thus in the play that is the Porcupine's Quill I have been cast as the Formidable Editor. I have myself cast Tim as Don Quixote, writing of him ". . . if one is going to tilt at windmills, who better to ride with than that gloomy aesthete Tim Inkster with his antique Zephyr laid?"

And Elke? Elke is the *éminence grise*, the Power Behind the Throne.

Such imaginary characters are as real and vital to the living press as the cold steel of the Heidelberg Kord 64 in the workshop's basement.

Beginning in 1991 the pace of the press was picking up so fast that we were under considerable pressure. Of the five titles shortlisted for the 1991 Governor General's Award for Fiction two were Porcupine's Quill books of short stories, *Blue Husbands* by Don Dickinson and *Quickening* by Terry Griggs. And the pressure never let up. To give the reader some idea of the pace, the House of Anansi over a period of twenty-three years and under five or six editors published about 160 books. Over a period of fifteen years, alone, I will have acquired and edited more than 100 books. By the year 2000 I was feeling tired and overworked.

I had a phone call one day in 2000 from Carmine Starnino in Montreal wanting to come up to Ottawa to chat. Was it all right to bring a friend? This meeting was momentous. The friend turned out to be the poet Eric Ormsby, whose work I was already familiar with. We felt immediately at ease with each other and fell into delightful conversation in which, mutually, nothing needed to be explained. It's most unusual to feel such immediate mutual attraction.

This lovely meeting was an event I think of almost religiously as the Advent of Ormsby.

Eric studied librarianship at Rutgers University and took a Ph.D. degree from Princeton in Near Eastern studies and Classical Arabic. He has worked as a curator in Near Eastern studies at Princeton. He has been a director of libraries at two research institutions: the Catholic University of America and, for ten years, until 1996, at McGill University where he is currently a professor of Islamic studies.

He has published four collections of poetry and a recent book of essays, *Facsimiles of Time: Essays on Poetry and Translation*.

John Updike wrote about Eric's poems: "He is a most excellent poet, resonant and delicately exact with words and objects. Ormsby's reverent attention to things as they are lights up his every page with a glow."

I soon persuaded Eric to turn his reverent attention onto the Porcupine's Quill and he now functions as poetry editor for the Press, taking some of the pressure off me. His first book for the Press was David Solway's *The Lover's Progress*, followed by Norm Sibum's *Girls and Handsome Dogs*. Norm and Eric celebrated the publication of this handsome book vigorously; Norm flaked out on Eric's couch. In the morning Eric's wife, Irena, came downstairs and Norm sat up and said brightly: "Good morning! May I give you a lift home?"

Starting in 1990 the short story collections started to flow: *Victims of Gravity* by Dayv James-French; *Quickening* by Terry Griggs; *Blue Husbands* by Don Dickinson; *Flight Paths of the Emperor* by Steven Heighton; *Man and His World* by Clark Blaise; *Bad Imaginings* by Caroline Adderson; *City of Orphans* by Patricia Robertson; *A Litany in Time of Plague* by K. D. Miller; *Lives of the Mind Slaves* by Matt

Cohen . . . the list flows on and on and all the work is of very high quality, all marked by an intensity and originality in the use of language.

When I started out in the sixties Hugh Garner was considered a heavyweight; Morley Callaghan reigned. The prose was bangers-and-mash. *My* story writers are mercurial, their prose an extremely delicate instrument indeed.

I feel rash enough to claim that most of what I've chosen stands above the ruck. I am ever more certain that a writer's use of language is the key to that choosing. I wolf through manuscripts and become immediately impatient if I do not feel the urgency of the writer's language, the compression, the precision, the suggestion. I receive endless letters of inquiry which explain to me that the proposed stories are about autistic children, child abuse, gay mores in Vancouver, the problems of female artists, hospital stories from a doctor's perspective, and as I sigh and groan and curse I think of Paul Fussell's comment on Evelyn Waugh: "Waugh is indispensable today because, for one thing, he is that rarity, a writer who cares about language. He knows that writing is an affair of words rather than soul, impulse, 'sincerity,' or an instinct for the significant. If the words aren't there, nothing happens."

But the delight when the words *are* there. When I open the manila envelope and read:

> One side of Aunt Ella's face was purple. One arm and one leg were, too. The purple skin looked rougher than the rest, and I wondered if it would feel hot if I touched it. She and her brother George, who was not purple anywhere, sipped their soup exactly together. First they raised their spoons to their lips, then they took the same shivery sip, then they lowered their spoons back down to their bowls. As if they'd practiced.
>
> K. D. MILLER

Or this:

> My parents were married in a high wind that was conceived in the tropics and born in a jet stream. As it crawled up the coast, playing with flags and sailboats, teething on cliffs and peninsulas, it

matured into a lusty and vigorous gale. A product of incompatible air currents—polar and equatorial, with a trace of African Simoon ancestry—it blew like a bastard, sweeping suddenly into the orchard where the wedding ceremony was proceeding at a lazy mid-August sun-sodden pace.

TERRY GRIGGS

Or this:

His most vivid childhood memory was of sickness, which he loved. He loved staying in bed all day, reading books, eating Jell-O, flesh broth, globs of honey and aspirin crushed between two spoons. He loved the natural disorders of his body—vomiting, diarrhea, infections, swellings, pale sleeps and altered appetites. Because his parents did not believe in TV and because he had a window, Morris watched weather. He saw blushing sunrises, curtains of rain holding in the night, snow in the blue afternoons. Morris missed prodigious amounts of school, was top of his class, and never wore a hat, in the hopes of catching something special.

ANNABEL LYON

We went on to publish *On earth as it is* by Steven Heighton; *Driving Men Mad* by Elise Levine; *Influence of the Moon* by Mary Borsky; *Help Me, Jacques Cousteau* by Gil Adamson; *Lovers and Other Strangers* by Carol Malyon; *Telling My Love Lies* by Keath Fraser; *The Garden of Earthly Delights* by Meeka Walsh; *Kiss Me* by Andrew Pyper; *Buying on Time* by Antanas Sileika; *If I Were Me* by Clark Blaise; *Small Change* by Elizabeth Hay; *Promise of Shelter* by Robyn Sarah; *Learning to Live Indoors* by Alison Acheson; *Love in a Warm Climate* by Kelley Aitken; *The King of Siam* by Murray Logan; *Aquarium* by Mike Barnes; *Devil's Darning Needle* by Linda Holeman; *Give Me Your Answer* by K. D. Miller; *One Last Good Look* by Michael Winter; *Walking in Paradise* by Libby Creelman; *How Did You Sleep?* by Paul Glennon; *Oxygen* by Annabel Lyon; *The One with the News* by Sandra Sabatini; and *Gambler's Fallacy* by Judith Cowan.

People often ask where and how I find the manuscripts we publish. Very few indeed get chosen from what arrives in the mail. I've only accepted six unsolicited MSS since 1989. This is simply because most are awful in horrible ways. I look at so much material that it should be obvious I can't read it all. Connolly's paragraph plus two more for good measure are enough to do the trick. Covering letters are also a good short cut; if the salutation is "Hi!" or "Hello, Porcupine's Quill" I read no further.

I laughed in delighted recognition a few years ago when I was reading Humphrey Carpenter's biography of Ezra Pound, a life entitled *A Serious Character*. The sentences that made me laugh concerned the writer and editor Ford Madox Ford.

> Pound delighted in Ford's brisk off-the-cuff literary judgements, which were nearly always right, and in his ability as an editor to detect the quality of a manuscript almost by its smell.
>
> ("I don't read manuscripts," Ford would say, "I know what's in 'em.")

I find manuscripts by glancing at what arrives in the mail, by reading the literary magazines, and by following up the recommendations of Porcupine's Quill writers. The writers obviously have a sense of what's going to appeal to me. Steve Heighton, Elise Levine, Caroline Adderson, Leon Rooke, and Diane Schoemperlen all pass along suggestions. I trust their eyes and ears and I welcome their help; it works towards making the press a shared venture, an aesthetic underground. I was going to use the word *network* but I think the word *web* is more precise. The filaments of the web stretch from coast to coast and sometimes, nearly invisibly, stretch far back into the past.

An example of that would be Mary Swan from Guelph. She sent me a letter of inquiry. Her track record in the magazines looked good. She sent me stories and an extraordinary novella entitled "The Deep." I accepted immediately. Some weeks later she heard that "The Deep" had won first prize in the *O Henry Award Stories* in the States. All this might seem completely random but wasn't. A filament was jiggling the web. Years before, Mary had been taught in Toronto by Alice Munro. They had kept in touch. Years later when

Mary had a collection ready Alice had recommended me as an editor; "Tough but fair," Mary said Alice had said.

Another example of the way the web works. In 1980 Clark Blaise and I edited *Best Canadian Stories 80* for Oberon. We were both charmed by a story named "Esso" by a new young writer called Linda Svendsen. Years later she published the magnificent collection *Marine Life*. Fast-forward again and she is teaching writing at UBC, head of the Creative Writing Department. I got a letter from her a couple of years ago saying she had a student whose work she thought might interest me. I wrote to the student and in return was sent a wad of stories. They were astonishing, exciting, odd, entrancing. We published the stories in 2000. The book was *Oxygen*, the author Annabel Lyon.

Sometimes I receive collections of stories or novels which I don't consider publishable in their submitted form but there may be in the MS a spark of language, a tension, that suggests that the writer is capable of a better book. In that sort of case I have to take a gamble. Will I be able to tease from this writer a different book, a better book? Will the writer accept a new direction? Have I the energy to enter into this manuscript? Is this going to work between us emotionally? Or should I simply reject the manuscript? Temperamentally, I incline to the gamble; I want to bet on what the writer *will* do rather than has done.

Gil Adamson's *Help Me, Jacques Cousteau* is an example of a book that evolved. Gil came to me as a result of a recommendation by Steve Heighton. She sent in a collection of stories that seemed to me disparate in style and subject matter, too much a grab bag. I wrote to her suggesting that the funniest and the most moving of the stories concerned families and that she should group these stories together and write some new ones, thereby creating a linked collection. I sensed that at some level these particular stories had an autobiographical impulse and were intensely felt. Gil at first resisted the book I could sense but gradually relaxed into writing it.

She wrote in the book's acknowledgements: "Any resemblance to persons living or dead is not only coincidental, but is also a damned lie, according to my mother."

For the last few years I've been teaching every summer at the Humber School for Writers at Humber College in Toronto. The course is usually in the last week of July. This is developing into another source of manuscripts. I have published from Humber, Sharon English (*Uncomfortably Numb*) and Mary-Lou Zeitoun (*13*).

One of the pleasures of that week at Humber is the company of Mark Leyner, Bruce Jay Friedman, Tim O'Brien, and D. M. Thomas. In 1999 Mordecai Richler taught there and was rather badly behaved. On the opening morning of classes Joe Kertes, the director of the course, dropped into Mordecai's room to see that all was well. Mordecai was sitting on the edge of the desk smoking a cheroot and staring out of the window. The class was sitting in strained silence. Nothing seemed to be happening. Joe said brightly, "So! Shall we make a start?" Mordecai shuffled himself around and said, "What would be the point?"

For the record, however, since the first time I met him in 1970, Richler treated me with great courtesy, kindness, and generosity. I still remember with acute embarrassment interviewing him in the early seventies in his study in his Westmount house to discover halfway through that I'd pressed the wrong buttons on my tape recorder. He confined himself to a sigh.

Last year Humber was enlivened by the presence of Roddy Doyle. Mary-Lou Zeitoun read the opening chapter of her novel *13* as class work; *13* is a story as told by a thirteen-year-old punk rocker. When she'd finished, Roddy Doyle said, "Fuckin' great!" I thought that would make an excellent blurb for the back of the book. He did write one for her but it was more decorous.

In 1993 in addition to the Sherbrooke Street setback the Press suffered another. I had wanted to link the Porcupine's Quill with a similar literary press in the States or England. Literary presses have always tended to be internationalist and my hope was that we could select half a dozen American authors, say, and promote them in Canada while the other press promoted some of our authors in the States. I hoped that we could have launches and reading tours for the Americans and that all this would lead to our literary worlds drawing closer together.

Tim and I got in touch with the publisher and editorial director of Gray Wolf Press, Scott Walker. The press is based in Minneapolis. We exchanged books and catalogues and discussed on the phone the idea of some kind of co-operation. Scott and a couple of his editors were to be in New York for a book fair and we agreed to meet there. As it was a warm, pleasant day we met in Central Park and spent a few hours discussing the price of paper, unit costs, and the non-viability of short story collections in the US market. It slowly became clear that they considered our list *too* literary. I thought theirs too commercial. And their unit costs were about a quarter of ours.

This venture cost Tim a lot of money in plane fares and hotels and restaurants and I've never heard the end of it. The taxi to La Guardia drove at such demented speed that when we reached the airport, a very shaken Tim had to have a little lie-down. And the most vivid memory for both of us is the small printed posters tacked to the trees in Central Park. They said: Please Do Not Feed the Rats.

Since this attempt and after probes at Carcanet Press in England I've come to the conclusion that small presses are *necessarily* individualist. I very much value my own freedom at Porcupine's Quill and I certainly wouldn't welcome an advisory board. I find the products of boards and committees generally *lumpy*—like the annual *Journey Prize Anthology*. Though I do still sometimes hanker after an American or British component I know the deal would founder on the rock of Tim's dedication to Zephyr Antique laid.

"Sure their books are cheaper," said Tim about Gray Wolf. "Nastier, too. Nasty paper. Perfect bound."

End of subject.

He was right.

In 1994, the books were brilliant but sales were not and Tim was on the verge of bankruptcy. He phoned me in deep despond and asked me to start dismantling the list by placing our writers with other publishers. Tim needed $14,000 to survive and couldn't raise it anywhere his pride would allow him to. I called Anna Porter at Key Porter Books and we talked around the problem for a while and then I baulked. Our list was building in 1994 in exactly the way I'd dreamed. We positively glittered. *Quickening* by Terry Griggs, *Blue Husbands* by Don Dickinson, *Flight Paths of the Emperor* by Steven Heighton, *Dance with Desire* by Irving Layton, *A Night at the Opera*, by Ray Smith, *Forests of the Medieval World* by Don Coles, *Bad Imaginings* by Caroline Adderson—I *could not* cast these pearls away.

And then a dream of salvation came to me.

Sometime earlier in Ottawa on my ceaseless rounds I'd dropped in at a used book store called Benjamin Books. The owner of the store, whose interests run more in Marxist-Leninist directions than in literary ones, said he had a box of books that might interest me. The books came from the libraries of Archibald Lampman, his wife, Maud (Playter) Lampman, his father-in-law, Edward Playter, his sister Isabelle who married Ernest Voorhis, and his daughter Natalie who married Loftus MacInnes, son of the poet Tom MacInnes.

The books had belonged to a member of the Lampman–MacInnes family.

It was a treasure trove of Canadian material. It included the dedication copy of Lampman's first book, *Among the Millet and Other Poems*; he had copied out the dedicatory poem "To My Wife" and inscribed the book "To My Beloved Maud." The highlight of the collection was a holograph book of Lampman's sonnets written a year before *Among the Millet* was published. There are 101 differences between the holograph versions and the printed versions. There was also a clutch of signed presentation books to Lampman by William Wilfred Campbell, Bliss Carman, Charles G. D. Roberts, and John Henry Brown. Masses of Duncan Campbell Scott all inscribed to Lampman's daughter, Natalie. There were completely unrecorded leaflets, poems, and pamphlets. There was even a signed photograph of Duncan Campbell Scott and Rupert Brooke dated August 1913 taken in the garden of Scott's house, now destroyed, on Lisgar Street in Ottawa.

The store's owner, Mordy Bubis, really wasn't paying sufficient attention and sold the books to me for $7,000. I added to this collection a lot of Duncan Campbell Scott material I'd collected over the years down to and including his Christmas cards which all carried poems, some of them unrecorded. It seemed obvious that all this material ought to be in the National Library. I offered it but they declined, saying they already had a lot of Lampman. I thought this was rather like the British Museum saying they already had lots of Shakespeare but the National Library is something of an intellectual morgue at the best of times. Eventually I sold the entire collection to Michael Gnarowski for $20,000 which was a figure absurdly low but I needed money to save the press.

The next problem was Tim's pride. I doubted he would simply accept $14,000 as a gift. I proposed, therefore, that he sell me the archives of the Press from 1989 onwards. The University of Guelph had been buying them previously but had informed Tim and Elke that although they were still interested in acquiring them they would no longer pay. Tim agreed to my proposal and I sent him a cheque. It amused me to think that Archibald Lampman and Duncan Campbell Scott were reaching out from the grave in continued support of Canadian literature. I bought from Tim a second batch of archives when I sold my Anansi collection to the National Library. I'm hoping that this rather vast archive, along with all the edited manuscripts and correspondence, will end up in McGill's Rare Book Room.

I felt from the beginning that the books we were publishing would not survive unless they existed in a critical context, unless they were discussed and compared and evaluated. Canadian history—and that includes its literature—is a sorry, insubstantial thing like the wake of a ship, churned foam continually flattening out and disappearing, leaving no track or trace. The books can only survive if people are reading them and that is why I wanted criticism addressed to the Common Reader even if the Common Reader is in short supply. The universities seemingly have little interest in contemporary writing and their professors have chosen to look inward and talk to each other in constipated jargon. I felt that what we needed was passionate and intelligent criticism from people for whom literature was part of life, from people who lived books, from people who wanted to share their passions. I also felt that it was not essential for me, editorially, to agree with all their opinions and arguments. The important thing, it seemed to me, was the current of passion itself, a current that would engage, introduce, reevaluate, provoke, disparage, praise.

We began the critical series in 1990 with *Volleys*, a debate amongst W. J. Keith, Sam Solecki, and me about the importance of the short story as a genre. In 1991 we published *An Independent Stance* by W. J. Keith and in 1993 *How Stories Mean*, a compendium of comment by writers on the genre. These books appeared under the series title Critical Directions under the editorship of J. R. (Tim) Struthers. The books are lively but sales were bleak. Again we let the series lapse.

Conscience nagged, however, and I knew we had a duty here and so I re-started the critical series with *Ripostes* by Philip Marchand in 1998. Phil had won my early enthusiasm and support for the intelligence and vigour of his reviewing in the *Toronto Star*. The book caused a mild uproar; he had called into question the reputations of Margaret Atwood, Timothy Findley, and Michael Ondaatje. He was irreverent about the Writers' Union of Canada, saying memorably of Lenore Keeshig-Tobias, then chair of the Racial Minority Writers' Committee, that she was "famous for her ability to weep in public." The book was, amazingly, soon sold out.

We continued in 2000 with T. F. Rigelhof's *This Is Our Writing*. In 2001, Eric Ormsby's *Facsimiles of Time*. In 2002, Stephen Henighan's *When Words Deny the World*, a book which sold out entirely in about a month. I have in the works major essay collections from David Solway, Carmine Starnino, and Michael Darling.

What accounts for the success of this critical series, I believe, is its thoughtful opposition to much academic and media opinion, opposition usually backed by devastating quotation. These books are a sustained attack on what Philip Marchand in one of his essays calls "our dogged Canadian willingness to be bored."

Terry Rigelhof on Robertson Davies suggests the tone:

> If Davies hadn't added two more volumes to turn *Fifth Business* into the first volume of the Deptford Trilogy and demonstrated that he was incapable of writing in anything other than a stilted style or inventing any voice, male or female, that wasn't Dunstan Ramsay's, I'd be more tempted to celebrate his achievement here.

I'm pleased with the impact of the critical series. It is impinging on the awareness even of those not much given to reading.

The lacklustre *Globe and Mail* columnist James Adams launched a counterattack recently in his *Weekend Diary*. He quotes the travel writer Pico Iyer:

> When a Canuck reads a sentence such as "Toronto is by official UN statistics the single most multicultural city in the world; it is also statistically the safest city in North American and, by the

reckoning of many, the one with the richest literary culture," he or she automatically tenses up and gets ready for the follow-through put-down.

Which had that sentence been written by John Metcalf, Stephen Henighan, Philip Marchand or another member of the Porcupine's Quill group, would have occurred.

Notice the pathetic implication—*as always*—that to criticize a Canadian book is to criticize Canada. Where does the newspaper *find* these stand-on-guard dorks?

In 1997 Tim Inkster acquired from Douglas Fetherling the journal *Canadian Notes and Queries*. Fetherling had shifted the journal away from academic concerns and towards being "a periodical of Canadian literary and cultural history." I took over the editorship with Number 51.1. We regard *CNQ* as a part of the critical component of the Porcupine's Quill. With our reviews, profiles, interviews, and essays we wish to intrude rudely on the bland mindlessness of Canadian literary life. Michael Darling is the book review editor. Carmine Starnino is the poetry editor.

In 2001 we published a brilliant essay by David Solway entitled "Standard Average Canadian or The Influence of Al Purdy." In essence, the essay described Purdy as the Stompin' Tom Connors of Canadian poetry and deplored his influence on younger poets.

Tim had been receiving a grant of $3,000 a year towards the magazine's expenses from the Ontario Arts Council. After the David Solway essay appeared, Lorraine Filyer, the Ontario Arts Council Literary Supremo, phoned Tim and informed him that she and her henchthingies, as Frank magazine would say, had decided to reduce his grant to zero. The reason she gave was the journal's "lack of editorial vision." Tim promptly secured financing for the magazine from the Upper Canada Brewing Company, a better class of people.

The most recent issue of the journal was a special issue on Norman Levine. Cynthia Flood contributed a definitive essay on Norman's style which is the very model of what literary criticism should be.

Norman wrote in the journal: "*Canada Made Me* was published by Putnam in November 1958. A long review by Paul West in the Christmas issue of the *New Statesman and Nation* was read by Honor

Balfour of the London office of *Time*. She interviewed me. When her piece appeared, the 500 copies that McClelland had went quickly. He wouldn't take any more. Nor would any other Canadian publisher. I had to accept that Canadian publishing was closed to my work."

Norman told me that when he was writer-in-residence at UNB in Fredericton he gave a reading at the Saint John campus and afterwards a professor came up to him and said, "Are you the Levine that wrote *Canada Made Me*?" Norman said that he was and the scholar spat at his feet and walked away.

Yet I've long held that *Canada Made Me* sits at the centre of Canadian literature. It is concerned with the essence of Canada: immigration, the lives of immigrants. How deeply that spitting scholar would loathe such an opinion! Not many readers have discovered the book yet but we have reprinted it and it is available. It sells three or four copies in a year. It will not go away. We do somewhat better with the reprint of *From a Seaside Town* but only because the Tate St. Ives buys copies regularly.

Norman is of singular importance to me. He is the very figure of the artist. He has worked quietly for decades forging a radical style. He has survived. He has survived the indifference of audience and he has produced stories which are at the centre of achievement in Canadian literature, "A Small Piece of Blue," "We All Begin in a Little Magazine," "Champagne Barn," "Something Happened Here" . . .

He has also had to endure the crassness of the Canadian literary world. I have already mentioned that Cynthia Good of Penguin Books Canada, who published *Champagne Barn* and, later, *Something Happened Here*, was quoted in the *Ottawa Citizen* as saying: "At the time, we considered Norman to be on a par with Alice Munro or Mavis Gallant. We weren't alone. That's how many people viewed him at the time."

At the time?

She is quoted later as saying that sales of *Something Happened Here* were "modest." Aha! Norman's fall from grace was linked to numbers, was it? She is equating sales with achievement. And in this she's not alone.

Jenny Jackson, the *Ottawa Citizen* books columnist, wrote in review of Clark Blaise: "The book is put out by Porcupine's Quill, the press of the unjustly forgotten, those with the PR epitaph 'a writer's writer'. . ." Her words attempt to be patronizing. She goes on to gloat that Clark never "broke through" to a "mass audience." Could one suggest that if writers are "unjustly forgotten" then it just might be the duty of a books columnist to *seek* justice for them. "A writer's writer" means that the writer is so good other writers are influenced by him or her. Isn't Jackson's job to connect that excellence with a readership? But it isn't really literature that is her subject matter. What she's really interested in is *exactly* PR. Recently she wrote in a review of Stephen Henighan: "His first four books of fiction have earned respectful reviews, if little money."

Sales.

Numbers.

What a squalid little mind she has! I despise her pat acceptance of the status quo. People who employ numbers arguments are usually coarse souled. I had thought of sending her a poker-work plaque, elegantly executed, of the old graffito: Eat Shit! Fifty Billion Flies Can't Be Wrong!

Sarah Hampson, continuing this trend of Levine-bashing, wrote a slighting and obtuse profile of Norman which was published in the *Globe and Mail* in July 2002. She concentrated on what she perceived as his eccentricity and his penury.

"Levine unlocks the door to his apartment; pushes it forward and gestures for me to enter first. The smell of time rises up from a soiled mauve carpet, a sagging floral-print sofa . . ."

She managed not to see his grandeur.

Inspired by Norman's anecdotes over the years about St. Ives and about the painters who were his friends—Peter Lanyon, Terry Frost, Patrick Heron, and Francis Bacon—Myrna and I decided to go there for a holiday to see the Alfred Wallis paintings in the Tate St. Ives. Wallis was a primitive painter so powerful that after you've seen the paintings you can only see St. Ives itself through his eyes. He died in 1942 and is buried in the cemetery above Porthmeor Beach in a grave covered with Bernard Leach tiles.

Holidays with Myrna are usually boot-camp affairs as she insists on climbing mountains, hacking across moors in knee-deep heather, squelching through bogs. On this occasion she wheeled me into walking the cliff path from St. Ives to Zennor, an expedition I now think of as the Zennor Death March. The distance is only about ten miles but the path follows the ups and downs of the headlands and the "walk" often becomes a vertiginous scrabble, the sea surging and sloshing hundreds of feet below; later, I read that that walk was rated as "severe." We did this without water or proper shoes and many hours later collapsed in Zennor into the one-roomed Tinners' Arms, a pub once frequented by Katherine Mansfield and D. H Lawrence, where we rehydrated with many pints of meditative ale. And caught the Land's End bus back to St. Ives.

Between 1989 and 2002 the Porcupine's Quill has published about twenty novels. I said earlier that I felt that most of what I'd chosen to publish stands above the ruck. I feel this more strongly about the story collections than I do about the novels. There are a few story collections, too, that I have reservations about but novels present real problems. They do everywhere. I wonder sometimes if Canada has ever produced a great novel. Possibly Mordecai Richler's *St. Urbain's Horseman.* I'm still not sure.

There are twentieth-century names against which we have to weigh all novels before we can talk lightly of "greatness" or "significance." Conrad, Joyce, Beckett, Naipaul, Waugh, Nabokov . . .

The recent Toronto media uproar about Dennis Bock's ill-written *The Ash Garden* is a perfect illustration of judgements passed without the felt weight of tradition. A perfect line for a critic is Spender's "I think continually of those who were truly great." What I am getting at is that there are thousands of novels but very few like, say, Graham Swift's *Waterland.* We ought to *know* the fate of most of "The New Face of Fiction." Most novels are fated to become literature's leafmould.

Leafmould. Concurrent with the writing of this book I've been editing for the Press, of course, and putting together an issue of *Canadian Notes and Queries* containing an essay on the House of Anansi and a bibliography of the press which runs from the founding in 1967 to 1989 when the press was bought by Jack Stoddart. Noting what was published year after year and trying to decide now what was worthy and what was a mistake has inevitably left me considering the value of what I am doing with the Porcupine's Quill. How much of the work is likely *not* to become leafmould? Anansi published forty-eight poetry titles; I'd say that seven are still of interest. Of the fifty-five fiction titles there are thirteen I can reread and commend.

It is not a criticism of the House of Anansi that so many of its books have become leafmould. The books of any literary press—of all presses—are of a time and place and it is inevitable that many will not be of lasting significance. But cherished by posterity or forgotten entirely, all these books are essential in the growth of a nation's literature. What is important is, in Dennis Lee's words, that we "wrestle with the mind and passion of our own time and place." What is important is that ambitious books are written and read, that new writers are launched, new readers won over, that the delight of reading and writing is handed on. The shape and significance of a literature take a very long time to reveal themselves.

There were reasons why the House of Anansi published so much that was fated to disappear. Anansi was a strident nationalist wake-up call to an almost comatose industry. The very act of publishing a Canadian book was for Anansi a political act. The press was also under enormous pressure to publish from the generation it was addressing. And publish it did—poets, hippies, ravers, practitioners of experimental prose, American draft evaders, cosmic weed smokers . . . Anansi was perhaps too much a part of the sixties ferment to be objective about its choices.

I have some hopes that the publications of the Porcupine's Quill will fare better. I haven't had to suffer the heated expectation of an entire generation as Anansi did; during the years I've been editing almost the reverse has been true. Literature has lost its sixties and seventies glamour, nationalism has languished, cultural ferment has subsided into apathy and indifference. Ideal conditions for making cool—and purely aesthetic—choices. Another factor in favour of the survival of Porcupine's Quill books is that I am much older than Dennis Lee was when he was making those choices, older and less driven. I like to think that age gives me a certain distance; I'm less likely than Dennis was to get involved in the moment.

All of which brings me circling back to the subject of novels. Most "mainstream" novels are fated to become leafmould and this is why I try to keep away from them. A nasty part of me rubs its hands with glee whenever I read in a review that a novel records the doings of two or three generations of whoever . . . *there's* one I won't have to bother with.

As I put this in "Travelling Northward":

> Six figure sums were routinely advanced to *artistes* who penned swollen sagas of powerful industrial families, of immigrant families rising from poverty to become powerful industrialists, of landowning families who diversified into powerful new industries and became more powerful than they'd been before but at the same time becoming riven by incest, insanity, possession by the devil, litigation and Alzheimer's, homosexual and lesbian inversion, poltergeists and hysterectomy, losing that guiding vision of their founder old Grandfather Ebenezer who used to kneel on the good earth running soil through his wise old fingers saying wise dawn things to little barefoot Mattie who never forgot a single utterance . . . and who went on to found an empire in oil, microchips, and laser-beam technology before renouncing the world and establishing an Ecological Foundation and Nature Reserve in memory of Grandfather Ebenezer where she cleaned up oil-fouled seabirds and imparted gentle wisdom to little barefoot Bobbie who three hundred pages later would corner the world market in extruded protein.

Working with Tim and Elke I'm able to publish novels which are eccentric and quirky, novels no commercial house would ever touch. I cannot write about them all but I delight in having published Alexander Scala's *Dr. Swarthmore*, Keath Fraser's *Popular Anatomy*, Susan Perly's *Love Street*, Leo Simpson's *Sailor Man*, Terry Griggs's *The Lusty Man*, Ray Smith's *A Night at the Opera*, and Harold Rhenisch's *Carnival*.

I don't claim that these are "great" novels but they're lovely performances and they all gave me great pleasure. Alexander Scala's *Dr. Swarthmore*, a darkly comic tale of divine revelation and capitalism, has a curious history. Scala wrote it after leaving Harvard when he was twenty-two. He submitted it to Penguin Books which rejected it on the quaint grounds of blasphemy. Scala was so insulted that he put the MS in a drawer for thirty years. Steven Heighton in Kingston, a friend of Scala's, read the MS and phoned me to commend it. I loved the book from its opening page.

A review said of it: "Assuredly the first novel of the new millennium in which the Second Person of the Trinity has a walk-on part in a cheap suit."

All of these novels received far less than their due because they are all unusual and demanding and we do not have enough money to publicize them in the way the commercial houses do. Brenda Sharpe, who created the Porcupine's Quill Web site, claims that Leo Simpson's *Sailor Man* is one of the best books the Press has ever published. It received, to the best of my knowledge, one review, and sold 368 copies.

Of all our novels *How Insensitive* and *Noise* by Russell Smith have provided me with the most fun. I received from Russell a letter of the utmost snottiness and a sample chapter of *How Insensitive*. The letter, as I recall it, described Canadian literature as being concerned with angst on farms. Canadian literature was written by boring middle-aged people for other boring middle-aged people. *His* book, in contrast, was by a young urban person and reflected Canada's *real* urban concerns and blah, blah. He concluded the letter by saying more or less that I probably wouldn't like the book because I was myself a boring middle-aged establishment fart. I was charmed by the sheer aggression of this letter and even more charmed by the writing itself. Russell has written scenes more brilliantly funny than any other Canadian writer. He is a master of dialogue. Comparison with Kingsley Amis would not be inappropriate. *How Insensitive* sold an astonishing number of copies—well into the thousands. *Noise*, a better book, sold far fewer copies. Inexplicable. Although *How Insensitive* was short-listed for the Governor General's Award, reviews of both books have been mixed and there is in general a grudging reaction to Russell's work. Part of this can be explained by the fact that Canadians tend to resist humour. They are made uneasy by sophistication and Russell is *very* sophisticated indeed. He is also an intellectual and his questing intelligence is displayed in the construction of his prose and in the narrative devices he invents.

I fell into his work with immediate relish because I recognized how supremely gifted he is and I also recognized—and deeply approved of—his influences—Waugh and Kingsley Amis. There is about Russell a very British quality which comes from his South African background and that too might explain Canadian unease with his sprightly writing.

Here's a snippet of two punks in a Swiss Chalet, from *Noise*; his work is crammed with such vignettes.

There were two punks with mohawks at the cash counter, waiting for someone to materialize behind it. James waited behind them for a minute. There didn't seem to be anybody working in the whole place. He shivered in the air conditioning. The Muzak breezed along. The punks were looking about, too. They had a glazed look. One of them had a T-shirt which read, "WHERE'S THE FUCKING MONEY YOU OWE ME?"

"What's with all these pictures of like Heidi houses?" said one.

The other one squinted at the blown-up posters on the walls. "Switzerland," he announced.

"Why Switzerland?"

"It's a Swiss Chalet, right."

James glimpsed movement through a hatch into the kitchen, and waved his arm at whatever it was.

"I don't get Switzerland," said the first punk, as slowly as if in a dream. "I mean it's never really turned me on, you know?"

"Yeah. It's not sexy."

"Exactly. Switzerland's not sexy. Fuck Switzerland."

"Fucking Swiss bastards. Fuck 'em."

The novels I choose for the Press are always fun but the main focus for me remains short fiction. The Press is already *the* press for the short story, so in 2002 I turned my attention to a related form, the novella. I suggested to Tim that we start publishing stand-alone novellas. The form is an awkward one for publishers; conventional wisdom is that novellas are too long for magazines and too short for books and if they're published at all they're published in collections of stories.

I wanted to take novellas out of their surrounding clutter and shine the spotlight on them in much the same way that museum curators have abandoned display cabinets crammed with jumbled objects and have highlighted a few exquisite artifacts in austere cases.

A single novella can live in one's mind and imagination as vividly as can a novel. There is no need to defend the idea. I simply look back at the years of pleasure given me by such novellas as Thomas Mann's "Death in Venice," Nathanael West's "Miss Lonelyhearts," Philip Roth's "Goodbye, Columbus," Evelyn Waugh's "Scott-King's Modern Europe" . . . We started our programme with two intense and sophisticated novellas by David Helwig ("The Stand-In") and Mary Swan ("The Deep").

Some people are curious about the process of editing. I have always felt editing to be mildly impertinent and arrogant and I only feel that I can do it because I am a writer myself and know that most of the writers I work with have read my fiction and have some regard for it.

Major editing involves rearranging the building blocks of a story, cutting passages, finding a more effective starting place, giving greater weight to pertinent images. This is emotional and intuitive work.

Minor editing, though vastly important, is line-by-line testing and probing. An aspect of this kind of editing more common than readers might suppose is forcing writers to be logical and precise. I edited two books for the Honourable Heward Grafftey, science minister in Joe Clark's brief government, because he was a neighbour and because I like him. I remember handing him a chapter scored with red ink marking lapses in logic.

"But, well," he sputtered, "I am by training a lawyer."

"Then I'm glad," I replied, "you're not representing *me*."

I once wrote jokingly that the essence of editing was to go through each typescript finding the word *careen* and crossing it out. Writers refuse to accept that the word means "to cause a ship to lean or lie on one side for calking, barnacle removal, or repair." It can (only just) have an extended meaning of leaning sideways but such a meaning is compromised by its "ship" connotations. The word derives from the Latin *carina*, the keel of a ship. Writers believe the word to mean "rapid motion" or "reckless motion" possibly confusing it with *career*, from the Latin *currere*, to run, with connotations of war chariots. Driving this through writerly skulls is difficult.

The ideal editor must accept the uniqueness of each text and deal with it on its own terms. I try not to impose anything of my own style but rather seek to understand a book's rhetoric and then work to ensure that the writer performs that rhetoric to the top of his bent. I also feel quite strongly that an editor can only *suggest* changes; the writer must be ultimately responsible for the work.

The level and depth of editorial meddling is dictated not by some abstract theory but by the typescript itself. Sometimes good editing is the ability to see when little or none is needed. There are some writers who are so painstaking and meticulous and who have so burnished their manuscripts that editing is more or less a formality. I'm thinking here of such writers as Keath Fraser, Caroline Adderson, Annabel Lyon, and Mary Borsky.

Editorial meddling also has national characteristics. The British generally tend to feel that getting a book *right* is the writer's problem; they are less likely than other nationalities to accept a flawed book and work on it. American editors, because they *are* editors and editors *edit*, are more likely to regard finished books as interesting *seeds* of possible books. Consider the editing career of Gordon Lish at Knopf and *Esquire*; his work on Raymond Carver was so extensive that some American critics have said that Lish's name should be on the books as co-author. When I came to Canada in the sixties there were editors but at the Ryerson Press they were usually ex-salesmen who had done well on the road and had been rewarded with a comfortable berth in Toronto; they seemed to favour books on antique cars. I also had an impression that many editors in Canada were from the UK just as trade union activists seemed to be exclusively Scottish.

Some writers operate in what I think of as "closed systems." You can't go inside them except in superficial ways. This is because they've perfected a style and vocabulary that is so idiosyncratic or mannered that an outsider, an editor, cannot really contribute. Terry Griggs would be a good Canadian example. Ronald Firbank springs to mind. How did Robert Bridges edit Gerard Manley Hopkins? All that an editor can usefully do with a closed-system writer is say, These stories are stronger than these, so let's drop the weaker ones. This was exactly the process with Terry Griggs's extraordinary collection *Quickening*.

At the opposite end of the scale are writers whose work cries out for intercession. This is not to be negatively critical. A writer's style is the outcome of, among other things, temperament. Some writers write in a passionate outpouring of words and that approach seems to them necessary and natural. Steven Heighton writes in this way and in my editing of his work I always attempt to prune his lushness, concentrate, suggest the dryness of *fino* rather than the sugar of *oloroso*, the marksman's rifle rather than the shotgun blast. He is always good-natured about my plaintive nagging. In the *New Quarterly* special issue on my editing work Steve reproduced a letter I'd sent him about a story which appeared in his collection *On earth as it is*. The story was "Townsmen of a Stiller Town" which takes place in a morgue, an important detail given my first quoted note.

I wrote in part . . . "P. 22. If Basil had been drinking rye his breath wouldn't be 'briny.' What about 'a breath as foul and harsh as formaldehyde'?

"P. 20, middle of page. 'Joliffe's pipe on its side, sifting ash over papers.'

"You *cannot* say this. 'To sift' is a precise action of riddling material over a grill—metaphorically, I suppose you could 'sift through archives.' But a *pipe* can't *sift*.

"*Please* please an old man and change this.

"Sorry to fuss so much but getting things *right* will mean that your work will live. Get them *wrong* and wild dogs will gnaw at your corpse."

Possibly the loving combat I'm always locked in with Steve comes from my own temperament, from my own neurotic writing methods. I write an initial sentence usually many times over until it strikes me as perfect in diction and rhythm. Then I do the same thing with the second sentence. But joining the second sentence to the first changes both and so I rewrite both. This slightly mad process goes on, sentence by sentence, for weeks.

Sometimes manuscripts beg to be reshaped or rewritten. It often happens that the energy level in a story drops in one or more places. A good editor can feel these lapses or collapses as easily as an electrician can check current with a voltmeter. Conversely the voltmeter can pick up an energy surge; sometimes a paragraph or a couple of pages will stand out from surrounding competence and proclaim themselves and it often turns out that that paragraph or those pages are the emotional core of the story demanding to be taken out and reshaped.

To return to the image of a voltmeter checking current. This is as real to me as sewing on buttons might be for someone else. And, for me, as commonplace. I remember performing tricks once at the Humber School for Writers. A student submitted a story to the class and I rather astonished her by saying, "This story you've totally invented just as you've invented the characters. It's all rather plodding, I'm afraid. The only place in the story where you've connected to any real emotion is in the description of the inside of the sheds in the garden. And those sheds are drawn from your own life and childhood." She agreed that this was true, so I sent her off to think more about sheds.

I am not saying here that the current surges because material is autobiographical or "sincere," or that the "real" is more real than the imagined. It is simply that the real, the sheds, came alive in her story because *nouns* were coming into play. She was looking at *things* rather than playing with Lego. Sometimes the voltmeter picks up a sentence or paragraph because the writer is not concentrating sufficiently on the imagined world. When writers wander from the concrete, the particular, the current always drops. As I work on this book, I'm working with an ex-Humber student, Judith McCormack, on a short story collection. One of the stories is called "The Cardinal Humours." Here is its opening sentence:

When Eduardo de Majia left Barcelona on an overcast, grey-yellow day in the fall of 1873, he left behind his wife and his two sons, and he took with him trunks and barrels of medicaments, bitter syrups, dried herbs, astringent tonics, white powders of various kinds, and sixty-three vials of tinctures.

I noticed that I wrote to her . . . "Page 1 'white powders of various kinds' is very weak after the more specific things which precede. Try one of: nostrums, infusions, lenitives, paregorics, carminatives, balsams—all words fitting to the tradition and period.

"'Bitter syrups' also sounds a bit dodgy. 'Syrup' is defined as 'any *sweet* thick liquid.' Rethink this one.

"And come to think of it, 'astringent tonics' sounds a touch unlikely."

Well, I admit.

It possibly *is* a strange way to spend one's days.

Of recent years, Tim and I have had to revise our vision of the Press. Our earlier conventional assumptions about nurturing careers crumbled under the increasing commercialization of the industry in Canada and the advent of agents. Our writers were being offered advances we couldn't come anywhere near meeting and they defected to Doubleday, Anansi, Key Porter, HarperCollins, McClelland and Stewart, Random House, and Knopf. I suggested to Tim that under his logo he print: *Purveyors to the Trade.* Tim, reviewing the list of publishers and authors, said rather grimly, "Well, I suppose we must be doing *something* right."

We sulked for a while but soon came around to realize that we couldn't expect young writers to turn down the chance of a reasonable income when all we can offer is an advance of $500. We understood that we'd have to see the function and purpose of the Porcupine's Quill differently. We had become, willy-nilly, a launching pad for careers, so we needed to stop thinking "defection" and to embrace the new reality. We needed to see ourselves as talent scouts and expansive impresarios. Tim, with his always wily business sense, recouped some of his expenses by selling authors' first books to the larger publishers of their second books for republication and then, with considerable chutzpah, advertising the fact on his Web site, thereby using the major publishers to aggrandize the Porcupine's Quill's reputation.

I want to end this section on the Porcupine's Quill on a celebratory note because I feel we have much to celebrate. The Press has achieved all that I'd wanted at the beginning. Our writers are elegant and sophisticated. They love language and flaunt it. Joan Harcourt's "carefully crafted reliquaries, little boxes in which are enshrined little memories" have been firmly suppressed. And the Press does indeed crackle with energy. There's little question we're the best literary press in Canada. Perhaps in North America.

Along with acquiring manuscripts and editing where necessary and with printing and binding, a press has to *sell* books. Launchings are an effective way of selling books and are necessary to an author's sense of occasion. We launched books in Toronto and Ottawa and I'll conclude with an account of the Magnum Reading Series and the celebration of Irving Layton's eightieth birthday.

That one evening can stand for the entire spirit of the Porcupine's Quill adventure.

In 1990 I was in Toronto visiting Tony Calzetta. Tony had an exhibition on at the Lake Gallery and we went together to look at the paintings. I was introduced to Fran Hill, the gallery's director. Chatting with Fran was a friend from university days, Lise Giroux. Fran and Lise had both studied art history at York University. Lise told me that she, too, was from Ottawa and was opening a bookstore there. I promised to drop in. The Magnum Readings and Exhibitions Series evolved from this chance encounter.

Lise Giroux and Yoni Freeman together ran side-by-side establishments, the Magnum Book Store and Opus Bistro. The bookstore was managed by Paula Black while Opus was managed by Lise. Yoni, originally from Israel, was the presiding culinary genius. Prior to opening Opus he had worked under Jamie Kennedy and Michael Stadtlander, two of Toronto's most acclaimed chefs, at the Scaramouche restaurant. When I reported to Myrna that Yoni was from Israel, she, as an ex-kibbutznik, claimed that the words *Israeli chef* constituted a perfect oxymoron but she was won over after the first mouthful.

The Opus Bistro quickly built a reputation as being one of the best restaurants in Ottawa. It was always packed with noisy and happy diners and reservations were necessary days in advance. *Where to Eat in Canada (1993)* raved about Yoni's cooking:

> His cooking may look simple and straight-forward, but actually it's about as simple as an ode by Horace. Try his black-bean soup with smoked pork, his blue-cheese salad with pears, his baked salmon with horseradish and sour cream—which we much

prefer to his blackened sole. The menu is constantly changing and dishes like liver with calvados, cellentani with fresh squid and mussels, salmon with pink peppercorns and roast duckling with sour cherries are now little but a memory . . .

It seemed obvious to all of us that good food and drink were the natural partners of good books and paintings. Our conversations circled around ways and means and motives. Lise had a vision of the Magnum Book Store becoming a cultural centre and a cultural force in Ottawa. Sitting at the commodious Opus bar we consumed many a meditative Gibson (two ounces of Bombay Sapphire gin, three drops of vermouth, two cocktail onions).

We were setting out, we realized, to build a community. We were tired of cultural events being ghettoized in universities and auditoria, tired of institutional battery-acid coffee in Styrofoam cups, tired of littered floors, tired of dragooned student audiences wearing reversed baseball caps. We wanted something more intimate and gracious. We wanted the audience involved in the whole venture, able to meet and mingle with the writers and painters and—which is just as important—with each other. We wanted everyone to share in a coffee, a beer, a glass of wine, and enjoy paintings and conversation in a relaxed atmosphere.

This idea of building a community was also pursued in the generous hosting of writers and painters at Opus Bistro for dinner on the Saturday preceding the reading on Sunday evening. But—central question in the arts—who was going to pay the bills? We had visions of corporate sponsors and of sponsorship by publishers but these visions remained visions. No corporate entity showed the slightest interest in what we were attempting. Inevitably, Lise and Yoni shouldered the burden; Fran Hill and I helped by donating our time and energies.

I suggested to Lise a mechanism that would allow us to pay the readers and give us at the same time a faint chance to recoup some of our costs. We would ask each reader to give us a piece of previously unpublished work. For this work we would give the reader $200— the same sum paid by the Canada Council for a reading. I would then make thirty Xerox copies of the piece and staple them into card covers. Each would carry the following statement of limitation:

*Here first published in a edition of thirty copies
of which
four are* hors de commerce *and
twenty-six are numbered and signed.*

This we did for every reading. We charged $25 for these limited editions. They cost about $100 to make, so adding that to the fee paid the reader brought the cost to $300. To break even we had to sell twelve. This never happened. Nor in nine years of operation at Magnum and at other venues did we attract a single student or professor from either of Ottawa's universities.

I stapled the Xeroxed sheets into blue card covers and gradually these expensive editions became known as "Blue Things." Some Toronto dealers had standing orders for multiple copies but the audience in general was unable to see the significance of the severity of the limitation. I saw one of the early "Blue Things," Leon Rooke's story "Daddy Stump," quoted in a rare book dealers' catalogue recently at $225.

To help in building the community and to publicize the readings and exhibitions we sent out a Xeroxed newsletter to a mailing list we were always building. Lise also listed the readings and exhibitions on the daily menus. We did this not merely as advertising but because we wanted to integrate literature and painting into daily life.

The newsletters typically had notes on the writers by me, comments on the exhibitions by the painters themselves, Paula Black's list of new and recommended books, and a recipe by Yoni—Fall Fruit Chutney, Barbecue Flank Steak Sandwich, Shrimp with Feta Cheese and Harissa . . . that last the beginnings of Yoni's obsession with extremely hot peppers.

The design and organization of the newsletter was taken over by Brenda Sharpe who, like all of us, donated her time and expertise to the enterprise.

The Magnum Readings and Exhibitions Series started in April 1991 with a reading by me and an exhibition by Tony Calzetta. Since then we heard Leon Rooke, Hugh Hood, Ray Smith, Dayv James-French, Terry Griggs, Diane Schoemperlen, Rohinton Mistry, Joan MacLeod, Douglas Glover, Irving Layton, Jane Urquhart, Mark

Frutkin, Don Dickinson, Clark Blaise, Norman Levine, Carol Shields, Steven Heighton, Gael Turnbull, George Elliott Clarke, Matt Cohen, Audrey Thomas, Yann Martel, Isabel Huggan, John Mills, John Newlove, and the adorable Caroline Adderson.

We hung exhibitions by Tony Calzetta, Andrea Bolley, David Bolduc, Alex Cameron, Richard Gorman, Gordon Rayner, Tony Urquhart, Peter Templeman, Blair Sharpe, Dieter Grund, Catherine Beaudette, and Clive D'Oliviera with a summer show of photographs of the readings by our "official" photographer, Micheline Rochette.

Right from the start there seemed to be something magical about the series. The first audience was about a hundred strong and we never dipped lower than thirty-five. Magnum Book Store had a small café area at the rear where Yoni served lunch four days a week. Those walls as well as space in the bookstore proper were hung with paintings. And the *kind* of interaction that I'd dreamed of actually happened. While the first show was up—works on paper by Tony Calzetta—two women were having lunch in the Magnum café. When finished, they asked the waiter for the bill and one of them, pointing at the pictures, said, "And I'd like that one and she'll take the pale pink one over there."

Perfect.

Exactly the way pictures should be bought.

Burt Heward, the *Ottawa Citizen* books editor, covered our activities faithfully in his Saturday column and Nancy Baele, the *Citizen* art critic, covered most of the shows. The CBC began to record the readings and interview the writers. Gradually we began to recognize the same faces in the audience and in the Opus Bistro afterwards. We began to put names to faces. We were beginning to grow into a community.

Because we developed a core of regulars and because those regulars came to trust my taste I was able to present at Magnum writers who were not well-known—in some cases Porcupine's Quill writers launching a first book—and give them the experience of a large and enthusiastic audience. I even dared to present five poets—Carol Shields, Irving Layton, Gael Turnbull, George Elliott Clarke, and John Newlove.

There were some wonderful moments at the Magnum Readings but the most moving of the weekends was that on which we staged a party for Irving Layton's eightieth birthday. The Porcupine's Quill had just released *Dance with Desire: The Love Poems of Irving Layton*. The first copies arrived at Magnum the day before the party. I had commissioned Richard Gorman to do drawings for the book and Rick had come down from Toronto to celebrate the occasion.

(While the book was in production I'd gone to Rick's house to pick up the drawings. It was a surreal morning. Rick had been up all night drinking brandy and painting. He showed me around. Kitchen. A living room draped in sheet plastic used as a studio. Bedroom. Then he opened a door onto a room entirely bare. He made no comment. Lying on the floorboards were three very dead Christmas trees.)

Lise had set up a big table in the bookstore café area and had festively set the table with a centrepiece of mimosa. Present were Rick Gorman, Fran Hill and friend, Doris Cowan, Ken Rockburn, Micheline Rochette, Randall Ware, Myrna and I, and, of course, Irving and his wife Anna.

Ken Rockburn ran a CBC radio show called *Medium Rare* which featured music and interviews with writers and musicians. He asked if he might discreetly record the dinner conversation. He later broadcast an edited version on his program.

I bought some hand-made paper and Myrna designed and printed special menus. We also contributed a couple of bottles of Veuve Clicquot to toast Irving and wish him many happy returns. What a splendid evening it was! What bits of it I remember. I've never dared listen to the tape.

IN HONOUR OF IRVING LAYTON
On the occasion of
Irving Layton's
eightieth birthday
and on the launching of
Dance with Desire: The Love Poems of Irving Layton
Saturday, March 7, 1993

Split Pea Soup with Smoked Pork
or
Avocado Salad with Salmon Caviar
(Konocti Fumé Blanc, Lake County, California 1989)

Baked Lamb Rack with Rosemary Sauce
or
Gulf Shrimps with Roasted Red Peppers and Garlic
(Vina Santa Rita Reserva, Maipo Valley, Chile 1988)

Chocolate Terrine with Fresh Strawberries

Ken Rockburn not only recorded conversation at the dinner but subsequently wrote a memoir. Here's a brief excerpt from his 1995 book *Medium Rare: Jamming with Culture*:

The evening began with a round of toasts to Layton, who, in turn raised his glass to his wife, Anna, for her "love, compassion and inspiration." He then proposed a challenge to the table that would be responsible for the progress of the remainder of the evening; he asked each of us to recall some strange and wonderful story, something which had happened to us personally that we could not explain, some odd occurrence or, better still, some eerie event or coincidence which illustrated the mystery of life.

"Because this is an unusual evening," he said, "where writers and painters and sculptors are getting together. You know, what the hell is literature all about, what the hell is poetry all about if it isn't about a defiance of reality? Reality smells, it stinks, unless it's gotten ahold of by the artists who transmute it into something strange and wonderful. So I want strange stories that show the remarkable and the magical in all our lives. Those of us who are lucky enough to have a line to our childhood know it's there."

As Layton spoke, his wife Anna, sitting beside him, would watch him carefully, picking up his napkin from the floor when it slid unnoticed from his lap, providing an appropriate word when one failed to come to him, or repeating in his ear the words of one of the other guests if Layton failed to hear. Her attention was unobtrusive and not in the least patronizing, which could easily have been the case for any other couple whose age difference was nearly 50 years . . .

"I will soon be 80 . . ."

"You are." From Anna.

"Anna is . . ."

Anna smiled. 'Thirty-two."

"Thirty-two. I am Jewish—listen carefully, take it in—Anna is an Acadian, a Catholic. In other words, her cultural background is quite different from mine. The disparity in age is quite clear."

All eyes tried not to be on Anna.

"I mean, 80," Layton shook his head. "A guy of 80 doesn't even dream of an erection anymore, you know."

"Oh, Irving," chided Metcalf, "stop telling these awful lies."

"Surely you dream?" I asked hopefully.

"Irving," offered Richard Gorman, "you won't be 80 until you're 110."

"God bless you for saying that," said Layton. "But you would say, if you were a sociologist, that the chances of the two of us having a happy and successful and wonderful marriage that has endured for nearly ten years, would be very slim. Very few would be willing to bank their savings on anything like this.

"Yet here are Anna and I, after ten years, as much in love, if not more, than we were at the beginning. And that's what life is all about, that's what poetry is all about, that's what the poets are always talking about. They're always trying to make people aware that there is magic about, the unpredictable, there's chance and there's beauty and there's love."

More food came, more wine was consumed and more stories were told. Myrna Metcalf told of a strange encounter at the neolithic stone ring at Avebury, the dishevelled Richard Gorman told a wonderful tale about giving the Rideau River offerings of tobacco, in the Indian fashion, for allowing itself to be the subject of a mural he was painting, and how the ritual had attracted all manner of wildlife to the spot; the brooding boyfriend of Fran Hill told a story that *seemed* to involve drug use and that weird state of consciousness between sleep and wakefulness, though everyone was too drunk by that time to understand whatever it was he was trying to say.

On Sunday, the scene at Magnum Books was pure Hollywood. People were lined up for a full block an hour before the reading was

supposed to start. We had engaged the services of an off-duty police-
man to handle the door and as the time ticked by we began to fear for
public safety. The bookstore was jammed with bodies. Every chair
was taken, people were sitting on the floor and standing three deep
around the walls. Fervent Layton fans had come from as far away as
Montreal and London.

We estimated that we crowded in about 190 people and we
turned away another 130 or so at the door, many of whom gathered
outside singing very loudly: *Happy birthday, dear Irving! Happy birthday to you!* After the reading we sold more than one hundred books.

I'd segregated Irving in the Opus Bistro so that he could sit down
and rest himself and so that, at the appointed time, he could make a
suitable entrance. Irving and Anna and Lise and I sat at the bar waiting. Irving sipped at a snifter of cognac. I numbered the Blue Things,
passing them over one by one for Irving to sign. That finished,
I glanced at my watch yet again. We all seemed to be feeling a little
nervous, unnerved almost by the numbers. At eight o'clock we
walked through the connecting passage into Magnum Books to face
the heat and expectation of the crowd.

I climbed onto the makeshift stage to introduce the evening.

Phil Jenkins, Ottawa author and columnist for the *Ottawa Citizen* wrote about the reading as follows:

"Give me a moment while I let the rum and Coke descend to my
toes," Irving Layton said, and the crowd at the poet's informal
eightieth birthday party at Magnum Books gave him the moment.

And what a crowd it was. A sea of respect jammed into a
space the size of a backyard swimming pool, with Layton down
at the front on the springboard, waiting to dive into the poems
of the new edition of *Dance with Desire*. (The original edition
appeared in 1986. This one, a classy volume with swirling charcoal drawings of bodies in love by ex-Ottawa resident Richard
Gorman, includes some extra poems chosen by John Metcalf.)

". . . I like to think I have joined the ranks of the great
amorous poets; Ovid, Robbie Burns, John Donne," Layton pro-
nounced as the rum and Coke reached his toes. Then he began to
read, and the room filled with poems tapped out on hip bones,

saintly wantons, breast strokes, taxi horns honking for Marilyn, sonnets scribbled in taverns, religious nudges, favoured erogenous zones and civilized seductions—and laughter, our laughter, at the thrust of his wit and the rolling of his rhythms.

He read for an hour, an act of stamina and gratitude that proved his love of performance and wish to please. He finished with a poem to his wife, *I Take My Anna Everywhere*, crossing the stage to stand before her and recite it like a suitor, The last two lines read:

> *All the men who see her*
> *want to live their wrecked lives forever.*

There were flowers and a standing ovation for our hero of the horizontal. "I'm grateful for the moment," Layton told us. Then, like a pub entertainer who is sure that the crowd is in love and ready for more, he took requests from the audience, six in all, that included a Bishop, an ode to his mother from whose speech cadence he claimed to get his "impeccable sense of rhythm," and a long, throat-tiring account of his first trip to Paris.

After the sixth there was a silence in which you could have heard a simile drop. "Perhaps we should stop here and move into the bar," John Metcalf wondered. Layton agreed with that, looked out over the sea of respect and gave us this entirely suitable closing remark.

"At 80, I'm in the prime of senility. All I worry about now is whether there will be anyone left to come to my funeral; whether my fly is up or down. And how the hell the world is going to get along without me."

L'ENVOI

I CROSSED THE BRIDGE and started up the steep little hill to Leon Rooke's house when I felt a deep stab of pain in my chest. I stood still looking back to the stream where a heron posed in the shallows. The pain stopped immediately and I went on my way to get of a couple of beers from Leon's fridge for Tim and me. Indigestion? Two rather greasy pakoras I'd eaten earlier?

It was September 1997, the Eden Mills Writers' Festival, the village dense with thousands of visitors. Every year Tim and Elke man a booth selling books and I always attend because the day is my annual "office day" with writers and publishers dropping by the booth to chat.

The next day I took the bus from Guelph to Toronto and arrived early at Union Station. To pass some time I thought I'd walk to Nicholas Hoare's bookstore on Front Street. Just outside the station that same pain, but agonizing, clamped me motionless. I could scarcely breathe. I managed to lean against the low wall, conscious only of legs and feet passing by.

It was, of course, angina. I was sent to the hospital for a stress test and in December had an angiogram which revealed a 95 per cent blockage in one artery. The surgeon said that normally they'd have carried on and performed the required angioplasty then and there, but that budget restraints under the Harris government meant that I'd have to join a waiting list. I waited until April of the next year for the angioplasty. They inserted into the artery a piece of tubing called a stent. Learning this new word was the only pleasing aspect of the whole terrifying business. The peculiar horror of the operation is that one is conscious while it is going on. When the operation is over, the patient has to lie still in bed with a sack of sand compressing the incision into the femoral artery in the groin up which they have fed the surgical equivalent of a plumber's snake.

"If you feel anything wet or hot," said the nurse, "press the alarm button. We'll only have seconds."

All this struck me as not far removed from having your arm sawn off in the cockpit of a ship of the line and the stump cauterized in boiling pitch.

For a while after the operation I felt tired and diminished. The anxiety of the eight months of waiting for the operation cost me sorely. Since then, life has been ruled by pills in the morning and pills in the evening. The sight of the Nitroglycerin Sublingual Spray is a daily reminder of mortality. My real priorities were being nudged aside by electrocardiograms and fasting blood tests.

Gradually, however, the world stopped contracting. The Press needed my attention. *Canadian Notes and Queries* needed stropping to a keener edge. Where in Canada, Michael Darling aside, could I find reviewers like Florence King whose review of *Parachutes and Kisses* by Erica Jong contained the sentence "Jong's sow-in-heat prose style is impossible to quote in a newspaper . . ." Two new novellas seemed to be ripening in my mind. One of them involving the ancient mistress of a G.D. Roberts–like poet whose ashes she brings back to Fredericton for interment in the cathedral and who ends up winning a parcel of moose steaks at a darts shoot-out in the Legion Hall. A new book of critical essays was also bobbing about.

But during this period of restricted action I was able to step back a pace or two from the daily onrush and hullabaloo of the Press and consider the profound changes in the literary scene since 1989 when I'd joined up with Tim and Elke. Rampant commercialization was making so much din that quieter voices were ignored or drowned out in the uproar. An aesthetic underground was never more necessary.

Steven Heighton said to me recently, "Literature used to be about literature. Now it's about money."

Money, and Prizes. Prizes proliferating. And along with them the manufacturing of celebrity by the manipulation of publicity budgets. Literature metamorphosing into Show Biz.

Writers were once validated by what they wrote; now they seek validation from journalists and TV personalities. Who would *wish* to be sandwiched between a poodle trainer and a lighthouse keeper, enduring the unctuosities of a Peter Gzowski, a Pamela Wallin or a Peter Mansbridge? Who would *wish* to discuss *le mot juste* with Jan Wong, a journalist who in her youth embraced the aesthetic subtleties of Mao's Cultural Revolution? Who would *wish* to be interviewed on Evan Solomon's TV show *Hot Type*, an experience I would imagine like being slobbered on by an enthusiastic Labrador? How could writers be lured by siren songs so *crummy*? It is the shallowness that appals. Yet the celebrity manufactured by these nonentities is what many writers seem to crave; for many this mindless exposure is a component of "success."

Under these conditions and with an unsophisticated readership, books turn into commodity, into "product," and they are packaged and sold as such. The ludicrous frenzy created over and around Ondaatje's *The English Patient* can serve as an example. Philip Marchand in the *Toronto Star* was the only critic to say publicly that the book was ill-written and tedious.

Prizes, too, have become a problem. There is something anti-literary about prizes. Literature is not a competition. Prizes deform a literature by focusing attention on a small clutch of books. The awards do not confer *literary* status; they are transparently marketing schemes. Media interest is less in theme and style than it is in the sum of money awarded. In Canada, prizes are celebrated in nationalistic rather than literary terms; *we won* is the national and media attitude rather than we read and experienced and enjoyed.

When the short list for the Booker Prize was announced in 2002 the *Globe and Mail* published two fascinating letters to the editor on the subject on the same day. One was an upswelling of smarmy Babbittry from Douglas Gibson, president and publisher of McClelland and Stewart Ltd. The other was an indignant outburst from Stephen Henighan, author most recently of a book of literary essays, *When Words Deny the World*.

Gibson wrote:

The news that three Canadian authors have been nominated for the Booker Prize must bring pride and pleasure to all of us. James Adams is correct to dwell on the remarkable international success of our authors in recent years.

In the past few months, we have read many pessimistic stories about Canadian publishing, centring on the financial failure of the General Publishing group. By happy contrast, now is a time to celebrate Canadian accomplishment and to recognize the far-sighted role played by our government agencies—specifically, the Department of Canadian Heritage and the Canada Council—in supporting our authors and nurturing the publishers that launch them.

If there were a writing Olympics, our men and women would be on the podium all the time, and our national anthem would be played so often that even non-Canadians would know the words.

Henighan wrote:

James Adams's claim of a "golden age" in Canadian literature (Some Day, They'll Call This the Golden Age—Sept. 25) over-looks the uncomfortable fact that the appearance of three Canadians on the Booker shortlist coincides with the judges' decision to shortlist more "fun" and "popular" books. This is a commercial, not a literary, triumph. The Booker shortlist confirms that the Canadian publishing industry has perfected a strain of easily exportable, no-name entertainment.

Mr. Adams himself underlines the commercial roots of his bias when he defines each book he mentions in terms of the prize money it has earned. "Golden age" is a gross misnomer. The metaphor Mr. Adams should have used comes from the history of American robber-baron capitalism. This is our Gilded Age. The difference is that, during the U.S. Gilded Age, writers stood outside the commercial glare and criticized it.

Journalistic engagement with our culture has sunk now to columns in the *Globe and Mail* with smartass titles like "Arts Ink," which on this day of writing informs us that Michael Jackson suffered minuscule burns while setting off fireworks at a charity concert.

Rarely do we hear sane voices rising above "hype" and "buzz." Rarely do we find people taking the long view, patiently comparing books from the present with books from the past. Rarely do we hear reference to the "crafte so longe to lerne." The universities, once a countervailing influence, seem to have abandoned any public role and teachers of literature either echo media endorsement or simply play with themselves.

Bloated bogus novels trumpeted.

Florid verbiage.

And an audience that can't seem to tell the difference.

We are in a mess.

But so, I am cheered to find, is Australia.

I read recently *Snakecharmers in Texas: Essays 1980–1987* by Clive James. In a review of Robert Hughes's *The Fatal Shore* written for *The New Yorker*, James looked back over Australian literature's recent past and I was astonished to find that what he had to say about Australia was almost identical to what I had said about Canada in *Freedom from Culture: Selected Essays 1982–1992*.

Clive James, author of a delicious three-volume autobiography which begins with *Unreliable Memoirs*, wrote of Australia:

> Ardent republicans would like Australia to be self-sufficient in the arts the way it is in minerals. The idea that any one country can be culturally self-sufficient is inherently fallacious, but in the forward rush of Australian confidence during Gough Whitlam's period of government, when grants were handed out to anybody with enough creative imagination to ask for one, reason was thrown into the back seat. For the last fifteen years, Australian artists in all fields, supposedly free at last from the imposition of being judged by alien—i.e. British—standards, have been judged by their own standards, and almost invariably found to be the authors of significant works. The glut of self-approval has been

most evident in literature, which in normal circumstances customarily produces a strong critical movement to accompany any period of sustained creativity but in Australia's case has largely failed to do so. The undoubted fact that some very good things have been written can't stave off the consideration that many less good things have been given the same welcome . . . In Australia, while literature is rapidly becoming a cash crop, a literary community has been slower to emerge. Criticism is too often, in the strict sense, tendentious. Scale is duly hailed, ambition lauded, but the direction of the book—does it point the way? does it give us purpose?—is usually the basis of assessment. There are not many critics detached enough to quibble over detail, and ask why so many great writers have produced so little good writing.

The relatively recent arrival of literary agents in Canada has accelerated the commercialization of the literary world. Agents want to make money and therefore take on as clients only writers whose books have commercial potential. Agents demand big advances for their writers. In most cases, the Canadian reading public is not large enough to buy a sufficient number of books to earn back the advance. If foreign sales are not made, the publisher is bound to lose. This situation will be tolerated while publishers are in competition to build lists but cannot be sustained indefinitely.

One possible effect of all this might be that books will be tailored with an international audience in mind. This, in turn, will probably tilt the work towards genre writing. The large publishers will become less and less interested in books likely to appeal only to Canadian experience; publishing power resides in New York and London and those arbiters are more familiar with martinis than they are with moose and Mounties.

If the large houses, as they are rumoured to be doing, start the practice of refusing to read un-agented manuscripts, then another layer of commercialization will have been put in place. Authors will have to be approved by agents whose *raison d'être* is to sell work with commercial potential.

In my 1987 Tanks Campaign pamphlet against the idea of subsidy I concluded with these words:

Publishing and all other aspects of the literary life in Canada need to be put on a commercial footing. I think that is the only way we can regain dignity and perspective.

Free from government aid and approval, our writing can better work its magic on readers. In *Required Reading*, Philip Larkin wrote: "I think we got much better poetry when it was all regarded as sinful or subversive, and you had to hide it under the cushion when somebody came in. What I don't like about subsidies and support is that they destroy the essential nexus between the writer and the reader. If the writer is being paid to write and the reader is being paid to read, the element of compulsive contact vanishes."

Despite the fact that sound commercial practice would leave us with a smaller—and much different—literary world, it would at least be *ours*, the possession of individuals. We would be free from Culture, free from nationalism, free from CanLit, and free for the first time in many years to begin the building of a literature in Canada, a literature, in Philip Larkin's words, of compulsive contact.

Having actually watched the process of commercialization over the fifteen years since I wrote those words, I have to admit that I was wrong. Commercial publishing in Canada has no place for the poetry of George Johnston or Eric Ormsby, no place for the essays of W. J. Keith, no place for the delicacies of Mary Borsky, Clark Blaise, or Libby Creelman. I still believe, passionately, in Larkin's "compulsive contact," still believe our literature needs to separate itself from the state. I have no idea how that can be effected. I have no answers other than the willing co-operation of individuals.

Reviewing in 1964 *Kipling's Mind and Art* edited by Andrew Rutherford, Evelyn Waugh wrote of Kipling's priorities—and politics—a few sentences which aptly describe mine too.

He believed civilization to be something laboriously achieved which was only precariously defended. He wanted to see the defences fully manned and he hated the liberals because he thought them gullible and feeble, believing in the easy perfectibility of man and ready to abandon the work of centuries for sentimental qualms.

I thought often during the writing of this book of the House of Anansi. The press was sold to Jack Stoddart of General Publishing in 1989, the same year I started working with the Porcupine's Quill. It was as if the Porcupine's Quill was assuming the task which must be taken up by new people every twenty years or so.

Dennis Lee said in an interview in the *Montreal Star* in 1969:

Literature is a whole dimension of being a citizen of a country, which we've generally been deprived of. Without it, you have something less than an adequate society. You don't have enough nourishment. It's an underdeveloped situation.

We give a hoot. It's a civilized act to wrestle with the mind and passions of our own time and place.

And if we don't do that, we're less than civilized.

Exactly so, Dennis.

And that is why, lofty tree or future leafmould, the wrestling must go on.

Bibliography

Books by John Metcalf

New Canadian Writing 1969. Clarke, Irwin. Toronto, 1969.
The Lady Who Sold Furniture. Clarke, Irwin. Toronto, 1970.
Going Down Slow. McClelland and Stewart, Toronto, 1972.
The Teeth of My Father. Oberon Press. Ottawa, 1975.
Girl in Gingham. Oberon Press. Ottawa, 1978.
General Ludd. ECW Press. Toronto, 1980.
Selected Stories. McClelland and Stewart. Toronto, 1982.
Kicking Against the Pricks. ECW Press. Toronto, 1982.
Adult Entertainment. Macmillan. Toronto, 1986.
Adult Entertainment. St. Martin's Press. New York, 1990.
Adult Entertainment. Random House of Canada, 1990. Paperback release.
What Is a Canadian Literature? Red Kite Press. Guelph, 1988.
Volleys (with Sam Solecki & W. J. Keith). Porcupine's Quill. Erin, 1990.
Shooting the Stars. Porcupine's Quill. Erin, 1993.
Freedom from Culture. ECW Press. Toronto, 1994.
Acts of Kindness and of Love (with Tony Calzetta). Presswerk Editions, 1995.

Books Edited by John Metcalf

TRADE BOOKS

Best Canadian Stories 1976 (with Joan Harcourt). Oberon Press. Ottawa.

Best Canadian Stories 1977 (with Joan Harcourt). Oberon Press. Ottawa.

Best Canadian Stories 1978 (with Clark Blaise). Oberon Press. Ottawa.

Best Canadian Stories 1979 (with Clark Blaise). Oberon Press. Ottawa.

Best Canadian Stories 1980 (with Clark Blaise). Oberon Press. Ottawa.

Best Canadian Stories 1981 (with Leon Rooke). Oberon Press. Ottawa.

Best Canadian Stories 1982 (with Leon Rooke). Oberon Press. Ottawa.

Here and Now: Canadian Stories (with Clark Blaise). Oberon Press. Ottawa, 1977.

First Impressions. Oberon Press. Ottawa, 1980.

Second Impressions. Oberon Press. Ottawa, 1981.

Third Impressions. Oberon Press. Ottawa, 1982.

Making It New. Methuen Publishing. Toronto, 1982.

The New Press Anthology: Best Canadian Stories (Vol. I) (with Leon Rooke). General Publishing. Toronto, 1984.

The New Press Anthology: Best Canadian Stories (Vol. II) (with Leon Rooke). General Publishing. Toronto, 1985.

The Bumper Book. ECW Press. Toronto, 1987.

Carry on Bumping. ECW Press. Toronto, 1988.

Writers in Aspic. Véhicule Press. Montreal, 1988.

The Macmillan Anthology 1 (with Leon Rooke). Macmillan. Toronto, 1988.

The Macmillan Anthology 2 (with Leon Rooke). Macmillan. Toronto, 1989.

The Macmillan Anthology 3 (with Kent Thompson). Macmillan. Toronto, 1990.

How Stories Mean (with J. R. [Tim] Struthers). The Porcupine's Quill Press. Erin, 1993.

The New Story Writers. Quarry Press. Kingston, 1992.

Cuento canadiense contemporáneo. John Metcalf (compilador), traducción: Juan Carlos Rodriguez. Universidad Nacional Autonoma de México. Mexico, 1996.

TEXTBOOKS

Wordcraft (Books 1–5). J. M. Dent and Sons. Toronto, 1967–77. (Vocabulary and comprehension books, Grades 7–11.)

Rhyme and Reason. Ryerson Press. Toronto, 1969. (Poetry textbook, Grades 8–10.)

Salutation. Ryerson Press. Toronto, 1970. (Anthology of world poetry. Grades 10–12.)

Sixteen by Twelve. McGraw-Hill. Toronto, 1971. (Canadian short stories. Grades 10–12.)

The Narrative Voice. McGraw-Hill. Toronto, 1971. (Canadian short stories. University text.)

Kaleidoscope. Van Nostrand Reinhold. Toronto, 1972. (Canadian short stories. Junior high school.)

The Speaking Earth. Van Nostrand Reinhold. Toronto, 1972. (Canadian poetry. Grades 9–11.)

Stories Plus. McGraw-Hill. Toronto, 1979. (Canadian stories. Grades 10–12.)

New Worlds. McGraw-Hill. Toronto, 1980. (Canadian stories. Grades 8–9.)

Making It New. Methuen. Toronto, 1982. (Trade and university text.)

Canadian Classics. McGraw-Hill Ryerson. Toronto, 1993.

For Oberon Press

At Peace. Ann Copeland. 1978.
Taking Cover. Keath Fraser. 1982.
The Elizabeth Stories. Isabel Huggan. 1984.
The Love Parlour. Leon Rooke. 1977
Cry Evil. Leon Rooke. 1980.

For Quarry Press, Macmillan and ECW Press

Hockey Night in Canada and Other Stories. Diane Schoemperlen. 1991.
The Man of My Dreams. Diane Schoemperlen. 1990.
Death Suite. Leon Rooke. 1981.

For the Porcupine's Quill Press

Cape Breton Is the Thought-Control Centre of Canada. Ray Smith. 1989.
The Improved Binoculars. Irving Layton. 1991.
Lunar Attractions. Clark Blaise. 1990.
Europe. Louis Dudek. 1991.
Endeared by Dark: The Collected Poems of George Johnston. 1990.
Victims of Gravity. Dayv James-French. 1990.
Volleys. Solecki, Metcalf, Keith. 1990.
Quickening. Terry Griggs. 1991.
Blue Husbands. Don Dickinson. 1991.
The Happiness of Others. Leon Rooke. 1991.
Portraits of Canadian Writers. Sam Tata. 1991.
An Independent Stance. W. J. Keith. 1991.
Flight Paths of the Emperor. Steven Heighton. 1992.
Dance with Desire. Irving Layton. 1992.
While Breath Persist. Gael Turnbull. 1992.
A Night at the Opera. Ray Smith. 1992.
Thank Your Mother for the Rabbits. John Mills. 1992.
Man and His World. Clark Blaise. 1992.
Forests of the Medieval World. Don Coles. 1993.
Bad Imaginings. Caroline Adderson. 1993.
How Stories Mean. John Metcalf and J. R. (Tim) Struthers. 1993.
Apology for Absence. John Newlove. 1993.
Mogul Recollected. Richard Outram. 1993.
Shooting the Stars. John Metcalf. 1993.
From a Seaside Town. Norman Levine. 1993.
Canada Made Me. Norman Levine. 1993.
Onlyville. Cynthia Holz. 1994.
City of Orphans. Patricia Robertson. 1994.
Thrand of Gotu. George Johnston. 1994.
How Insensitive. Russell Smith. 1994.
A Litany in Time of Plague. K. D. Miller. 1994.
Lives of the Mind Slaves. Matt Cohen. 1994.
Popular Anatomy. Keath Fraser. 1995.
On earth as it is. Steven Heighton. 1995.
Driving Men Mad. Elise Levine. 1995.

The Lusty Man. Terry Griggs. 1995.

Influence of the Moon. Mary Borsky. 1995.

Help Me, Jacques Cousteau. Gil Adamson. 1995.

Lovers and Other Strangers. Carol Malyon. 1996.

Sailor Man. Leo Simpson. 1996.

Telling My Love Lies. Keath Fraser. 1996.

The Garden of Earthly Delights. Meeka Walsh. 1996.

Kiss Me. Andrew Pyper. 1996.

The Porcupine's Quill Reader. Eds. Tim Inkster and John Metcalf. 1996.

Dancer. Shelley Peterson. 1996.

Buying on Time. Antanas Sileika. 1997.

If I Were Me. Clark Blaise. 1997.

Small Change. Elizabeth Hay. 1997.

Sleeping Weather. Cary Fagan. 1997.

Jacob's Ladder. Joel Yanofsky. 1997.

Promise of Shelter. Robyn Sarah. 1997

Collected Poems (Vol. 1). P. K. Page. 1997.

Collected Poems (Vol. 2). P. K. Page. 1997.

The Schemers and Viga Glum. George Johnston. 1997.

Learning to Live Indoors. Alison Acheson. 1998.

Love in a Warm Climate. Kelley Aitken. 1998.

The Bubble Star. Lesley-Anne Bourne. 1998.

Belle of the Bayou. Joanne Goodman. 1998.

The King of Siam. Murray Logan. 1998.

Mixed-Up Grandmas. Carol Malyon. 1998.

Ripostes. Philip Marchand. 1998.

Noise. Russell Smith. 1998.

Aquarium. Mike Barnes. 1999.

Devil's Darning Needle. Linda Holeman. 1999.

Give Me Your Answer. K. D. Miller. 1999.

Old Flames. Kim Moritsugu. 1999.

Abby Malone. Shelley Peterson. 1999.

The Man Who Loved Jane Austen. Ray Smith. 1999.

One Last Good Look. Michael Winter. 1999.

Crossing the Salt Flats. Christopher Wiseman. 1999.

Southern Stories. Clark Blaise. 2000.

Kurgan. Don Coles. 2000.

Walking in Paradise. Libby Creelman. 2000.
How Did You Sleep? Paul Glennon. 2000.
Oxygen. Annabel Lyon. 2000.
Carnival. Harold Rhenisch. 2000.
This Is Our Writing. T. F. Rigelhof. 2000.
Great Expectations. Grant Robinson. 2000.
The One with the News. Sandra Sabatini. 2000.
Love Street. Susan Perly. 2001.
Facsimiles of Time. Eric Ormsby. 2001.
Gambler's Fallacy. Judith Cowan. 2001.
Dr. Swarthmore. Alexander Scala. 2001.
Pittsburgh Stories. Clark Blaise. 2001.
A Kind of Fiction. P. K. Page. 2001.
Dove Legend. Richard Outram. 2001.
Holy Writ. K. D. Miller. 2001.
The Lover's Progress. David Solway. 2001.
13. Mary-Lou Zeitoun. 2002
When Words Deny the World. Stephen Henighan. 2002.
Seasoning Fever. Susan Kerslake. 2002.
A Tourist's Guide to Glengarry. Ian McGillis. 2002.
The Understanding. Jane Barker Wright. 2002.
The Stand-In. David Helwig. 2002.
The Deep. Mary Swan. 2002.
Uncomfortably Numb. Sharon English. 2002.
The Syllabus. Mike Barnes. 2002.

Reading Series Publications

THE MAGNUM BOOK STORE READINGS

Acts of Kindness and of Love. John Metcalf.
Daddy Stump. Leon Rooke.
Sixty Billion Humans. Hugh Hood.
A Night at the Opera. Ray Smith.
Contacts. Dayv James-French.
Tag. Terry Griggs.
Trouble. Diane Schoemperlen.

Passages. Rohinton Mistry.

Extracts from Works-in-Progress. Joan MacLeod.

An Excerpt from the Redeemer. Doug Glover.

A Selection of Poems. Irving Layton.

Fragment of a Novel-in-Progress. Jane Urquhart.

An Excerpt from In the Time of the Angry Queen. Mark Frutkin.

An Excerpt from a Novel-in-Progress. Don Dickinson.

I Had a Father. Clark Blaise.

For Gods and Fathers. Steven Heighton.

From a Family Album. Norman Levine.

Keys. Carol Shields.

Dusters. Gael Turnbull.

Provençal Songs. George Elliott Clarke.

Waiting for Angel. Matt Cohen.

An Extract from Graven Images. Audrey Thomas.

Seven Stories. Yann Martel.

How I Got Started and Why I Can't Stop. Isabel Huggan.

Extract from Black Nightingale. John Mills.

Poems. John Newlove.

THE FOOD FOR THOUGHT READING SERIES

The Lady and the Servant. Norman Levine.

Landscape with Poisoner. Caroline Adderson.

The Boy from Moogradi. Leon Rooke.

Lieutenant Lukac's Cat. John Metcalf.

Hiram and Jenny. Richard Outram.

Provence and Mystery Stories. David Helwig.

Delirium. Cynthia Holz.

Our People. Carol Shields.

Berry Season. Patricia Robinson.

Acknowledgements

My thanks are due to the many Canadian writers who have granted me permission to quote from their work. Especial thanks to Patrick Toner (*If I Could Turn and Meet Myself*), Ray Smith ("Ontological Arseholes: Life with Montreal Story Teller"), and Robert Giddings (*You Should See Me in Pyjamas*), who granted me also ghastly flashes of my younger self.

Photos by Sam Tata and the author courtesy of the John Metcalf fonds in the Special Collections of the University of Calgary. I have kindly been given permission to reprint from the following: P. J. O'Rourke, *Age and Guile Beat Youth, Innocence, and a Bad Haircut*, copyright © 1995, reprinted by permission of Random House Canada; John Mills, review of Morley Callaghan's *Close to the Sun Again*, from *Queen's Quarterly*; Keath Fraser, *Le Mal de l'air*; Leon Rooke, introduction to *Macmillan Anthology (2)*; Barry Cameron, introduction to *On the Edge: Canadian Short Stories* for *The Literary Review* (Fairleigh Dickinson University); the Tanks Campaign, from William Hoffer's catalogues; Michael Darling's review of Rohinton Mistry's *Tales from Firozsha Baag*, in *Macmillan Anthology (1)*; Mistry, *Such a Long Journey*; Lisa Moore, quoted in *Quarry Magazine*, 1992; Hoffer, "Cheap Sons of Bitches: Memoirs of the Book Trade," written for *Carry On Bumping*; Mark Abley's review of George Johnston's *Endeared by Dark*; Don Coles, "My Son at the Seashore, Age Two"; Richard Outram, "Techne"; Steven Heighton, *The New Quarterly*; the Porcupine's Quill Press and K.D. Miller; Terry Griggs; Annabel Lyon; Russell Smith, *Noise*; Judith McCormack, "The Cardinal Humours"; Ken Rockburn, *Medium Rare*.